Teaching

Instructional Design

Instructional Design
New Alternatives for Effective Education and Training

Kerry A. Johnson
Lin J. Foa

nucea

National University Continuing Education Association
American Council on Education Macmillan Publishing Company
NEW YORK
Collier Macmillan Publishers
LONDON

Copyright © 1989 by American Council on Education and
Macmillan Publishing Company,
A Division of Macmillan, Inc.

All rights reserved. No part of this book may be reproduced or transmitted in any form or by any means, electronic or mechanical, including photocopying, recording, or by any information storage and retrieval system, without permission in writing from the Publisher.

Macmillan Publishing Company
866 Third Avenue, New York, N.Y. 10022

Collier Macmillan Canada, Inc.

Library of Congress Catalog Card Number: 88-36696

Printed in the United States of America

printing number
1 2 3 4 5 6 7 8 9 10

Library of Congress Cataloging-in-Publication Data
Johnson, Kerry A.
  Instructional design : new alternatives for effective education
and training / Kerry A. Johnson and Lin J. Foa.
     p.   cm. — (The American Council on Education/Macmillan series
in higher education)
  Includes index.
  ISBN 0-02-897191-4 (Macmillan)
  1. Instructional systems—Design.   I. Foa, Lin J.   II. Title.
III. Series: American Council on Education/Macmillan series in
higher education.
LB1028.35.J64   1989
371.3—dc19   88-36696
                                                               CIP

Contents

EDITORS' PREFACE	ix
ACKNOWLEDGMENTS	xii
ABOUT THE AUTHORS	xiv

SECTION I: ANALYSIS AND ASSESSMENT

CHAPTER ONE: THE FOUNDATIONS OF INSTRUCTIONAL DESIGN   3
    Theoretical Foundations   4
    Historical Development   6
       Social Science   6
       Management/Engineering Science   9
       Information Science   10
    Research Findings   12
    The Differences Between Instructional Design and
       Traditional Instruction   12
    Conclusion   14
    References   14

CHAPTER TWO: WHAT IS INSTRUCTIONAL DESIGN?   16
    A Family of Designers   18
       A Common Process   18
       A Common Product   19
       Uncommon Skills   20
       Summary   21

Instructional Design: The Process, the Products, and the Instructional Designer   21
   The Process: Instructional Systems Development   21
   The Products: The Instructional Design   26
   The Instructional Designer   28
   Summary   30

CHAPTER THREE: ASSESSING THE NEEDS   32
Significant Trends Affecting Future Learning Needs   33
   Demographic Changes   33
   Technological Innovation   35
   Global Competitiveness   37
Shifting Knowledge Demands and Emerging Learning Constituencies   38
Education for an Information Society   38
Implications for the Future Design and Delivery of Programs for Adults   44
References   46

CHAPTER FOUR: INSTRUCTIONAL DESIGN AND LEARNER MOTIVATION   47
Adults as Motivated Learners   48
Instructional Design and Learner Motivation   49
Motivation Models   51
Motivation and Computer-Based Education   55
Learner Control   58
Conclusion   59
References   59

SECTION II: DESIGN AND IMPLEMENTATION

CHAPTER FIVE: INSTRUCTIONAL DESIGN AND THE NEW TEACHING TECHNOLOGIES   63
Instructional Design: Basic Applications   64
   Elaboration Theory   64
   Component Design Theory   66
Instructional Technology and Innovation   66
Uses of Technology for Teaching   68
Conclusion   70
References   70

CHAPTER SIX: POWER AND POTENTIAL: THE UNIVERSITY AND INSTRUCTIONAL DESIGN   72
Gathering Pressures for Change   73
   The New Learners   74
   Changing Knowledge Structures   75
   Applied Learning   76
   Faculty Development and Part-Time Faculty   78
   Off-Campus Sites and Program Comparability   79
   Accountability and Assessment   80
   External Linkages   82
Conclusion   83
References   83

CHAPTER SEVEN: INSTRUCTIONAL DESIGN: A TEMPLATE FOR CHANGE   85

   Historical Perspective   85
      The University Becomes Involved   86
      State Board Initiatives   87
   Current Status   88
      Curriculum Development Today   88
      Strategic Planning   90
      Special Projects and Innovation   90
      General Education Revisions   90
   Conclusion   91

CHAPTER EIGHT: INSTRUCTIONAL DESIGN FOR DISTANCE LEARNING   92

   The Challenges for Instructional Design   93
   Instructional Design Strategies: Extension or Transformation   94
   Instructional Design in Theory   97
   Instructional Designers in Distance Learning Programs   98
   Broader Influences on Instructional Design   99
   Trends and New Challenges   101
   The Role for Instructional Design in a Changing Environment   102
   References   103

CHAPTER NINE: INSTRUCTIONAL DESIGN IN INTERACTIVE VIDEO DEVELOPMENT:
       A BRITISH PERSPECTIVE   106

   Significant Developments in Open Learning and
      Distance Delivery in the U.K.   107
      Open College   108
      Enter the Computer (Sometimes Bearing Gifts)   109
      From Television to Video   109
      VCR   110
      Summary   110
   The Present Situation   110
      Interactive Video in the U.K.   110
      New Technology in Instructional Design   111
      Instructional Design Solutions in Interactive Video   113
      The IV in Schools Project   114
   Guideline Questions   114
   Toward International Cooperation   119
   References   119

CHAPTER TEN: BUILDING AN INSTRUCTIONAL DESIGN ORGANIZATION   121

   What Is an Instructional Design Organization?   121
   When Is an Instructional Design Unit Necessary?   123
      The Ad Hoc Approach to Addressing Instructional Design
         Needs   123
   Benefits of Having Your Own Instructional Design Capability   124
   Benefits of Buying Instructional Design Services from Outside
      Sources   126
      Comparing the Costs of Each Approach   127
      Summary   127

How Is an Instructional Design Organization Structured, Staffed, and
    Managed? 127
  Structure 128
  Organization and Management 129
Conclusion 136
References 136

SECTION III: EVALUATION

**CHAPTER ELEVEN: EVALUATING THE INSTRUCTIONAL DESIGNER: A CASE STUDY OF
    A PERFORMANCE APPRAISAL SYSTEM**   139

Roles of the Instructional Designer 141
What Is Performance Appraisal and Why Is It Needed? 143
Developing a Performance Appraisal System 144
Costs and Benefits of Performance Appraisal 147
Conclusion 147
Reference 148

**CHAPTER TWELVE: THE ROLE, METHODS, AND WORTH OF EVALUATION IN
    INSTRUCTIONAL DESIGN**   157

The Role of Evaluation Within Instructional Design 158
Evaluation Methods in Instructional Design 161
  Project Documentation 162
  Assessment of the Worth of Project Objectives 162
  Formative Evaluation 164
  Immediate Effectiveness Evaluation 165
  Impact Evaluation 166
  Cost-Effectiveness Analysis 167
Evaluating the Worth of Instructional Design 168
  Evaluating the Process by the Product 168
  Six Common Dimensions 169
Conclusion 177
References 177

CHAPTER THIRTEEN: CHAOS, CONNECTIVITY, AND COMPUTERS   182

The Nature of Scientific Thought 182
Chaos as a Scientific Approach 184
Connectivity—"The Society of Mind" 185
Graphics and Learning 185
Artificial Intelligence and Learning 186
Computers as Design, Delivery, and Management Tools for the
    Future 187
  Design Tool 187
  Delivery Tool 188
  Management Tool 190
Conclusion 190
References 191

GLOSSARY   193

INDEX   195

Editors' Preface

The scope of education and training targeted at adults is being rapidly transformed. Changing technologies, changing demographics, and changing goals mean that our universities, industries, and government agencies must work together in an interactive triad to restructure and redirect our notions of what people need to learn, and when. The scale of change means that we must look to education and training to provide structural, rather than individual, solutions. Educational developers, managers, and policymakers in these three sectors must learn not only to work together but also to communicate clearly with each other. Instructional design theory and techniques can help achieve this communication and collaboration.

For our immediate purposes, instructional design can be described as both a systematic process and a body of knowledge. (See Chapter Two for a complete definition.) As a process, instructional design creates efficient and effective instructional programs based on an analysis of learners, content, and the learning environment. As part of this formal process, the degree to which the design efforts are successful is evaluated, and necessary corrections are made.

Instructional designers select appropriate instructional strategies and media to fit learning requirements. These strategies may range from traditional stand-up delivery by an instructor to self-paced learning delivered via interactive videodisc. The use of technology and media is frequently recommended in instructional design, but it is by no means a necessary condition for its success. Instructional design has developed in tandem with developments in technology, using them where appropriate, but its theory and process are equally useful in traditional teaching.

As a body of knowledge, instructional design includes variations on this systematic, yet flexible, process. Instructional designers must also be familiar with both learning theory and evaluation theory, and be able to apply the principles of learning theory to specific instructional situations. Finally, they must be familiar with the attributes of learning technologies, so that they can use them cost-effectively.

Instructional design has been perceived as successful in creating training curricula—particularly in the areas of science and technology, where development funds have been readily available. However, rapid advances also are being made in designing courses in such fields as ethics, art history, and writing. There are no inherent limitations on the subject matter used in the process, but because instructional design projects can be costly, the requirements of scale and significance must be considered. Thus, cost effectiveness rather than subject matter frequently becomes the deciding factor in project selection.

The historical foundations of instructional design are multiple. (See Chapter One for a more complete history.) It has evolved over the past forty years as an outgrowth of new discoveries and theories in psychology, management and engineering science, and information science. The work of researchers and scholars in behavioral psychology and cognitive development (such as Skinner, Piaget, and Bruner) contributed to new theories of learning and have provided another stimulus to the thinking about instructional design.

In the 1960s, instructional designers in the military coupled these theories with recent advances in engineering and management, such as systems analysis and operations research, to create the formal instructional systems design (ISD) process. This is still the standard upon which all instructional design variations are judged. Systems thinking has allowed educators and trainers to apply technology sensibly to large-scale instructional projects.

In the past decade, advances in the field have centered particularly on developments in communications theory and audio-visual media. The general trend in these areas has been toward greater individual control and power in the use of various media, and a blending of media into a single interactive, visual system. Because learning takes place in each medium in different ways, the task of today's instructional designer is to combine into one seamless product the structure of the information to be learned, what is known of learner characteristics and styles, and knowledge about media production techniques.

Today, concepts and applications of instructional design are changing our ideas of what education and training are, and what they can do. In this book, we introduce instructional design to those who only vaguely—or never—have heard of it. We will also suggest new implications and challenges in the field to those who are already experienced practitioners.

Because instructional design theory and practice influences learning in so many diverse areas—from corporate management training, to military basic skills training, to collegiate distance education offered internationally, to improvement of traditional faculty classroom efforts—we have sought to include chapters by authors from diverse backgrounds. Because of its breadth and variety, instructional design offers the potential to produce new and more effective collaborations between and among industry, government, and the university. However, its kaleidoscopic complexity has led to considerable controversy, and our authors have not been reticent about exploring the challenges that exist. As well as examining current definitions, needs, and uses of instructional design from the educator's and trainer's viewpoint, we include current opinions about its use and effectiveness from the manager's and policymaker's perspectives.

In this regard, we can paraphrase a quote used by one of our authors and say, "Instructional design would be worth it just because it makes you think so hard about what you're doing." It is not only an educational tool, then, but a management tool—and we will see how the theory and processes can be applied to subjects ranging from strategic planning to performance appraisal.

In a more immediate sense, we have borrowed from the instructional design process itself to structure this book. The chapters are organized in three Sections, the first being concerned with the *analysis and assessment* stage of instructional design. Proceeding from a discussion of the foundations of the field in Chapter One, we move to a detailed definition and analysis of instructional design in Chapter Two. Following that are two chapters that assess the need for instructional design—first on the macro, or societal, level in Chapter Three, and then on the micro, or more individual, level in Chapter Four.

Once the definitions of, and needs for, instructional design are clear, we move to Section Two—the *design and implementation* phase. Chapter Five introduces the reader to one of the major questions facing all teachers, but particularly instructional designers: the implications and appropriate use of technologies in teaching. Chapter Six then examines the broad roles that instructional design can play in colleges and universities, and how its implementation can lead to effective collaborations with corporations and government agencies.

Chapters Seven through Ten then provide specific case studies, and evaluate the use of instructional design as a planning tool, in community colleges (Chapter Seven), in the international development of distance education (Chapter Eight), and as the basis for a British interactive video center designed to serve industry (Chapter Nine). Chapter Ten brings the section on implementation and applications to a close by analyzing how an instructional design unit can be organized and managed.

With a sense of the versatility of instructional design applications, we then move to Section Three to examine the final phase of the process—*evaluation*. Continuing the analysis begun in Chapter Ten on the organization of an instructional design unit, Chapter Eleven explores the special skills needed by designers to succeed in a functioning unit, and how managers can evaluate their performance. In Chapter Twelve, we come full circle to the most fundamental of questions asked by those involved in any way with instructional design: *How can we evaluate the quality of the product, and does instructional design advance the goal of all instruction—student learning?*

Because instructional design is a field in the process of dynamic development, we conclude with a look at the future. Unusual recent developments in the physical sciences, and especially in computer science, may lead to new and exciting possibilities in instructional design. These frontiers are sketched in Chapter Thirteen—a fitting conclusion for discussion of a field that has only begun to reach its potential.

Acknowledgments

We gratefully acknowledge the interest and patient support provided by Kay Kohl, executive director of the National University Continuing Education Association; Lloyd Chilton, our editor at Macmillan; and especially the encouragement and editorial assistance offered by the editor-in-chief of this series, Milton R. Stern, dean of University Extension at the University of California, Berkeley.

We also offer our profoundest thanks to another group of people without whom this book could not have been completed. Frequently working under stressful conditions, Victoria Erdly, Melissa Lange, Maria Dacquel, Kelly Jones, Renee Lyles, Andy Shaw, and Martha Smith admirably accomplished the necessary word processing, telephoning, and mailing of chapter drafts. Marj Crane also cheerfully provided another much-appreciated pair of editorial eyes in the final stages of the work.

Finally, our thanks to family and friends for their tolerance and good wishes throughout this project.

About the Authors

Jocelyn Calvert is Director of Administrative Studies and Social Sciences at the British Columbia Open University. Her responsibilities encompass development and delivery of courses and programs in an educational system that stresses regional collaboration and promotes international cooperation. She was educated for this role in a doctoral program in social psychology at the University of Wisconsin (Madison).

Angus Doulton is Director of the British National Interactive Video Centre in London, England. NIVC is an entirely independent entity promoting appropriate use of interactive technologies by all potential users. Prior to holding this position, Doulton worked for fifteen years as an educational publisher.

Joyce K. Elsner, Dean of Instruction at Rio Salado Community College in Arizona, has held that position since 1978. She is responsible for the instructional and student-services programs, including instructional design and curriculum development. Elsner received her doctoral degree from UCLA with an emphasis in community college administration.

Lin J. Foa is a Project Officer with the Annenberg/CPB Project, a funder of television-based courses and innovative uses of technology in higher education. Previously, she has held positions as Executive Assistant to the Chancellor at The University of Maryland University College; and as chief administrator at an independent elementary and middle school and at a satellite campus of the Evergreen State College, where she also was a member of the faculty. Her Ph.D. in Interdisciplinary Studies is from Emory University's Institute of Liberal Arts.

Kerry A. Johnson is Senior Project Manager for Omega Performance Corporation. He was formerly the Director of the Center for Instructional Development and Evaluation at The University of Maryland University College. CIDE designs and produces a wide range of instructional programs for education and business using varied media, including computer-based and interactive video instruction. Johnson has also taught instructional design at The University of Maryland, College Park. He holds a Ph.D. in Instructional Design, Development and Evaluation from Syracuse University.

Richard Lent is Director, Design and Development Services for Omega Performance Corporation. Omega is the leading provider of training services to the banking industry. Prior to joining Omega, Lent managed the custom training and interactive video development business for Digital Equipment Corporation. He received his Ph.D. in Instructional Design, Development and Evaluation from Syracuse University.

Thomas C. Reeves has been involved in the development and evaluation of new training technologies, primarily interactive videodiscs (IVD), since completing a Ph.D. in Instructional Technology at Syracuse University in 1979. An Assistant Professor of Instructional Technology at The University of Georgia, Reeves also is coauthor of a book summarizing evaluations of IVD, and a consultant for MetaMedia Systems, Inc. on the design of the National Science Center for Communications and Electronics. For two years the editor of the *ADCIS News*, a publication of the Association for the Development of Computer-Based Instructional Systems, Reeves became President of ADCIS in November, 1988.

James Van Patten is a senior consultant in the customer services division of Omega Performance Corporation. He is responsible for the analysis, design, and management of custom training programs for the financial services industry. Before joining Omega, Van Patten managed the custom interactive video production group for Digital Equipment Corporation. In addition to overseeing those professional designers, writers, and video producers, Van Patten designed and wrote over 150 hours of computer-based instruction. He also has considerable experience consulting with various companies and universities concerning instructional design theory and techniques. Van Patten received Bachelor's and Master's degrees in Music, and his Ph.D. in Instructional Design, Development, and Evaluation, from Syracuse University.

Mary Lindenstein Walshok is Associate Vice Chancellor for Extended Studies and Public Service, and an Adjunct Associate Professor of Sociology, at the University of California, San Diego. A sociologist of work, Walshok is the author of *Blue-Collar Women* (Doubleday, 1981) and numerous articles on sociological trends affecting work and education. She has been a Kellogg National Fellow from 1984–87 and investigated the effects of technological innovation in the workplace.

Janet L. Whitaker is Associate Dean of Instructional Technology at Rio Salado Community College in Arizona. She is responsible for using technologies for distance education, library/media services, and the college's audio teleconference network. Whitaker completed her Master's degree in Educational Media at Indiana State University, and two years of postgraduate work in instructional design and evaluation at Arizona State University.

Marcia A. Whitney is Associate Director of the Center for Instructional Development and Evaluation (CIDE), The University of Maryland University College. At CIDE she has directed many projects, ranging from continuing education for European-based military health professionals to interactive videodisc development for the U.S. Navy. Whitney received her doctoral degree from The University of Iowa, with an emphasis in educational psychology, measurement, and statistics; and has considerable experience in educational evaluation.

Raymond J. Wlodkowski is a core faculty member with Antioch University–Seattle. A licensed psychologist with experience as a therapist with adolescents and families, his areas of specialization are human development and motivation. Wlodkowski also serves as a consultant to numerous local and national organizations, and is the author of several books—the most recent of which is *Enhancing Adult Motivation to Learn,* published by Jossey–Bass, which won the Frandson Award for Literature in 1986. He has also been the recipient of a university award for teaching excellence.

Instructional Design

SECTION I
Analysis and Assessment

CHAPTER ONE

The Foundations of Instructional Design

Kerry A. Johnson

> Deep understanding of a domain of knowledge requires knowing it in various ways. This multiplicity of perspectives grows slowly through hard work and sets the stage for the re-cognition we experience as new insights (Howard E. Gruber, 1981).

As children we are natural learners continually analyzing, synthesizing, and evaluating our environment. We build thinking skills by exploring, sensing, feeling, trying on, expressing. Our minds fill. We build mental structures, scaffolding for thought. We build learning tools.

As we become adults, we encounter more and more complex learning situations. We face greater accountability. We must integrate new knowledge and learning skills much faster, and presumably much better, into the framework we have already built. And, as society becomes more complex and demanding, the information we require to prosper and grow becomes more difficult to process and assimilate. We require better, faster, more efficient learning tools.

Instructional design involves organizing and using tools of the mind and tools of learning, to improve the conduct of education and training. It has a history both long and short, in that it has evolved from other disciplines. In its most essential form, however, instructional design involves thinking creatively about teaching and learning.

The tools that we develop as individuals to think creatively, to observe, to solve problems, to ponder, to invent, are variations on our original child-tools. They are enhancements of, and refinements on, the themes of analysis, synthesis, and evaluation.

Instructional design is based on the ideas that (a) the common goal of education and training is the development of human potential; and (b) there is sufficient knowledge about the nature of learning to improve the process of developing that potential. Instructional design, broadly defined, provides a process with which to identify as goals what people need to know and do, to set out to achieve those goals, and to understand whether or when they have been achieved. According to Gagne and Briggs (1974), the purpose of the systematic design approach is that it encourages setting objectives, and provides a way to know when they are met. This process, combined with a growing body of learning theory, provides a set of tools that allow us to maximize individual learning potential.

It is useful to compare instructional design to other fields, such as architecture (as Van Patten does in Chapter Two), to better understand the complexity and promise of the field. The architect planning a new house applies processes grounded in the gathering, organizing, and presenting of information. But whereas the architect designs environments for living, the instructional designer creates environments for learning—psychological or intellectual environments that facilitate, and provide resources and incentives for, learning. Whether it is a well-designed seminar or a self-contained, computer-based package, designers shape the structure of instruction to meet learner needs. Basing their work on evolving instructional theory, they organize the strategies for learning into effective instructional events (Gagne and Briggs, 1974).

THEORETICAL FOUNDATIONS

The theoretical foundations of instructional design demonstrate a tension between "pure" science, on the one hand, and practical application on the other. Unlike scientific theories, which claim to truthfully represent the phenomena of a given field, the theories of instructional design are practical (Scheffler, 1985). They integrate knowledge of several disciplines and suggest action and outcomes. Instructional design, therefore, reflects a faith both in science as process, and in pragmatism (Richey, 1986). It is structured, in the sense that there are procedures that can be followed and guidelines that can be applied, but it is flexible in that there are many ways to use the procedures or follow the guidelines.

The foundations of instructional design are in the behavioral and social sciences—in particular in behavioral, developmental, social, and cognitive psychologies. Instructional design also draws upon the management sciences and engineering, having been influenced by such fields as systems analysis, operations research, management theory, and organizational development. Finally, instructional design has roots in information science, broadly interpreted to include communications, audiovisual media, information management, and computer science. (see Figure 1.1).

This ancestry, with its range and variety, both frees and limits the field of instructional design. It is freed in the sense that its several sources provide a

Figure 1.1. *Origins and components of instructional design and development.*

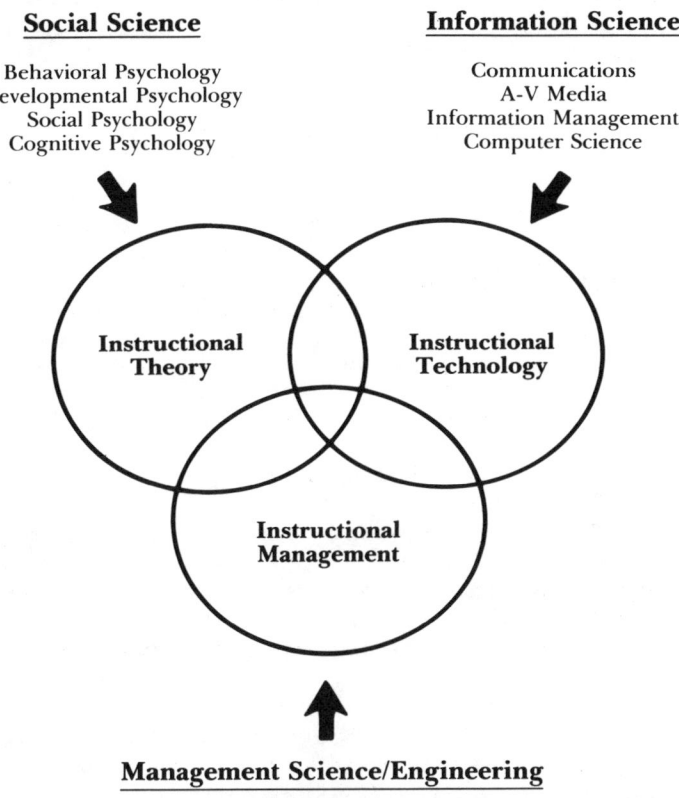

tremendous breadth of substance and form with which to build a new discipline. It is limited in the sense that many critics, and in some cases designers themselves, view instructional design as totally derived from a single discipline, and thus narrow in perspective (Schiffman, 1986).

Those who continue to view instructional design as primarily a behavioral science linked directly to Skinner and other behaviorists consider it to be overly simplistic, relying totally on observable learning outcomes gained at the expense of more complex and indirect learning. Those who view the field as arising from media and communication argue that designers generally choose a media-based solution to most education and training problems. Lastly, the contribution of systems analysis to the design process has been criticized as an attempt to apply rigid scientific approaches to an essentially dynamic human activity: learning.

Unfortunately, criticism that fails to recognize the integration of several fields into the new field of instructional design, also generally denies both the uses and the benefits of instructional design approaches. A great strength of instructional design is that it expands potential—potential to call on a wide range of perspectives on learning and human behavior as well as on how that information can be creatively combined within a broader social and organizational context.

HISTORICAL DEVELOPMENT

Although the discipline of instructional design has not developed in a clear chronology, with specific milestones, there is a general evolution that provides a sense of its maturity. Figure 1.2 seeks to show that evolution. It should be noted, however, that the influences of the various other fields on instructional design continue after their first impact. Instructional design is an amalgam of these other fields. Ultimately, it integrates and applies instructional theory, instructional technology theory, and instructional management theory in combination.

Social Science

The fields of behavioral, developmental, social, and cognitive psychology have contributed a set of learning theories to instructional design within a complex history of overlapping time lines. Certainly instructional design benefited from the work of Skinner and his associates during its earlier years, although Skinner's work was an extension of prior, less applicable behaviorist research.

Behavioral psychology prevailed in most American universities' psychology departments during the 1940s, 1950s, and 1960s and directly influenced early instructional design theories. Concepts such as reinforcement, contingency management, and behavior modification became popular throughout much of education, particularly at the K–12 level. More importantly, the concept that learning could be controlled, if not understood, by controlling the learning *environment* became central to many learning theories.

A major result of applying this behaviorist approach was the fairly widespread use of programmed instruction (PI). PI is characterized by specific and careful decomposition of the material to be learned into small "chunks." Learning each chunk, and being reinforced for learning each chunk, eventually led the learner through the carefully constructed path of material until the whole of it was mastered. Among the lasting general contributions of behavioral psychology to instructional design is, in fact, the notion that large bodies of knowledge can be analyzed into component parts and reorganized on the basis of a learning schema as opposed to a knowledge structure schema.

However, two serious limitations of behavioral psychology led designers to look also to other branches of psychology. The first limitation was that behaviorism provided little guidance for more complex mental tasks—for example synthesis, analysis, or evaluation. The second limitation, and perhaps the more serious one, was that it appeared to treat both the learner and learning as passive. Current theory, in contrast, considers learning as active, energetic, and internally motivated.

In Europe developmental psychologists, led by Piaget, responded to the recognition that learning is active. Piaget's work with children was founded

The Foundations of Instructional Design 7

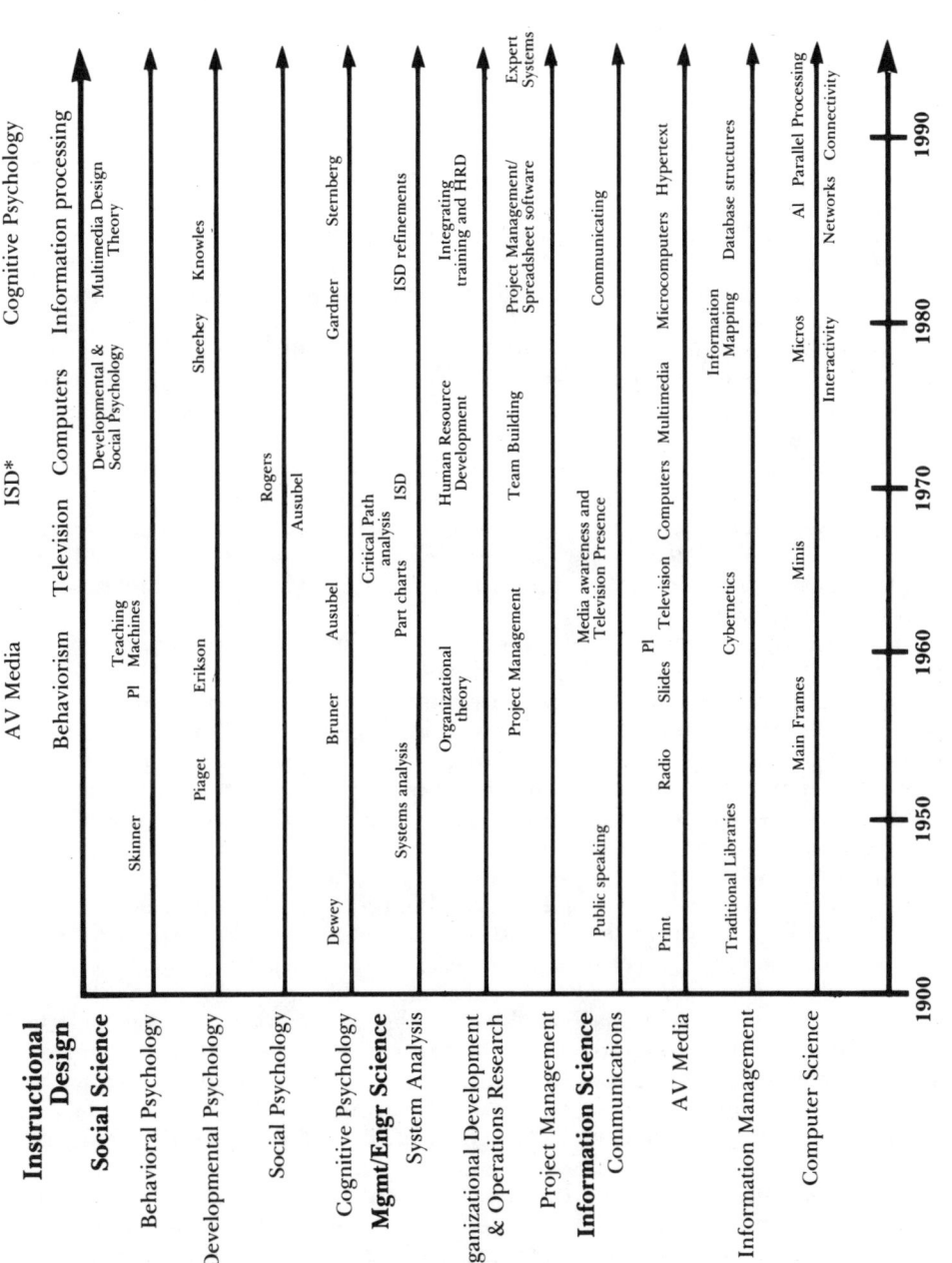

Figure 1.2. Historical foundations of instructional design.

* Instructional Systems Design

on the concept that children are continually probing and constantly organizing and reorganizing their observations of their environment. He also suggested that as children mature they develop more complex and abstract structures for understanding their observations—that children evolve through a predictable and universal series of developmental stages. Piaget's notions of active learning and developmental stages have been extended by others to adult learning and development, and have become a central theme for much of adult learning theory. That is, adults are active learners, and there are predictable, if not well-understood, stages of development in adulthood.

In the United States there was an even earlier tradition supporting active learning that was popular before being overshadowed by behaviorism. Dewey, in the first decades of this century, and later Bruner, both viewed learning as active and learners as exploring, manipulating, and analyzing the learning environment. Both of them attempted to understand more clearly the cognitive processes that contribute to learning. They also brought an awareness of the social aspects of psychology to the learning process by acknowledging the importance of experiential learning, of learning in groups, and of learning from others.

In the 1960s and 1970s, Ausubel provided insight into the way that individuals organize information, and contributed much to adult learning theory through his work in social psychology and (in particular) behavior modeling. Ausubel's theories, combined with Dewey's early work on motivation and Bruner's emphasis on discovery learning, formed a powerful set of guidelines for instructional design.

More recently, Gardner (1985) has advanced cognitive psychology by suggesting the conclusion, based on both physiological and psychological research, that there are multiple intelligences—intelligences that call on different skills for each of us. He argues that these multiple intelligences need to be considered in planning, designing, and implementing education and training programs. His work verifies in some ways what has been intuitively clear for years. It also extends intuition into practice by suggesting ways that knowledge of the complexity and richness of the mind's mechanisms can be acknowledged and accommodated when designing instructional systems.

Sternberg (1985) has proposed a "triarchic theory of human intelligence" that also holds great promise for instructional designers. It comprises three subtheories—*contextual, experiential,* and *componential*—each of which are particularly relevant in describing adult learning.

The *contextual* subtheory specifies how intelligent behavior adapts to, selects from, or shapes an existing environment. Sternberg suggests that the context within which the individual operates influences intelligence in specific ways. He also suggests, however, that this contextual influence, this ability to analyze and understand the context of experience, only explains part of intelligent behavior.

The *experiential* subtheory proposes that each individual brings to a given context a set of specific prior experiences. Intelligence and learning ability are influenced by the degree to which that experience can be applied to the new situation. Making connections between prior experiences and new situations is, therefore, a specific and significant form of intelligence.

The *componential* subtheory suggests that there are underlying mental or cognitive structures that determine intelligence. This subtheory is most closely related to Gardner's work in that it can be further specified to include various forms of cognitive structures.

Taken together, the three subtheories provide not only an important conceptualization of intelligence, but a useful viewpoint for design practice. Sternberg's triarchic theory points clearly to the need to (a) understand the environment, the context for learning, in relation to the subject matter to be learned and to the learner; (b) understand the learner's experience relative to that context; and (c) understand the cognitive structures relevant for that particular learning task.

The influence of these various approaches to learning theory has led to more cohesive and effective instructional design theories and practices. Understanding more about how the mind works should allow designers to create learning environments that extend and enhance the natural active learning behaviors of childhood. Adult learners, after years of conforming to educational norms, in many ways need to reacquire some of the energy, excitement, and responsibility for learning that they possessed as children. Carefully designed instruction, based on solid learning theory and delivered in an engaging manner, will likely improve the possibility of that reacquisition.

Management/Engineering Science

Systems analysis has also had a major influence on the development of the instructional design process. It places a strong premium on careful initial analysis: If one understands the problem, the solutions will be more appropriate, and generally less costly. Systems analysis has also provided some of the overall management strategies that control particularly large-scale instructional design projects. Those systems strategies, developed and tested by the military and the space administration as well as the business sector, provide a means of tracking and monitoring project progress and assessing project effectiveness.

As a result of the successful use of systems analysis to manage large military projects during World War II, systems and systematic approaches to problem solving and project management were used on a more and more widespread basis for peacetime projects. By the early and middle 1960s, instructional specialists were developing the process as a means of managing large curriculum and instructional projects, such as those in the "new mathematics" and "new physics." Later in the decade, university researchers conducted formal projects for the military, detailing the instructional design process as a special case of systems analysis. The military version of this process, generally referred to as Instructional Systems Development (ISD), is the basis of most present-day design approaches.

Among the benefits of systems analysis for instructional design is that large, complex projects can be broken down into smaller, more manageable components. By doing so, designers are better able to identify strategies, approaches, activities, and methods that are likely to enhance the student's learning experience. This occurs for at least two reasons: (1) the intricacies of the content relative to the learner's aptitudes are more carefully analyzed; and (2) better assessment of available and required learning resources expands the likelihood of integrating innovative instruction into the learning package.

Another benefit of the systems approach is that there is a general assumption that complex instructional problems are best solved by combining the knowledge and ability of a team of specialists rather than depending upon an individual instructor as designer, producer, and deliverer. This team approach more urgently requires a specific process than would a single instructor working on a single, idiosyncratic course. It requires a full set of management tools to keep the team on task, to make deadlines, and to ensure the integrity, quality, and consistency of instructional approaches and products. It is this management orientation and the understanding of the entire design process that provides designers with the necessary tools and benchmarks to keep complex projects on target.

Specific tools and techniques for project management have continued to evolve from the basic systems perspective. For example, designers now regularly use microcomputers to track, analyze, and manage project progress. A number of useful project management programs allow designers to predict resource needs, assign staff, and manage team activities throughout the process. Many of these tools build on specific planning processes such as PERT charting and critical path analysis—tools that have been used for twenty to thirty years to analyze large military and space-agency projects. These tools can also assist in evaluating project success from a cost-benefit perspective, an area that still needs considerable development.

Information Science

From another relatively new science, information science, instructional design has gained insights into the structure, organization, and management of information. This is particularly true in relation to the use of media. Recent research on the design of media, especially in the use of graphic and video materials, as well as research on the design of computer-based information systems, has led to a more reasoned and effective use of technology for teaching.

A principal lesson from past experience has been the awareness that characteristics of a given medium affect both its perception and its use by the learner. Salomon (1981) argues, for instance, that each medium consists of its own unique symbol system for representing information, and that different media encourage the development of unique and varied information-processing skills. Not only is this message structured through the medium, but so are the learner's thought processes (Morariu, 1985). As a result, because the attributes of each medium differ, each requires different design considerations. Of greatest significance in this regard is the gradual acceptance of the concept that a single medium or mode of instruction will not necessarily solve complex learning problems that involve varied audiences. Present thinking is moving away from hasty media selection, although it is still typical of many education and training programs. In fact, with many new technologies, such as interactive workstations, media selection becomes the learner's task as various media are integrated into a single comprehensive learning system.

A new field within computer science is also contributing to the development of instructional design theory: artificial intelligence. Trying to make machines that think has shed new light and brought new appreciation for the complexity of human thought and learning. Seemingly simple learning tasks, or tasks that appear "natural," such as language learning, have proven even more complex than previously thought.

The concepts involved in creating complex computers, computers that mimic human processes, are beginning to include rough biological modeling of the human brain as well as logical modeling. For example, the basis of parallel processing, which is the latest major approach to computer architecture, builds on what is known about the neural structure of the brain, the interconnected web of separate neurons that collaborate in thought.

Changes in computer technology are significant for instructional design in that they provide a greater range and flexibility for computers used as learning tools. Early use of computers for teaching was limited by the technology to relatively mundane topics, simplistically approached. New computers, however, provide opportunities to develop complex models and simulations. They allow students to explore difficult concepts in science, social science, and the humanities at a level that allows Bruner's discovery techniques to be applied more generally in higher and continuing education. They also allow students to communicate with faculty, fellow students, and colleagues in powerful new ways, sharing ideas within and between universities or departments of a corporation. In some cases, for instance, corporations are using computers to facilitate and manage staff development by providing assessment, counseling, and instruction to employees at any location in a worldwide learning network.

On a grander scale, large communications companies are exploring the worldwide distribution of instruction through a learning network that will operate like a utility. One example, called the Education Utility, is being developed by the National Information Utilities Corporation (NIU) in conjunction with AT&T (Gooler, 1986). The concept of the Education Utility is to gather a "massive and dynamic reservoir of information and educational programming" from which individual teachers and learners can draw at will where they work or study. The information is delivered electronically in a variety of forms from computer software to video programming, and from information systems to electronic mail. The design challenge and the opportunity for colleges, universities, and corporations involves integrating such a powerful resource into the curriculum. The challenge for the utility involves understanding the design implications and the user needs that will make the system effective.

Of even more significance to instructional design is the contribution that computer science is making to understanding the ways in which information must be sequenced and assembled for optimal use. The amount of information that individuals need—either to prepare for employment in a modern technological setting or to keep their jobs—is growing rapidly. Computer science research is addressing these issues, and the results of that research contribute directly and indirectly to instructional design theory and practice. Information-mapping techniques, for instance, provide ways in which information can be organized in print format for easier access and use. These techniques derive directly from computer science, yet are being applied indirectly in varied new ways by instructional designers.

In terms of overall historical development, the foundation fields of instructional design obviously contribute to the discipline most significantly through their relationship to each other. The synergy that evolves through the grouping and regrouping of knowledge from each field encourages new perceptions. It is as if, by combining with each other, each field provided a new platform from which to view one of the most complex human activities—learning. Yet the results of this creation are practical, because instructional design guides real outcomes.

RESEARCH FINDINGS

Instructional design, then, is an emerging, applied, and creative science. It has evolved from a varied scientific foundation that values the development and validation of underlying principles. It argues for systematic gathering of information about learning and learners, and the formulation of theory and practice based on observation. The explicit assumption of instructional design is that its use will yield better instruction—more effective education and training (Richey, 1986). This means that it produces more learning, in less time, with greater learner satisfaction—a difficult argument to prove. There are ample endorsements for, but few solid research results directly supporting the use of, the instructional design process.

Many instructional design theorists have suggested that the field's lack of definite research findings results from a theory and a process that have too many variables and interactions to study under controlled conditions (Driscoll, 1984). Others have posited that it is the experimental research methodology itself that is too narrow. As has occurred in such fields as anthropology, they suggest that other kinds of research and evaluation, ranging from "explanatory observational studies" to "instructional treatment modeling" to "systems-oriented evaluation" need to be used to prove the effectiveness of instructional design (Reeves, 1986). This argument moves toward the concept, held by many educators, that education ultimately is art. Just as we cannot precisely and quantifiably analyze why a particular combination of color and form makes a great painting, so the complex and often intuitive leaps made by educators, whether working as instructional designers or classroom teachers, cannot be accurately and completely measured.

Whatever philosophic stance drives the argument, it seems clear that research about the effectiveness of instructional design has suffered from rapid growth, and consequent changing demands put on too few practitioners. Ironically, despite the lack of such validation, it is the enthusiasm of managers and training directors that has led to snowballing requests for instructional design, thus resulting in even *less* research.

The situation is analogous to the state of family practitioners in medicine. That field has grown so rapidly since its introduction to medical school curricula in the early 1970s that, while residents and graduates are much in demand, no one has stopped to validate through research whether they actually practice better medicine than the more traditional internists and pediatricians. Only as such fields enlarge, and sufficient numbers enter them over expanded periods of time, will the documenting research be developed. Until then, empirical data will have to be sufficient.

THE DIFFERENCES BETWEEN INSTRUCTIONAL DESIGN AND TRADITIONAL INSTRUCTION

The principal difference between instructional design and traditional approaches to education and training is philosophical. It relates to perspective, or point of view. It is a difference between viewing instruction from the learner's perspective or from the perspective of the content—an audience orientation versus a subject-matter orientation. Instructional design consciously and conscientiously keeps learner needs first among seemingly equal priorities. The resulting difference might be characterized as one between an audience-driven approach and a captive-audience approach.

This audience (or market) perspective consciously guides and influences all instructional design activities. It is also often visible in the outcomes. The essential perspective of the instructional designer promotes the following questions: *What does the learner know now? What does the learner need to know? What conditions will affect and facilitate his or her learning? How will you know when he or she learns it?* The answers to these questions are formulated as measurable goals and objectives. Those, in turn, are translated into instructional strategies and delivery systems. Finally, student performance is measured in relation to the goals and objectives.

In contrast, traditional instruction, typically based on a subject-matter perspective, asks different questions: *What is important about the content? What makes sense in the content? How can the instructor best present the content so the student will understand its place in the disciplines?* Answers to these questions generally yield something like a syllabus, or content outline, that ties content to a time line. The syllabus also refers students to related content. It rarely outlines learning strategies, however, and it almost never expresses expected student outcomes in measurable terms.

The significance of instructional design's consciously focusing on the learner does not suggest, of course, that effective instructors don't do that. In fact, a major characteristic of effective instructors is that they are constantly aware of student needs and student progress, and that they monitor student reactions throughout a course. However, as the diversity of student populations grows, this awareness is more difficult to put into practice. It is also difficult for an institution to maintain consistency across multiple sections of the same course, given the different styles and sensitivities of its faculty in regard to student needs.

A second major difference between instructional design and a traditional approach is that the designer consciously uses a systematic process to create instruction, whereas most traditionalists do not. According to McCombs (1986), Andrews and Goodson (1980) and Dick (1981) argue that the generic process consists of some variation on the following ten steps:

1. Needs assessment
2. Specification of broad goals and detailed objectives or learning outcomes
3. Development of criterion-referenced tests for assessing goals and objectives
4. Analysis of goals and objectives to determine types and sequencing of skills
5. Analysis of learner characteristics
6. Specification of instructional strategies based on task and learner analysis
7. Selection of media to implement strategies
8. Development of courseware based on strategies and media selected
9. Formative evaluation and revision of materials
10. Installation and maintainence of programs

(In Chapter Two, Van Patten formulates these steps into an operational process, tying it to outcomes and time lines.)

In whatever combination, instructional design is a creative, flexible, dynamic process; it is not rule-dependent, but fluid and responsive. McCombs (1986) even suggests that familiarity with the process, an intimacy with it, is essential to successful instructional design implementation. Without the intimacy, the process can become rote and less effective, much in the way a lack of an "inner voice" (to use Stephen Spender's phrase) limits the effectiveness of the poet (John-Steiner, 1987).

Subject matter, especially in scientific and technical fields, is expanding exponentially. To expect instructors to keep current in their own field, to understand new developments in learning theory and learning technology, *and* to be intimate with a coherent instructional design process, is unreasonable, given the typical reward structure and career path in education and business. In higher education, instructors are rewarded *first* for scholarly research, *second* for teaching. In corporations, instructors generally find themselves in front of a classroom because they were successful at their jobs. Corporate instructors typically know little about instruction and learning, and generally return to their regular jobs after a short teaching experience.

In contrast, the designer focuses on structuring and sequencing the events of instruction, and creating conditions that foster learning. This approach can actually enhance the integrity of the subject matter, because it views it in relationship to the learner, in terms of what the learner knows and what must be learned. Sequences are mapped according to the way a learner can comprehend the new materials in light of previous learning. Content is organized to be consistent not only with the principles of the subject area, but also with the principles of learning theory. Thus, while—initially—instructional design and traditional instruction may seem to be at odds, their distinctive emphases can in fact support and enhance each other.

CONCLUSION

Instructional design is an evolving discipline. Drawing on social science, management science, and information science, it is becoming both a body of knowledge about learning and learners, and a process for organizing and managing the development of complex instructional programs.

Given its history and orientation, particularly in relation to instructional technology, instructional design has made significant contributions to the uses of video and computers in education. More important, however, it has provided guidelines for the organization and presentation of all instruction—from lecture to independent study, from laboratory to library. Instructional design has caused educators and trainers to stop and think—to review their goals, to explore new delivery formats, and to reconceptualize traditional learning models. It makes educators and trainers more conscious of their instructional decisions, and helps to focus their instructional expectations.

REFERENCES

Andrews, D. H., and L. A. Goodson. 1980. A comparative analysis of models of instructional design. *Journal of Instructional Development* 3: 2–16.

Dick, W. 1981. Instructional design models: Future trends and issues. *Educational Technology* 7: 29–32.

Driscoll, M. P. 1984. Alternative paradigms for research in instructional systems. *Journal of Instructional Development* 7 (4).

Gagne, R. M., and L. J. Briggs. 1974. *Principles of instructional design* (2d ed.). New York: Holt, Rinehart & Winston.

Gardner, H. 1985. *Frames of mind: The theory of multiple intelligences.* New York: Basic Books.

Gooler, D. D. 1986. New York *The education utility: The power to revitalize education and society.* Englewood Cliffs, NJ: Educational Technology Publications.

Gruber, H. E. 1981. On the relation between 'aha experiences' and the construction of ideas. *History of Science* 19: 41–59.

John-Steiner, V. 1987. *Notebooks of the mind: Explorations of thinking.* New York: Harper and Row.

McCombs, B. L. 1986. The instructional systems development (ISD) model: A review of those factors critical to successful implementation. *Educational Communications Technology Journal* 34: 67–81.

Morariu, Janis. 1986. "Evaluating interactive videodisc instruction/training programs: A procedural evaluation model." The Proceedings of the Association for the Development of Computer-Based Instructional Systems. 27th International Conference, New Orleans. February 1986, pp. 171–174.

Reeves, T. C. 1986. Research and evaluation models for the study of interactive video. *Journal of Computer-Based Instruction* 13 (4): 102–106.

Richey, R. 1986. *The theoretical and conceptual bases of instructional design.* New York: Nichols Publishing.

Salomon, G. 1981. *Interaction of media, cognition and learning.* San Francisco: Jossey–Bass.

Scheffler, I. 1985. *Of human potential.* Boston: Routledge and Keagan Paul.

Schiffman, S. S. 1986. Instructional systems design: Five views of the field. *Journal of Instructional Development* 9: 14–21.

Sternberg, R. J. 1985. *Beyond IQ: A triarchic theory of human intelligence.* New York: Basic Books.

CHAPTER TWO

What Is Instructional Design?

James Van Patten

I remember my excitement when I was accepted to an instructional design doctoral program. I quickly got on the telephone to call my "significant others" and give them the good news. My enthusiasm slowly turned to confusion during each conversation as I began, "I've been accepted to the instructional design department!" "My goodness!" said my mother, "I didn't know you knew anything about buildings." My father wondered aloud, "Gee, can you make a living at it, or is it one of those things where all you'll be able to do is teach instructional design to someone else?" My best friend asked, "So, you'll be designing bridges and roads and things like that?" My wife-to-be was enthusiastic: "Oh good," she said, "I've never been very good at picking out furniture and colors and things like that."

My initial attempts to differentiate instructional design from other design disciplines failed. Mostly, I believe, because I wasn't too sure of exactly what instructional design was, and how it differed from other design sciences. I knew it was housed in the school of education, and that it combined many of the disciplines I enjoyed: photography, writing, psychology, and design. As I began my studies, I hoped the faculty could help me not only become an instructional designer, but also understand when instructional design was needed, for what situations, and by whom.

I remember my excitement upon graduation from the instructional design doctoral program. Years of disciplined inquiry had armed me with myriad facts, concepts, principles, and procedures concerning instructional design, psychology, media, statistics, and educational evaluation (though you'd never have known it, given the way I was roughed up during my dissertation defense). I took part in semester-long investigations of the differences between educational evaluation and descriptive research; of the application of *modus tolens* logic to research design; of how Hannah Arendt's notion of "the human condition" can be applied to educational systems; and of the fact that "data" is plural. More germane to the actual practice of instructional design, I also learned about writing instructional objectives, working with subject matter experts (SMEs), conducting task and content analyses, and managing instructional design projects.

I found it very interesting that, while at the university, most of my fellow students asked the same basic question I asked: "What exactly is instructional design?" When asked, the faculty often answered with some obfuscatory phrase, like "It depends on your perspective."

Armed with a desire to begin using my knowledge and skills, I sought employment as an instructional designer with various colleges, universities, and companies. As might be expected in 1981, I found few advertisements for "instructional designers." Most higher-education positions were advertised as "Curriculum Specialists," or "Media Specialists." These institutions had decided that instructional design was somehow related to one's expertise in a particular discipline (e.g., "I need someone to design the new creative writing curriculum. What short stories have you published?") or a particular technology (e.g., "We need someone to make instructional films and videotapes. Do you have a demo reel I can see?"). Business and industry usually advertised for "Technical Writers," "Trainers," or "Instructors." These companies had defined instructional design either as related to one's skill in a particular area (e.g., "We need someone to write up the documentation for our new products. What do you know about multiplexed 32-bit parallel processors?") or related to one's skills in front of a class (e.g., "We need someone to train our salespeople. What kind of stand-up training have you done—and, by the way, where did you sell?").

Without exception, my interviewers were unimpressed that I was skilled in writing objectives and in task and needs analysis, or that I could draw content out of SMEs and organize it into effective and efficient instruction, or that I could manage an instructional design project. They became particularly suspicious when I assured them that I could create "whatever solution the education or training problem required" regardless of the fact that I had no expertise in the content area. Again and again I was asked, "If you don't teach, aren't an expert, and don't really write, what exactly is it that you do?" I realized that my livelihood depended on my ability to answer that nagging old question, "What exactly is instructional design?" Luckily for me, I found an answer—and have been gainfully employed as an instructional designer ever since.

In the intervening years, I've met many instructional designers in industry, government agencies, and educational institutions. I make it a point to ask *them*, "What exactly is instructional design?" Though I don't get a consistent answer, primarily because the field is such a complex amalgam and is changing so rapidly, I have seen a pattern emerge. Rather than present an answer to "The Question," most designers respond by providing their description of three dimensions of instructional design: the *process*, the *products*, and the *skills* required by the designer.

A FAMILY OF DESIGNERS
A Common Process

Instructional design is a member of a large family of design sciences. Other members of this family include medicine, architecture, industrial design, and the various other engineering disciplines (such as mechanical and electrical engineering). One of the similarities among these design sciences is the process they use to borrow scientific principles, mix those principles with other information, and apply the result to meet human needs.

The first dimension common to all instructional designers is this process, which has been called the engineering process or systems model. Using this model, a specific goal is met by prescribing, designing, and implementing a carefully designed intervention. Using this definition, a physician engineers a patient's health, an architect engineers a client's space, and an instructional designer engineers a client's knowledge and skill.

There are three main components to the overall design/engineering process: *identify the problem, design a solution, and implement the solution.* Though there is little agreement among designers when specific activities occur in the process (e.g., "Exactly when do I write behavioral objectives?"), there is little disagreement concerning the overall process. The engineering process is really only disciplined common sense in that it is necessary to identify a problem before one can design and implement its solution.

The information required by the various design and engineering disciplines is also similar. In general, all designers/engineers use three types of information: (1) *what they know;* (2) *what they observe;* and (3) *what they feel.* What designers/engineers know is the body of scientifically generated theories, principles, and facts they can apply to the problem. What they observe is the specific problem at hand and all the interrelated variables that define it. What they feel is their intuition (gained from experience), which they use to elevate a good, technically sound solution to a great, "artistic" solution. (For the remainder of this chapter, *design* and *designer* should be considered synonymous with *engineering* and *engineer.*)

We can summarize the process of designing by stating that it uses knowledge, observation, and intuition to identify a problem, and then to design and implement a solution. For example, physicians take the facts and principles generated by the various biological sciences (such as morphology or pharmacology) and relate them to their knowledge of a particular patient, and their experience with similar patients. They then *design* a solution to that specific patient's needs, and implement it. Similarly, architects take the facts and principles generated by such various sciences as geometry, anthropology, or metallurgy and relate that information to their knowledge of a particular client and their experience with similar clients. They then design a solution to that specific client's needs, and implement it.

Instructional designers follow the same general process. They take facts and principles from such sciences as psychology or linguistics and relate that information to knowledge of a specific client's needs and their experience with similar clients and needs. They then design and implement a solution. Whereas physicians engineer health, and architects engineer space, instructional designers engineer human performance.

Therefore, a partial answer to "The Question" is, "Instructional designers *engineer* solutions to performance problems."

A Common Product

The second common characteristic of designers is that they produce solutions to problems or needs. There are two criteria for successfully "engineered" solutions: *effectiveness* (the solution must meet the need, close the gap, or solve the problem) and *efficiency* (the solution must bear an acceptable cost). In general, designers maximize the effectiveness of their solutions by maximizing all the "positive" components of an engineered solution. They maximize the efficiency of their solutions by minimizing all the "negative" components of a solution (for example, by minimizing required time, dollars, lost opportunities, ill will, pain and suffering, and political "black eyes"). Therefore, to design the best possible solution, designers must know three things: (1) as much as possible about the problem or need; (2) the impact of the problem or need; and (3) an acceptable level of cost, given the problem and its effects.

Let me cite an example. When an architect wins a bid to design a warehouse, he or she must get three important pieces of information: (1) What need is the building supposed to meet? (2) How does this need affect the client? (E.g., What happens if the client doesn't build the warehouse?) (3) What's an acceptable cost, given the need and its impact? The warehouse must be designed to meet these criteria. Similarly, designs generated by instructional designers or physicians must also meet identified needs for acceptable costs, given the effects.

In the design process, the first step is identifying the need. Given that effective and efficient products are required, this means that, to identify needs, designers must also identify the impact of needs, and the acceptable costs of solutions. Unfortunately, neither a need, its impact, or its costs are very well understood at the beginning of most design projects. And, because most design projects have neither the time nor the money for an in-depth research phase to get the required information, the project begins anyway. Because of this, most initial designs are usually somewhat uninformed—and, if implemented as originally conceived, probably prove not particularly effective or efficient. To remedy this problem, designers use the engineering process to provide the required need, impact, and cost information throughout the project.

Therefore, when one is asked what the products of design are, one possible answer is: "Designers create a *series of products* throughout the design process. Each of these products is evaluated to generate the required need, impact, and cost information. In this way, designers increase their understanding of the solution's effectiveness and efficiency requirements and fine-tune each subsequent 'product' in the process." Most important to remember is that the series of products is generally the same whether the designer is a physician, engineer, architect, or instructional designer.

Given the general design process of identifying the need, designing the solution, and implementing the solution, there are three basic products—one for each phase. Though the terminology may differ between design disciplines, the function of each product is similar: (1) identify the need with an analysis report; (2) design the solution with a design specification; and (3) develop and implement the required solution.

For example, to produce a house, an architect analyzes the need, impacts, and costs by interviewing the client, researching the site, and gathering other basic information. He or she returns with an analysis report that lists the required characteristics of the house (e.g., square footage, ceiling heights, general construction materials), a floor plan, and probably a pen-and-ink rendering of the exterior. The architect then helps the client evaluate these first products—as in this imaginary scenario: "How do you like the four bedrooms and two baths?" "What?" asks the client. "I want three bedrooms and three baths!" "So, you're not planning on any more children, or expanding a bedroom into a study?" queries the architect. "Well now," responds the client, "you may have a point there. What would it cost to have four bedrooms and three baths?"

The architect takes additional information gleaned from the first products, and creates a blueprint (the design specification). He or she returns to the client and then, together, they evaluate the blueprint. (For example, the architect observes, "I've specified 2 × 6 walls for R19 insulation, but that will raise the cost by $3,000." "I think that's money well spent," states the client. "Can we save the $3,000 somewhere else?" "Yes, I think so," replies the architect. "I believe we can come down a few levels in quality on the carpeting in the children's rooms and in the family room, as long as we increase the quality in the pads." "Fine, let's do it.")

The architect revises the blueprints, clears all decisions with the client, and begins building the house. Even though the house is under construction, the architect requests and receives more information at specific times, such as the color of the rugs, the placement of the wall outlets, or the size of the deck. In this way, the eventual product (the house) meets both effectiveness and efficiency requirements. The interim products (the floor plan and the blueprint) are used to gain more information about needs, impacts, and costs while the project is under way.

Given the products of design, a refinement to answering "The Question" is: "Instructional designers engineer efficient and effective solutions to human performance needs."

Uncommon Skills

The third quality common to the design sciences is the varied, even eclectic, skills required of their practitioners. Architects, physicians, engineers, and instructional designers are required to operate from different frames of reference at different times. Sometimes they are artists, their creative solutions inspired by something more than facts and observations. At other times they are craftsmen, constructing and polishing a solution based on their skill and the feedback they receive about their interim products. Designers often are project managers, directing the work of others as their designs are implemented. Sometimes they are scientists, employing rigorous scientific methods to evaluate information or to validate a component of their design.

Designers must maintain a high level of skill and knowledge in many different areas to successfully engineer and implement a solution. Skill inventories and job descriptions for physicians, architects, engineers, and instructional designers read too much like the Boy Scout Oath (trustworthy, loyal, . . .) to be of much practical use. But because all designers are in the business of creating solutions, their most critical skill must be their ability to precisely understand the need, its effects, and its costs. To do this, designers use two basic skills: gathering relevant information, and evaluating it in terms of what they "know" to be right, what they "hear or see" to be right, and what they "feel" to be right.

Designers' solutions contain a mix of scientific knowledge (what they know), observation (what they see and hear), and intuition (what they feel). These three types of information loosely define the science, craft, and art of design. As designed solutions are composed of some level of each of these three types of information, so too are designers part scientist, part craftsperson, and part artist.

Therefore, the final refinement to answering "The Question" is, "Instructional designers generate and evaluate information to engineer efficient and effective solutions to knowledge and skill needs."

Summary

Instructional designers are members of a larger family of designers who use an engineering process to create solutions. As part of this process, this family of designers creates a set of products throughout the life of a project that generate and evaluate information concerning the need, its impact on a client, and the acceptable costs of the solution. Designers use scientific principles and theories, as well as observation and intuition, to create the most effective and efficient solutions possible. The crucial skill of the most successful designers is their ability to identify and meet a need by generating and evaluating information.

INSTRUCTIONAL DESIGN: THE PROCESS, THE PRODUCTS, AND THE INSTRUCTIONAL DESIGNER
The Process: Instructional Systems Development

The most widely accepted process for designing instruction is the Instructional Systems Development (ISD) model. Basically, this model assumes that designers will never know all they need to know at the beginning of a project. So, the project is constructed to generate the required information at the required time. One might say that the unspoken motto of ISD is, "Make sure the right questions get answered by the right people at the right time."

To do this, ISD breaks the development process into a set of specific phases, each with its own "deliverable," or product. At the end of the phase, the deliverable is evaluated and revised before moving on to the next phase. The evaluations that occur after each phase are called "formative" evaluations, because their results will be used to formulate subsequent steps. The evaluation that occurs at the end of the entire process is called a "summative" evaluation. Though most institutions involved with instructional design have their own version of the ISD model, all ISD models are based on the following four-part sequence: (1) identify the need; (2) design the solution; (3) implement the solution; and (4) evaluate the solution.

Most differences among ISD models seem to be due to the nature of the final product. For example, when creating computer-based instruction, it is often useful to create the course "on paper" first. This paper course is evaluated and tested. Similarly, when creating instructional videotapes or films, designers usually create a storyboard that is evaluated. When creating paper-based instructional materials, these steps are not needed. Here is an example of an ISD process used to create paper-based instructional materials:

Phase	Deliverable	Created by	Evaluated by*
Analysis	Analysis Report	Designer/Evaluator	Client
Design	Specification	Designer	Client/SME
Development	Draft materials	Developer/Designer	Client/SME
Pilot test	Test results	Designer/Evaluator	Client/SME
Revision	Final materials	Developer/Editor	Client/SME
Production	Camera-ready	Editor/Graphics	Client/SME
Duplication	Inventory	Graphics/Printer	Client/Administrator
Implementation	Training begins	Instructor/Administrator	Client
Maintenance	Periodic Evaluations	Instructor/Designer Administrator/Evaluator	Client

*The client is usually a collection of people including the person who "owns" the need. Others involved as clients include managers, administrators, funders, and outside "experts." One of the first jobs of the designer is to find out who the real "client" is. Similarly, the subject matter expert (SME) is also usually a collection of people including the "expert" as well as high performers (i.e., examples of desired performance), managers, and even low performers (i.e., examples of undesirable performance). One delicate task of the designer is to find out if the "expert" is really that. Also, and more importantly, the designer must find out which SMEs are committed to the success of the project. There's nothing worse than an ISD project with a fuzzy client and an uncommitted SME.

Phase 1: Analysis

The analysis phase is conducted to define as precisely as possible the nature of the training problem. Because it happens first, it is sometimes called the "front-end" analysis. It is undertaken not only to describe the problem, but also to "add value" by helping the client to understand the issues affecting performance, and by separating the instructional issues from other issues (such as motivational or organizational issues). The analysis report contains a pragmatic look at the audience, their performance discrepancy, the content required to eliminate the discrepancy, the organization, the available resources, and anything else that will affect the design of the solution. The table of contents for the analysis report might look like this:

The Challenge

The performance discrepancy, its effects on the organization and/or individual, and the available resources

Audience Description
Current Skills
Learning History
Motivational Supports/Impediments to Success
Organizational Supports/Impediments to Success

Task/Job Description or Educational Goals

The skills and/or knowledge required to eliminate the performance discrepancy

What Is Instructional Design? 23

Implementation Issues
Facilities/Environment
Faculty/Instructors
Administrative Support

Evaluation Plan

The analysis report is reviewed by the client and evaluated for the accuracy of its descriptions and definitions. No "solution" is described in the analysis report—only the need, its impacts, and the resources available to meet the need are described.

Phase 2: Design

The design phase is where the designer first attempts a solution by creating a design specification. Using the architect analogy, this is where the designer creates the "floor plan" and the "pen-and-ink rendering." The table of contents for a design specification might look like this:

Summary of Needs

Course Goals/Objectives

Content Description
Task Description (hierarchy or flow chart)
Content Description (taxonomy or network concepts)
Attitude Inventory (e.g., safety, teamwork, appreciation)
Content Outline (a list of content topics and general instructional sequence)

Course Description
Length
Class Size
Design Strategy (e.g., expository, discovery, simulation)
Delivery Strategy (e.g., lecture, film, self-study)
Testing Strategy
Remediation
Special Features

Implementation Requirements
Facilities
Equipment
Instructors
Instructor Training
Administrators

Evaluation Plan

The design specification is evaluated by the client and SME for the effectiveness and efficiency of the solution it describes. Because design specifications are almost always revised, it is important that the content revisions find their way throughout the document, specifically into budget and time lines.

Phase 3: Development

After the design is evaluated and revised, the content is fleshed out. Again, using the architect analogy, the floor plan is expanded into a blueprint. For the instructional designer, this means the design specification is expanded into draft instructional materials. Though many designers argue about the composition of instruction, it is safe to say that all instruction has at least four elements—*definitions, examples, practice,* and *everything else*. Therefore, there are often four subphases to the development phase:

1. *Develop definitions for each content topic.* The definition for each concept, fact, principle, and procedure identified in the design specification is written, usually by the SME. Each definition is two to three sentences long. Because the definitions are the "meat" of the instruction, they often are reviewed and revised by the client and SME before the rest of the instruction is developed.
2. *Develop examples for each definition.* At least two examples are written for each of the defined topics, again usually by the SME. Each example, two to three sentences long, is also reviewed and revised.
3. *Develop ways of practicing each content topic.* Specific practice exercises are written so that students can remember and apply the definitions and examples. As with the other phases, the practice exercises are reviewed and revised.
4. *Develop everything else.* All of the other components of instruction are developed, such as advance organizers, transitions, summaries, synthesizers, and mnemonic devices.

After all the instruction is fleshed out, the final document is reviewed and revised. If the design includes film, then the final development document contains scripts and storyboards. If the design calls for computer-based components, then it also includes a flow chart.

Phase 4: Pilot Test, and
Phase 5: Revision

These two phases occur in an iterative loop until the instruction is judged "good enough." During the pilot test, the draft materials are used by members of the target population—whose performance, in turn, is evaluated.

The formal pilot test report—which, in general, is the final "formative" evaluation point in the project—should be submitted and reviewed. The purpose of the report is to make sure that all required changes are made *before* the spending of a lot of money via putting the instructional materials into production. The table of contents for a pilot test report might look like this:

Project Description
Summary of Needs
Summary of Course Goals/Objectives
Summary Course Description

Pilot Test Description
Goals
Evaluation Issues
Methods

Pilot Test Results

Recommendations

Revised Project Plan (If Required)

Phase 6: Production

The instructional materials are put into final production. If the materials are text based, then all graphics are drawn, all text is edited and pasted up, and a single camera-ready master is produced. All additional media are produced as well, such as computer programs, overhead transparencies, films or videotapes, and models or exhibits. The client conducts a final review of all materials in order to decide whether or not to begin duplication.

Phase 7: Duplication

When the "camera ready" master materials generated in the production phase are accepted, the course materials are duplicated as necessary, resulting in an inventory of materials. The size and nature of the inventory is evaluated by the client and/or by an administrator.

Phase 8: Implementation, and
Phase 9: Maintenance

Implementation and maintenance occur in a "summative" iterative loop, much as the pilot test and revision occur in a "formative" iterative loop. After duplication, course materials are distributed and instruction begins. If instructors and course administrators are required, then training is provided. Implementation is an ongoing activity that lasts until the skill and/or knowledge need is met, or the course materials become outdated. During implementation, it is important to ensure that the course is maintained so that it is still as effective and efficient as originally planned. Periodic midcourse corrections may be taken as required. This process should be as formal as possible, triggered by a scheduled evaluation of the instruction's success.

The end product of the ISD process is a set of materials that will effectively and efficiently meet a skill or knowledge need. The ISD process is focused on managing information and decisions to ensure that the need is correctly identified and met. However, the process does not necessarily require instructional designers as project managers; it only requires good project managers.

Though (as we saw earlier) most instructional designers spend their time somewhere within the instructional system's development process, that process is not specific to instructional design. What really differentiates instructional designers from other designers is the nature of what they design—the elements of the instructional designers' end product.

The Products: The Instructional Design

Though we have a pretty good definition of what instructional designers create (efficient and effective solutions to knowledge and skill needs), we do not know exactly what instructional designers *design*. That is, if one were to pay a designer "by the pound," what would the designer deliver? The seductively simple answer is: "Why, designers make designs!" And while this answer is true, it is far from complete.

As with all other designers, instructional designers create designs. That is, they design solutions. Just as engineers create design specifications, and architects create blueprints, and physicians create treatments, instructional designers create design specifications. It is what instructional designers include in their designs that makes them different from other designers. So, what do instructional designers design?

Most of the attributes of an instructional design are determined by the specific theories, principles, and facts that the designer uses to create the design. There are two types of scientific information, *descriptive* and *prescriptive*. The main difference lies in their goals. Descriptive science aims to describe a system. Prescriptive science aims to prescribe actions that can be taken on that system to yield a desired result.

For example, where the descriptive science of biology describes the components and functions of an organism, the theories and principles of the prescriptive science of medicine prescribe a medical intervention. That is, biology describes organisms, whereas medicine prescribes cures. Similarly, where metallurgy describes the tensile strength of steel, architectural principles prescribe how steel can be used to support a skyscraper or build a bridge.

In this same manner, instructional designers use the descriptive principles of psychology that describe the components and functions of learning. Instructional designers also use the prescriptive principles of instructional science that prescribe an instructional "cure." Where physicians' cures are constructed from drugs, exercise, diet, and surgery, instructional designers' cures (depending on whose principles and theories you use) are constructed from definitions, examples, practices, and everything else.

In each of the design sciences, scientific information generated by basic research is combined with information generated by applied research in that field. The goal of descriptive sciences, such as psychology, is to *describe*—the more accurately and in detail the better. The goal of prescriptive sciences, such as instructional science, is to *prescribe*—the more efficiently and effectively the better. Thus, the product of instructional design is created from prescriptive and descriptive scientific principles as well as from observation and intuition. Even with this definition (perhaps because of it), however, one doesn't really know what any particular designer will come up with at the end of the design phase. What is required is a common set of attributes for instructional design.

What Is Instructional Design? 27

To have a design, one must have two things: (1) a set of elements that require designing; and (2) a principle with which to organize (design) them. For example, when designing a piece of music, the composer selects a set of tones and spaces, and a principle for designing them. Over the years, groups of tones have been identified (e.g., modes and scales) along with useful organizing principles (e.g., sonata or rondo).

Similarly, architects design buildings from sets of solids and spaces, and principles for organizing them. There are types of spaces (communal areas, sleeping areas, kitchens, bathrooms, storage areas, heating/cooling areas, etc.), and types of organizing principles (a baroque church, a Cape Cod house, an office building).

As we shall now see, instructional designers also have a variety of instructional elements and organizing principles they can choose from.

The Instructional Elements

It is not easy to identify the list of instructional elements, because not many designers agree on what should be listed. Though most all agree that composers deal in tones, architects in spaces, and physicians in "life style" (recall that a physician's design is made up of drugs, nutrition, exercise, etc.), what is it that instructional designers deal in? Which elements compose the design?

Borrowing from cognitive psychology and instructional theory, one can posit four basic elements: definitions, examples, practice, and everything else. The definitions, examples, and practice are the electron, proton, and neutron of the instructional atom. Everything else is the gravity, nucleic forces, and electrical charges that make the whole thing work. As with the atom, we know something about the electrons, protons, and neutrons, but we don't know that much about everything else—or even if we've found everything else.

Definitions are the "meat" of instruction. They are what we want people to understand and use when they are done. In the final analysis, the rest of the instructional elements are methods to help people to learn and apply the definitions. Because research and common sense suggest that examples and practice increase the efficiency and effectiveness of instruction, they are included as primary elements of instruction.

The fourth group, everything else, is comprised of the other instructional devices that also contribute to efficiency and effectiveness. Some of these are tables of contents, summaries, advance organizers, and synthesizers. Whether or not designers choose to include some or all of the everything else in their designs is a matter of personal preference.

To summarize: Instructional designers deal in definitions, and in the examples and practice and everything else that increases the efficiency and effectiveness of learning and using the definitions.

The Organizing Principles

Once a designer has identified the set of definitions, examples, practice, and everything else that needs to be designed, he or she must select an organizing principle to create the design. As with the instructional elements, there are different opinions regarding appropriate organizing principles. In general, the instruction is constructed so that it is consistent with one of two existing structures: a structure based upon the learner, or a structure based upon the content.

In general, instructional designs that use organizing principles based on the learner try to capitalize on the learner's existing knowledge structure and to fit the instruction into it. A second type of learner structure is based on the structure of the learner's performance. These designs are organized according to how learners will use the content—not how they will learn or remember it.

Instructional designs based on content capitalize on the content's existing structure. These designs may use relational nets, concept taxonomies, or historical sequence to organize the elements.

Selecting the appropriate organizing principles and elements represents the heart of the instructional designer's job. For example, this is where the designer uses his or her *scientific information* to select the number and nature of examples for a concept classification problem. This is where the designer uses his or her *craft* to create a polished set of tasks for creating a "forward chaining" instructional sequence. This is also where designers use their *art* to specify just the right practice session that simulates a group decision-making process.

What designers make, then, are design specifications. But these design specifications specify the selection and organization of appropriate definitions, examples, practice, and everything else that maximizes the effectiveness and efficiency of a solution to a knowledge and/or skill need.

The Instructional Designer

Because I was a newly graduated Ph.D. in instructional design looking for work, I was repeatedly asked, "If you don't teach, aren't an expert, and don't really write, what exactly is it that you do?" I realized that if I were in the position of my interrogators I wouldn't know why I should hire a person like me either. After all, what value did I add to the organization? And even if I did agree that the "selection and organization of the appropriate definitions, examples, and practices that maximize the effectiveness and efficiency of a solution to a knowledge and/or skill need" were valuable, how would I know if someone was actually good at it?

Paradoxically, (perhaps because task analyses are our stock-in-trade), instructional designers haven't been able to come up with a useful task analylsis of instructional design. (If we try, we violate a basic rule: "Don't let the subject-matter expert do the design. SMEs don't know where to start or where to stop." We'd probably be better off letting a mechanical engineer do a task analysis of instructional design.) Most of the competency studies get into too much detail, or are too specific to a particular industry or context (e.g., what it takes to create lecture courses at a university; or the skills required to design interactive video).

What I will do here is describe what I think makes designers successful. I will not attempt a taxonomy or competency list. I will present a set of general *knowledge, skills,* and *attitudes* I'm glad I have (or wish I had). In general, I believe successful designers know how to generate, evaluate, and communicate information. They have good questioning, listening, speaking, and writing skills, and they are curious about the content and really care whether or not the learner is successful with it.

Knowledge

Instructional designers are required to generate and organize large amounts of information. This information comes from many different sources and exists in many different shapes. Most of it comes in the form of memos, reports, inventories, manuals, and other training materials. Additional information usually is required, and must be generated through phoned and live interviews, library research, or other fugitive-information sources. Perhaps most important, information concerning clients' and SMEs' feelings and concerns about project deliverables must be ferreted out. Instructional designers must also have knowledge of available design alternatives. For example, designers should be able to develop at least three different types of task analysis, so they can match the type of analysis with both the client and the instructional context. These types might include a learning prerequisite analysis, a part-to-whole analysis, and a flow-charted information-processing analysis.

It is important for designers to evaluate all the information they receive. This is done in many ways, from formal research projects to off-the-cuff cross-checking. Perhaps the greater part of the information to be evaluated is the content information that designers receive from SMEs. Most of this evaluation concerns separating the "nice to know" from the "need to know." It is important that none of the SMEs' assumptions go unchallenged. In addition, designers should not discount an information source because it is deemed not credible by others: It is often the learners who know best which training goals are appropriate. Unfortunately, most clients and SMEs refuse to ask them or don't believe them.

After information is generated and evaluated, it needs to be communicated to three different groups of people: (1) clients/SMEs, in the form of formal deliverables—such as a design specification or informal memos or presentations; (2) learners, in the form of instruction; and (3) project team members, in the form of directions, formal deliverables, and hallway conversations.

Skills

Because of the informational nature of instructional designers' activities, all communication skills are important. Specifically, designers are required to have excellent (1) questioning skills, to squeeze the content out of the SME; (2) listening skills, to evaluate what they hear (e.g., does what people tell you make sense? Is it really what they mean?); (3) speaking skills, to present design specifications, explain content hierarchies (and to try to explain instructional design to a client); and (4) writing skills, to create the project deliverables and—because most instruction is still written—to create the instruction.

I doubt that specific instructional design skills are really that important in themselves. These skills result from knowing alternatives and then, with other skills, creating a design in the mode of one of the alternatives. For example, one's task analysis skill is the result of (1) knowing what type of task analysis to choose, given a particular context; and (2) one's ability to question/listen with an SME to create the chosen task analysis.

Most "instructional design skills," such as task analysis, writing objectives, or sequencing content, are fairly easy to acquire. What is difficult is knowing which type of objective, analysis, or sequence to use in a given situation.

Attitudes

Attitudes are usually given only perfunctory discussion in instruction or in job analyses. However, the attitudes of instructional designers are important in determining their success. In addition to the attitudes that separate good employees from average ones (e.g., discipline, a willingness to take responsibility), there are three important attitudes separating good instructional designers from great ones: (1) a feeling that a process is as important as an outcome; (2) an interest in ensuring that people actually learn something and succeed; and (3) a general curiosity.

It is important for designers to be comfortable with the ambiguity often found early in the ISD process. This ambiguity about goals, needs, effects, and costs can be resolved only through the ISD process itself. If the designer is too much "goal oriented," many of the important project questions may never be answered. Therefore, designers must appreciate the importance of a design meeting wherein their first draft designs are torn apart. Similarly, because instruction is a process the learner uses to become competent, the designer must appreciate the "slow changes over time" that an instructional process facilitates. It is this process, after all, that the designer creates.

It is easy to create a design to answer the requests of the SME and the client. It is seldom easy to create a design that meets the needs of the SME, the client, *and* the learner. Often, unfortunately, the only advocate for the learner's point of view is the instructional designer. If the designer doesn't care about the learner's situation, the instruction will probably not succeed. For example, a client decides to train 4,000 people using thirty-five hours of computer-based instruction (CBI). I've never known anyone to sit through one week of seven-hour training days of CBI and remain cogent. Therefore, the designer must question the client's decision, perhaps wondering aloud to the client, "I wonder how these people will feel after five straight seven-hour days of CBI?"

Finally, instructional designers should have a general curiosity about things. That is, they need to get excited about the content, regardless of what it is. Designers need not be experts about the content, they need only to be interested in it. For example, they should get excited about how bankers sell noncredit services. Or, they should really want to find out how potline operators siphon the aluminum from a Hall pot, or what is the important difference between a rondo and a sonata. Though these examples may seem somewhat extreme, they typify projects in which any designer might be involved.

Summary

So, what is instructional design? It is a process and a set of products, brought about by a designer with specific skills. The process concerns the generation and evaluation of information for engineering efficient and effective solutions to knowledge and skill needs. The products of instructional design are project-specific in that they are design specifications for a particular knowledge or skill need. They specify the selection and organization of appropriate definitions, examples, practice, and everything else that maximizes the effectiveness and efficiency of a solution to a knowledge and/or skill need. Designers are people who know how to generate, evaluate, and communicate information. They have good questioning, listening, speaking, and writing skills. They are curious about the content of each instructional situation, and personally care whether or not the learner successfully acquires the necessary knowledge or skill.

CHAPTER THREE

Assessing the Needs

Mary Walshok

On September 10, 1987, *The New York Times Magazine* included a special advertising supplement, paid for by the National Alliance for Business, on the growing demand for education—education for youth and minorities lacking basic skills; for a work force in need of retooling; for adults unprepared for the changes resulting from technological innovations and a global economy. It was time for those of us who are formally responsible for adult and continuing education and training in the United States to reflect on the trends giving rise to new demands for knowledge on the one hand, and new constituencies for learning on the other.

In a book on applying instructional design and new technologies to the teaching/learning enterprise, it is important to consider early the larger questions of what we need to teach, and to whom. Even if one were to agree that instructional design can provide the key to more effective education and training, why bother with it? Following the instructional design process, will a needs assessment demonstrate compelling reasons to motivate our corporations, government agencies, and educational institutions to investigate and develop new and more effective educational methods? To find out, we need to focus on North America's emerging knowledge needs and the diversifying constituencies seeking and needing education.

Such a discussion must of necessity be placed in a context of broader social and economic change. Recurrent change has characterized the postindustrial world. New policy directions and organizational transformations may have to take place to serve the new knowledge demands and the newly emerging groups needing education. These issues concern not only postsecondary education but also many sectors of our society, as the *Times* advertising supplement so dramatically demonstrated. Employers in 1987 spent an estimated $210 billion on formal and informal education and training—an amount almost equal to U.S. expenditures on formal education in our schools. However, there is little articulation between the educational efforts of employers and those of formal school systems. Even worse is the poor articulation between the various levels of formal schooling—K–12; community and junior colleges; four-year colleges and major universities; and adult, continuing education, and extension services.

This chapter seeks to assess the teaching and learning challenges we will confront in the decades ahead as a consequence of important social, political, and economic trends. As such it also opens the door to a more focused discussion of how instructional design methodologies and technologies can meet these challenges, the central goal of this book. After a brief overview of trends affecting future learning needs, we will move to a more detailed discussion of the knowledge demands and learning constituencies emerging as a result of these trends. The chapter will conclude with some suggestions about how managers, educators, and policymakers can develop the organizational and technical capacities to respond to these recurrent needs for education. While the discussion that follows will focus on the United States, the impact of many similar changes will be felt in most postindustrial nations.

SIGNIFICANT TRENDS AFFECTING FUTURE LEARNING NEEDS
Demographic Changes

Social and economic changes affecting this country, and perhaps the entire globe, have profound implications for education. In the United States, Harold Hodgkinson of the American Council on Education has been conducting demographic analyses of individual states that project the profile of the American population by region, age, race, and income into the twenty-first century. His summaries provide a picture that differs significantly from the population profile of this nation through most of the twentieth century. In numerous speeches, Hodgkinson has asserted that as far as population is concerned, the future is already here. The proportion of minorities in the U.S. population is rapidly approaching 30 percent, and among children and young adults in California it is already 50 percent. A map, which appears in many of his reports and is reprinted in Figure 3.1, dramatically demonstrates the changing population mix in this nation.

These data show that the socioeconomic characteristics of most minorities in the United States are quite different from those of traditional college students and adults in continuing education and extension programs. High-school dropout rates are much higher, especially for Hispanics and blacks. College completion rates are much lower, and the overall economic and social hazards of being a black or Hispanic youth in the United States are startling when one looks at other hard data. One child in five lives in poverty today, and children in poverty are one-third less likely to graduate from high school. Fifty percent of all black females are pregnant by age twenty, and the percentages for white and Hispanic females are rising. The high-school dropout rates are close to 25 percent nationally, and as much as 50 percent in some cities. The aforementioned *New York Times* supplement adds to these disturbing figures by citing as a major danger sign the fact that 50 percent of all new jobs will require

Figure 3.1. *Minority enrollment as percent of public elementary/secondary school enrollment, by state.*

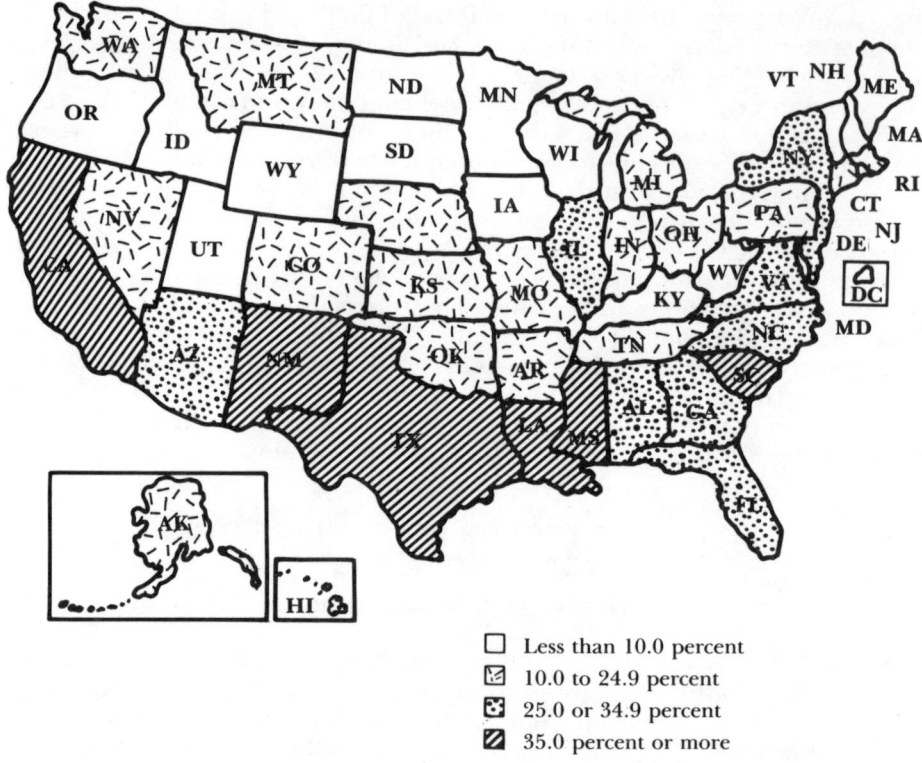

☐ Less than 10.0 percent
▨ 10.0 to 24.9 percent
▩ 25.0 or 34.9 percent
▨ 35.0 percent or more

Percent minority enrollment in public elementary secondary schools was generally greatest in the Southern and Southwestern States and in California. The percent black enrollment was highest in the Southern States while the percent Hispanic enrollment was highest in New Mexico, Texas, California, and Arizona.
(The Condition of Education, 1984 edition. A Statistical Report by the National Center for Education Statistics.)

education beyond high school, and 30 percent will require a college degree. Yet it states:

- 23 million adults are functionally illiterate in America today. Another 47 million are borderline illiterates.
- 80 percent of the new entrants to the labor force will be minorities, women, and immigrants, traditionally the populations least prepared to work.
- Over 1 million youths drop out of school each year. Dropout rates of many urban schools are close to 50 percent.
- The youth unemployment rate is triple the overall unemployment rate.

It goes on to point out that:

- 75 percent of those who will be working in the year 2000 are already in the work force. [Yet:]
- 11.5 million American workers lost their jobs between 1979 and 1984 through job shrinkage.
- 20 to 40 percent of dislocated workers are functionally illiterate.

In any review of demographic trends, data on both population profiles and job-market shifts also point out that 80 percent of the new workers by the year 2000 will be women, minorities, and immigrants. The majority of these new workers will not have been the beneficiaries of traditional educational experiences and preparation for work. In fact, a report recently released by the Labor Department, *Workforce 2000: Work and Workers for the Twenty-First Century*, points out this fact and notes that only 15 percent of all new workers between now and 2000 will be native white men. Given this changing labor pool, employers will have to forego their historic preference for giving the best jobs to white men. This in turn implies the need for a higher investment in the education and training of *all* groups, as the better jobs will increasingly require more skills and education.

A final demographic factor must affect our assessment of the need for more effective education and training. The life expectancy of Americans is being extended while the birth rate, particularly among white Americans, is declining. The ratio of elderly to young at the beginning of this century was one to eight, but by the end of the century it will be one to two. Close to 50 percent of that latter group of youth are likely to be from a minority racial, ethnic, or linguistic group. Unless some major and rapid changes are made in education and training policies and practices, these minority groups will be least able to function in our increasingly technological economy.

Educators have tended to focus on birthrates when tracking population trends, but, as the preceding data suggest, birth rates tell only part of the story. Demands for learning, and the rise of new constituencies needing education, are equally affected by regional, racial, ethnic, and social-class issues. The coming profound changes in all these dimensions raise important questions for what we teach and how we most effectively deliver that teaching.

Technological Innovation

A second important trend affecting knowledge needs and constituencies for learning can be observed in profound transformations in the work place, and in the economy resulting from technological innovation. For example, new technologies have increased productivity in agriculture and traditional heavy manufacturing to the point where these sectors employ relatively few people. This change has been accompanied by the growth of new employment sectors, such as high technology, and an increased demand for business, retail, and personal services. As a result, there are significant changes in the goods and services being produced, and in how they are being produced and delivered to customers and clients. The organizational capacities and the individual skills of workers, professionals, and managers must evolve parallel to the changes in productivity and technology.

These rapid transformations mean that the technology transfer process (the means by which new inventions or research discoveries come to be applied as processes or products), as well as business development cycles, have been accelerated and complicated. New jobs continuously arise from these new developments. Jobs for computer operators, programmers, and maintenance and repair workers exist today that twenty-five years ago were hardly imagined, while other occupations have become obsolete. New demands for increased services in such diverse professional fields as accounting, law, education, and health have emerged, as well as seemingly insatiable needs in the clerical, retail, maintenance, and food services.

Dramatically underscoring the rise in technological and service jobs, the April 1986 issue of *American Demographics* provides two interesting graphs describing job-growth sectors in the decade ahead (see Figures 3.2 and 3.3). Yet even these graphs are only based on currently existing technologies. What will emerging fields, beyond biotechnology for example, produce in terms of job opportunities by the year 2010?

In addition, the *Times* piece indicates that workers will change jobs five to six times during their lifetimes. It can no longer be said, "Once an auto worker, always an auto worker", or "Once an aerospace engineer, always an aerospace engineer." Technological changes, coupled with demographic changes, disrupt the orderly transitions in the world of work we used to expect, inducing shorter, and often chaotic, cycles of change.

We can no longer wait for a new generation to come along to change the way we do business. Current generations are being called upon increasingly to adapt and change. Over the next 10 years, for example, an estimated 5 million to 15 million manufacturing jobs will require new and different skills,

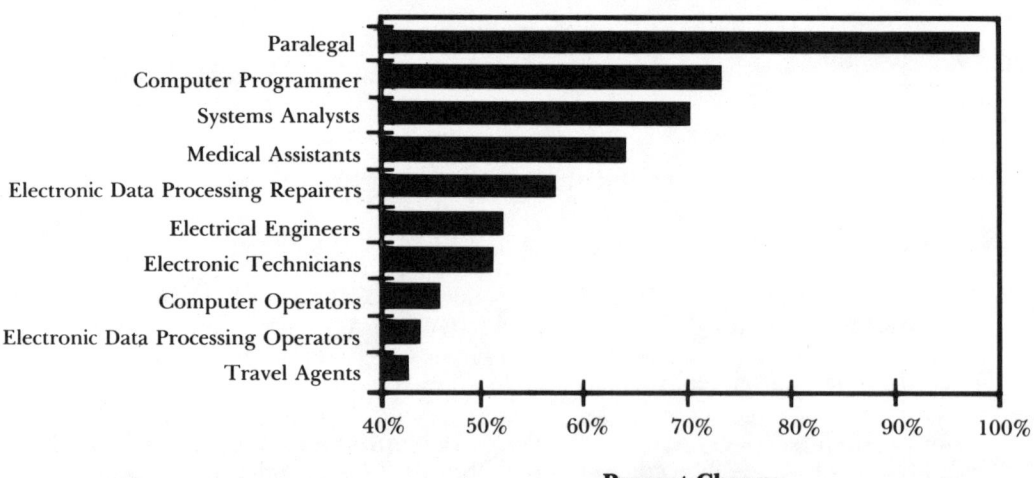

Figure 3.2. *Fastest-growing jobs in technical areas (fastest relative growth, 1985 to 1995).*

Source: *American Demographics,* April 1986.

Figure 3.3. *Most new jobs in traditional occupations (fastest absolute growth, 1985 to 1995).*

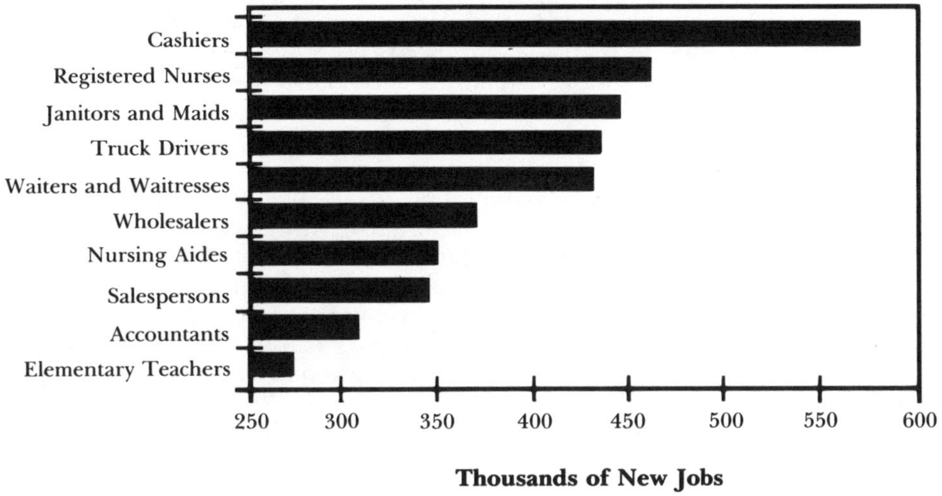

Occupation	Thousands of New Jobs (approx.)
Cashiers	~570
Registered Nurses	~460
Janitors and Maids	~445
Truck Drivers	~435
Waiters and Waitresses	~425
Wholesalers	~370
Nursing Aides	~350
Salespersons	~345
Accountants	~305
Elementary Teachers	~275

Source: American Demographics, April 1986.

while an equal number of service jobs will become obsolete. As the *Times* article reveals, already about 1.5 million workers are *permanently* displaced each year and require retraining or assistance to reenter the work force.

Global Competitiveness

A third major trend worthy of note is the increasing internationalization of trade, manufacturing, commerce, language, culture, and politics. Whether as citizens, as family and neighborhood members, or as workers and professionals, the vast majority of us now live in a context affected on a daily basis by international forces. This fact poses profound and far-reaching challenges, in terms of the content of our traditional school curricula—in history, politics, literature, language, business, and health—as well as of the students we serve. Our nation has been steeped in the history, traditions, arts, religious practices, political ideologies, and bureaucratic philosophies of Western Europe. We have a long way to go to equip our citizens, our labor force, and our leadership to function in a world where the Orient, central Asia, and Latin America represent major economic and political forces.

These new demands for knowledge—arising from demographic, technological, and global trends—will affect education in the years ahead. Typical of "front end" analysis in the instructional design process, this brief introduction sets the stage for the development of a needs matrix. This matrix can interrelate the demands for new knowledge, as well as the new constituencies demanding knowledge. These needs, once acknowledged, will require business and governmental policymakers and educational leaders to use imagination and innovative processes in both the design and the delivery of learning.

SHIFTING KNOWLEDGE DEMANDS AND EMERGING LEARNING CONSTITUENCIES

Discussions of education and training needs, particularly for adults, traditionally have tended to focus on the social circumstances and personal requirements of either individual learners or homogeneous groups. However, the changing conditions of life in the last decade of the twentieth century may require a broadened approach.

These changes have produced needs that are more structural than individual in character. Demands for new knowledge are intersecting with new constituencies of learners demanding knowledge. More people need to know more and different things. Sociology, rather than social psychology, must now serve as the impetus for developing continuing education and training programs, because broader institutional and economic needs and forces are supplanting the desires of individuals. Especially on the international level, we must remain sensitive and open to the changing requirements for education. Instructional design, with its innovative use of technology, is appropriate and attractive because of its capacity to deliver specific skills and knowledge efficiently and effectively to precisely targeted but large constituencies.

EDUCATION FOR AN INFORMATION SOCIETY

The following matrix summarizes the intersecting knowledge needs and learning constituencies that educators must plan to serve indefinitely as a result of changing societal forces. Items 1–3 reflect the knowledge demands and learning populations currently served by traditional institutions and, for the most part, by traditional means: face-to-face classroom instruction. Demographic trends suggest that the constituencies for these first three types of learning are changing substantially. Thus, the way we organize and deliver even basic education will need to change.

Items 4–9 pinpoint emerging and currently underserved sectors of educational need. I will argue momentarily that a more imaginative marshaling of institutional resources, and a more creative use of new technologies, can substantially increase both the quality and quantity of educational services provided in the near future.

Shifting Knowledge Demands
1. Basic education for a culturally, economically, and socially diverse population

Emerging Learning Constituencies
- K–12 age group
- Compensatory adult education for dropouts and the passed-over
- Adult basic literacy for the underprepared
- Non–English-speaking immigrants seeking second language skills for work and citizenship

2. General education in the traditions/values of the culture and the development of critical thinking skills	• Young adults seeking associate or baccalaureate degree education • Working adults in part-time postsecondary degree programs • Mature returning students seeking to complete a college degree or to secure a second college degree
3. Education for credentials and certificates for the world of work	• On-the-job training for service, paraprofessional, and technical workers • Apprenticeships and vocational school-based programs for skilled and semiskilled workers • Specialized business and management education at the work site, through proprietary schools, or in traditional colleges and universities • University and college-based advanced professional education in law, medicine, education, human services, etc.
4. Developmental continuing education for purposes of job retention, elaboration, mobility	• Cohorts needing continuing professional education in such fields as health sciences, management, engineering, education, law, finance, etc. • Workers and professionals needing to broaden their knowledge or skills—i.e., management for engineers, computers for artists • Workers and professionals seeking knowledge that is additive to that initially required by their jobs—i.e., foreign-language proficiency for bankers, word processing for secretaries, computer skills for auto workers

5. Reeducation and new training in response to workplace changes and dislocation	• Cohorts needing new technical skills in response to dying, changing, or emerging jobs—i.e., robotics in manufacturing; new diagnostic machines/medications in health; new printing technologies in newspapers and publishing • People needing crossover skills in order to be assigned to new skill areas or knowledge areas—i.e., teachers developing math and computer competencies, or skills in Asian languages • Groups finding themselves in need of new institutional and interpersonal skills—i.e., teachers of multiethnic students; managers supervising racially or gender-mixed work groups; doctors and health-care workers dealing with the elderly • Home-based workers needing specialized new skills—i.e., telecommunication sales, word processing
6. Knowledge brokering across fields and industries	• Practitioners and problem solvers in social and economic contexts requiring interdisciplinary knowledge and skills—i.e., occupational health and safety workers; engineers seeking management skills; not-for-profit administrators needing financial skills • Alliances of individuals or social groups interested in complex interdisciplinary problems such as alcohol and drug issues or regional economic development • Focused dialogues between researchers and practitioners in areas of practice where research findings change rapidly—i.e., molecular biology in fields such as agriculture or pharmaceuticals; clinical and human subject research and

	treatment in areas such as human nutrition, fitness, drug and alcohol dependence; innovations in research on magnetic recording for fields such as computers; scholarly discoveries in black history or women's history for the teaching of K–12 social science
7. Technology	• Consumers and users of basic research interested in applying findings for new products or production processes, such as industry-based R&D personnel in aerospace, computers, pharmaceuticals, medical instrumentation, consumer electronics • Constituencies interested in the marketplace and in the potential of basic and applied research, such as venture capitalists, bankers, attorneys
8. Education for local, regional, and international citizenship	• School-age children and young adults • Targeted influentials such as teachers/journalists • Adult decision makers: voters, legislators, community leaders • The general public's need for a more informed understanding of ever-changing issues in science, health, ecology, or international affairs
9. Quality-of-life enhancing education	• Adults with discretionary leisure time for such things as enrichment in the arts, humanities, culture • Specialized constituencies for learning, such as retirees or the voluntarily nonemployed

Examination of the less traditional categories listed in items 4–9 shows that our society is missing, or too slowly responding to, important areas of educational need. Until recently, for example, what colleges and universities defined as "noncredit" education often was seen as a trivial adjunct to the more serious and demanding "credit" programs—conventional classes leading to a terminal degree, such as a B.A. or an M.A. Save for a few pioneers, only in the past decade have most educators and human-resource managers begun genuinely to appreciate the important social and economic value of providing developmental continuing education (item 4). Continuing professional education for relicensure, such as that needed by doctors or accountants, has a longer history. But only recently have we begun to assume that every employee who already has an intellectual base and some kind of certification for the world of work nevertheless requires continuous involvement in the process of education—be it for purposes of job currency, retention, elaboration, or mobility.

The University of California extension system alone serves a quarter of a million people annually with noncredit programs of study in such diverse fields as toxic and hazardous waste management, executive development for scientists and engineers, professional writing and publishing skills, landscape design, and alcohol counseling and advising. These are carefully planned programs of study taught by highly qualified faculty and professional practitioners, many of them incorporating self-paced programs of study created with instructional design techniques.

Yet a great deal remains to be done. The National Center for Education Statistics reports that, by 1980, three out of four colleges and universities were offering some form of "noncredit" study and that more than 12 million registrations in noncredit courses were reported. This does not include those adults registered in continuing education programs at their work places or community centers, or through their professional societies, for whom accurate registration totals do not exist. But even if we double the 12 million college and university registrations, approximately four-fifths of the adult population is still excluded.

Until recently, traditional educators also ignored the need for item 5, reeducation in response to workplace changes, leaving the matter to the individual student or employer. Then we began to discover that many of the graduates and professionals we had previously certified as qualified were no longer so, either because of rapid changes in knowledge or because of our earlier, more limited views of the knowledge and skills needed. Some brief examples may be appropriate. Although the science of nutrition has been with us for many decades, an appreciation of the relationship between nutrition, exercise, and health has only recently been taught in schools of nursing and medicine. Previously trained physicians and nurses are now returning to universities to learn more about the positive effects of nutrition and exercise on disease prevention and treatment.

The phenomenal changes in the field of biology as a result of the research breakthroughs in molecular biology and DNA have made obsolete much of the early biological education that public-school (particularly lower- and middle-school) teachers received. Changes in mathematics, and the introduction of computers as tools not only for processing information but for modeling problems and exploring alternative solutions, have resulted in a national effort to bring practicing teachers back into university classrooms—not for degrees or recertification, but for the essential new knowledge that teachers need to educate young people and prepare them for college and the world of work.

Knowledge brokering and technology transfer, items 6 and 7, may seem more obscure—yet, for those colleges and universities that have created small business development programs, the need is apparent. Oftentimes, people with knowledge and skills in one area of endeavor can't realize their potential without making a connection with people who have knowledge and skills in another vital sector. In a society whose new business startups are more often tied to the "exploitation" of ideas and new technologies than of natural resources, the dual need to accelerate the technology transfer process and the development of the relationship between ideas, capital, and markets becomes very important. Research universities, colleges, and community colleges can play important roles in addressing this contemporary economic need, just as agricultural extension has traditionally served the complex economic development needs of the agricultural sector of our economy.

Increasingly, educational institutions are establishing industrial liaison programs through their schools of engineering and departments of biology. These technology transfer centers provide research seminars and technical briefings for industry-based scientists and engineers. Similarly, entrepreneurial development programs educate leaders of startup enterprises on the financing, marketing, personnel, and legal issues about which they must be knowledgeable to make a success of their technology.

All these activities are educational. They currently involve lectures, panels, and the exchange of papers between experts and practitioners. They involve books, laboratories, and directed learning—all activities that could use the instructional design process and appropriate technologies to reach greater numbers of people more efficiently and effectively. None of these programs relates directly to either the undergraduate curriculum or the awarding of college degrees, so they will be freer to experiment with alternative teaching methodologies.

Education for citizenship is included in the matrix because the requirements for citizenship are constantly changing with changes in technology and global relations. The tradition of research and scholarship characterizing the colleges and universities of the United States uniquely equips them to be ongoing centers of citizen education, or to work collaboratively with business and organizations committed to citizen education. An example may again be useful. The effects of technology on the military capacities of modern nations and their storehouses of arms raise important questions about war and peace, the need for deterrence, the potential for nuclear annihilation, the desirability of nuclear disarmament, the level of defense spending, and so on. The discussion of such issues has significant scientific, economic, historical, ethical, and moral dimensions.

The very complexity and interdisciplinary character of these issues suggests a role for institutions of higher learning and for instructional design. Throughout the United States, centers of international research on issues of global conflict and cooperation are springing up, many of which have a citizen education mission. This mission can be served through on-campus programs, but can also be achieved through the design of instructional materials for community discussion groups.

Finally, the expansion of "life enhancement" education, which we once saw reserved for only the idle rich or the allegedly "bored housewife," will become a more important part of our educational mission as demographic changes and transformations in the workplace result in larger constituencies of retirees and the voluntarily unemployed. As vital and active members of the community, and as an increased percentage of the total population, they will demand increased educational services. Here again, the traditional interest in degrees and programs of study that certify one for the world of work will not be the objective. In fact, programs already in place in many institutions suggest that this cohort is vitally interested in education focused on history, current affairs, the humanities, and the arts. It may well be that traditional educators, working collaboratively with museums, community organizations, and instructional designers, could develop programs that would serve much larger numbers than currently make their way to the campuses.

Thus, we need to be concerned about the extent to which we as a nation think comprehensively about the lifelong educational needs of all citizens, particularly given the importance of knowledge to our economy. Our failure until recently to begin to grasp the size and complexity of the various constituencies for learning (beyond those interested in conventional K–12 education and traditional credit- and degree-oriented programs in colleges and universities) has resulted in vital areas of national economic and social concern being underserved. Notable examples in the mid-1980s have been the problems of unprepared teachers in science and math, and the slowing of the technology transfer process in vital and internationally competitive fields such as computers and robotics.

The broadened definition advocated here does not automatically imply a quantum increase in the costs of delivering education. The secret lies rather in leveraging existing resources and in calling upon existing university, community, and industry-based programs to develop institutional mechanisms for broadening their service base. Instructional design and many of the technologies described in this book represent a dynamic and virtually untapped reservoir for maximizing those existing resources.

IMPLICATIONS FOR THE FUTURE DESIGN AND DELIVERY OF PROGRAMS FOR ADULTS

What choices and decisions will our policymakers—be they in educational institutions, business, or government—have to make to respond to these diversifying and expanding needs and opportunities? I return to the categories of challenge laid out by the National Alliance for Business: the need among all races and social classes for basic skills, the need among all categories of workers for retooling, the need among professionals and citizens to adapt to rapid advances in technology and knowledge. To respond to such a far-reaching and continuous set of educational needs through reliance on existing classrooms, tenured faculty, and on-campus schedules is neither feasible, economical, nor intellectually appropriate.

Traditional institutions of learning, as well as proprietary and corporate-based education programs, need to broaden their concept of who (or what) can do the teaching, in what contexts and for what constituencies. University-based degree programs with full-time science and engineering faculty may provide the traditional launch for an electrical engineer. But updates in the field may be more efficiently provided through courses delivered to the work site by instructional television or by well-designed, self-paced computer packages that cover new applications of new technologies.

Five or ten years after graduation, the engineer may find that he needs management education offered in an interdisciplinary sequence of weekend courses and seminars. The cross-cultural knowledge he needs to represent his company successfully with a Japanese firm may be available through a carefully designed self-paced program of reading and interactive video. A single individual may participate in education in a variety of ways for a variety of purposes, but the critical question remains: How do we as educators increase our capacity to serve these various needs and purposes?

We need more professional staff whose primary concern is the provision of both this wide range of "noncredit" programming and of more effective learner-focused programs in basic and general education. This professional staff must include persons with the skills to broker the essential relationships and access the essential knowledge, both in developmental education programs for the growing "underclass" and in technology transfer and applied learning for economic development. Equally important is the growth and development of staff who have grounding in their disciplines, augmented by a sophisticated understanding of the learning process. Only then can educators and trainers understand and support the development, production, and delivery of well-designed learning packages, whether in print and audio cassette, or via television, interactive video, computer—or combinations of new technologies still to come.

In addition to people with such interdisciplinary, outreach-oriented, and technical skills to complement the existing intellectual resources in the faculty, there needs to be a commitment of university facilities and sophisticated equipment to allow for the design and delivery of programs. Finally, there has to be some change in the current expectation that virtually all college and university education, other than traditional courses for credit and degree-related offerings, will be "self-supporting." Parallel concerns exist in business and government, where equally innovative instructional programs are needed.

The educational needs outlined in this chapter are *recurrent* in an information age, and *vital* to a participatory democracy and a healthy economy functioning in a global geopolitical context. Leadership must stop relying exclusively on the financial resources of the oftentimes short-term training concerns of industry, or the motivation for upward mobility that propels self-paying middle-class professionals. In the face of a teaching cadre sorely in need of retooling, of a manufacturing core sorely in need of revitalization, of an engineering and scientific labor pool substantially smaller than that of many of our international competitors, we need to make a broader social investment in education. For such far-reaching social and economic ends, a substantial investment in new personnel, in new methodologies, and in innovative delivery systems is called for—not at the *expense of* existing programs, but *in addition to* them.

The subsequent chapters in this book represent some of the best current thinking in the field about methodologies and technologies available to us as lifelong educators. They need to be read with a clear awareness of the knowledge demands and learning constituencies they can best serve. These ideas and their potential will never be realized, however, without the political will and visionary leadership that can enable us as a nation to redefine our educational priorities and to adopt a more comprehensive educational strategy for the decades ahead.

REFERENCES

Aslanian, C. B., and H. M. Brickel. 1980. *Americans in transition: Life changes as reasons for adult learning.* New York: College Entrance Examination Board.

Botkin, J., D. Dimancescu, and R. Stata. 1984. *Global stakes.* New York: Penguin Books.

Etzioni, A. 1983. *An immodest agenda: Rebuilding America before the twenty-first century.* New York: McGraw-Hill.

Gessner, Q. H. 1987. *Handbook on continuing higher education.* New York: ACE/MacMillan Series on Higher Education.

Johnston, W. B. 1987. *Workforce 2000: Work and workers for the twenty-first century.* Indianapolis, Indiana: Hudson Institute.

Leontief, W., and F. Duchin. 1986. *The future impact of automation on workers.* New York: Oxford University Press.

Lynton, E. A. 1984. *The mission connection between business and the universities.* New York: ACE/MacMillan Series on Higher Education.

———, and S. E. Elman. 1987. *Individuals.* San Francisco: Jossey-Bass.

National Alliance for Business. 1987. "Is America Ready for the 21st Century?" Advertising supplement in *The New York Times Magazine* (September 10).

National Governors Association. 1987. "Making America Work: Productive People, Productive Policies." Washington, DC.

Oxford Analytica. 1986. *America in perspective: Major trends in the United States through the 1990's.* Boston: Houghton Mifflin.

Reich, R. B. 1984. *The next American frontier.* New York: Penguin Books.

Schwartz, G. G., and W. Neikirk. 1984. *The work revolution.* New York: Rawson.

The United Way of America. 1987. "What Lies Ahead: Looking Toward the '90s." Alexandria, VA.

CHAPTER FOUR

Instructional Design and Learner Motivation

Raymond J. Wlodkowski

As a field of study, motivation is what was once called a "no man's land." There may be an easy way into it, but there is no sure way out—at least not with the certainty and predictability desirable for scientific understanding. Motivation deals with the quintessential question of all the social sciences, "Why do human beings behave the way they do?" Currently several disciplines offer enlightenment regarding the answer to this query, but little that could actually be called a precise or definitive reply. Yet industrial managers and educational administrators are constantly confronted with the need to plan and make decisions based on a sensitive understanding of people's motivation. The success of managers in every organization is anchored to how well their leadership serves and fits the motivation of those being led.

As a concept, motivation is problematic because it is a hypothetical construct that provides a possible concrete causal explanation of behavior (Baldwin, 1967). Therefore, it cannot be directly measured; and, as long as this state of affairs lasts, there will be many different opinions about what it really is. Like intelligence, another popular hypothetical construct, motivation helps us to approach a better understanding of human behavior—but with few, if any, final conclusions. Nonetheless, some comprehension of why people behave as they do is vitally important to helping them learn, and psychology has made many inroads upon the knowledge and skills useful for this purpose. Most psychologists concerned with learning and instruction use the word *motivation* to describe those processes that can energize and give direction or purpose to behavior. Relative to these processes are a rapidly growing number of well-researched findings that can be applied to instructional situations.

Motivation appears to be a cause, a mediator, and a consequence of learning (Walberg and Uguroglu, 1980). It is common knowledge among instructors that when people are motivated to learn what is being offered, they begin the task more smoothly and enthusiastically, as well as continue to work longer, harder, and with more vigor, than when they are not. Because time spent actively involved in learning is definitely related to achievement, the influence of moderate-to-high levels of motivation should be positive for most learning activity (Levin and Long, 1981). Enjoyable and rewarding learning experiences frequently increase the motivation of people to continue these activities, or similar pursuits, beyond the instructional situation (Maehr, 1976). Whether it be toward an intriguing novelist, or an athletic skill, or a computer program, human beings develop many attractions and interests as outcomes of positive learning experiences. The variety of courses available in most university programs for both undergraduates and returning adults can offer numerous opportunities for students to deepen these interests that can then become lifelong pursuits.

ADULTS AS MOTIVATED LEARNERS

Probably one of the most widely accepted views in the field of education is that adults are highly pragmatic learners. Research consistently shows that vocational and practical education that leads to knowledge about how to do something is chosen by more adults than any other form of learning. Adults have a strong need to apply what they have learned, and to be competent in that application (Knox, 1977). That is why the emphasis in instructional design on applied learning, or practice and outcomes evaluation, lends itself so well to adult education and training.

Another important view of adults, one that is largely developmental in both a physical and cultural sense, is that they are mature, responsible people who are capable of autonomous functioning in life and work. Thus, adults engage in learning as a result of their own volition. It may be that sometimes the circumstances prompting this learning are external, such as job loss or divorce, but the decision to learn is theirs (Brookfield, 1986). In fact, most adults are experienced, self-directed learners (Tough, 1979). When they do choose to learn on their own, instead of taking a formal course, their ability to self-determine such issues as learning pace, style, flexibility, and structure seems to play a large part in their decision (Penland, 1979). Thus, when adults see themselves as responsible for their learning, and when that learning is helping them to be effective at something they value, they are much more likely to be intrinsically and positively motivated (Wlodkowski, 1985). Seen from this perspective, some motivation theories are far more applicable to adult instruction than others. Psychological theorists such as Weiner (1980), McClelland (1985), de Charms (1968), Bandura (1977), and Deci and Ryan (1985), who embrace competence as a central assumption, support the idea that human beings actively strive for understanding and mastery.

Although instructors deal with many people who seem to have an innate need to be competent, effective, and self-determined, they also work with a significant number of adults who are dependent, lacking in self-confidence, and/or largely unmotivated for the learning tasks at hand. (This problematic state of affairs occurs most often in remedial and compulsory learning situations, of course.) More than a few good reasons can explain this difficulty among adult learners, but the problem has become increasingly more common in industrial communities reacting to rapid technological change.

Some adults have poor educational backgrounds or academic histories replete with problems and failure. Others see themselves as too old to begin new learning activities and to wrestle with the inevitable changes that such situations demand (Carp, Peterson, and Roelfs, 1974). Then there are those who don't expect to succeed, as well as those who feel threatened by the exposure to new learning that contradicts established beliefs and habits (Smith, 1982). Probably one of the largest groups of reluctant adult learners are those who feel forced or pressured into taking courses or training because they need the jobs, promotions, or salaries for which these learning experiences inevitably are requirements (Wlodkowski, 1985). In their eyes, they may be only surviving, or merely taking the absolutely necessary step to get ahead. And yet, even within the actual experience of any of the groups in such circumstances, human beings still have an innate need for self-determination and competence.

Helping these adults to become effective at what they value, and to take ownership of their learning, is not only a way to enhance their motivation for immediate learning, but also one of the few means possible to build their self-confidence for future learning. If the course or training is required, then the motivational goal of instructional design is *to make this learning worthy of the adult learner's choice*—to help that person eventually to think, "I may not have wanted this to begin with, but I do want it now." This cognitive shift can produce an emotional transformation from resistance to acceptance, with benefit to both the learner and the instructor.

INSTRUCTIONAL DESIGN AND LEARNER MOTIVATION

As we saw in Chapter Two, instructional design is prescriptive. Its primary purpose is to prescribe optimal methods of instruction. As a discipline, it analyzes sets of conditions and desired outcomes, and then offers those instructional methods that will optimize the given desired outcomes under the given conditions. As an activity, instructional design seeks to develop an architect's blueprint that prescribes which instructional methods should be used for a particular learning objective and a particular group of learners at a particular time (Reigeluth and Stein, 1983). Two important questions facing instructional designers are: (1) "How should the instructional events be sequenced over time?" (For example: In what order should concepts be taught? When should practice take place?) and (2) "How should learning content be synthesized?" (For example: How do two ideas relate? Can three principles fit into the same model?) Instructional designers place instruction into a stable and precise pattern. However, seldom do they thoroughly integrate human motivation into this tidy and exact diagram (Reigeluth, 1983).

When instructional design attempts, in effect, to produce a photograph of how to teach, motivation remains out of focus and beyond shutter speed. As we have seen, as a concept, motivation is too unwieldy. As a human condition, it is extraordinarily unstable. Motivation involves conceptual consideration of energy and volition. That means it must attempt to quantify and predict such things as feelings and desires, the messy stuff that continues to defy scientific reliability. People not only frequently change their mind about what they want to do, but they also usually vary in how they feel, and in how much effort they will expend when they finally do what they have chosen to do. For adults, this is as true for learning as it is for work or play. If one were to reliably measure motivation, one would need an instrument much more akin to an emotional thermometer than to any paper-and-pencil diagnostic.

Yet progress has been made, and a number of promising directions have emerged regarding the inclusion of motivational components within an instructional design approach to teaching and training. Because something cannot be clearly seen or easily stabilized does not mean it cannot be better understood. The fields of astronomy and biology have demonstrated this beyond question.

One of the aspects of instructional design that directly and positively relates to the motivation of adult learners is its precision about the outcomes of effectiveness and efficiency (Reigeluth, 1983). Effectiveness is usually measured by the level of student achievement, and efficiency is usually measured by effectiveness divided by student time and/or by the cost of instruction. In general, instructional design seeks to maximize learner achievement at the minimal rate of student-invested time. Because time is such a limited and valued commodity in the workplace and because competence is also so highly valued both by managers and adult learners, the field of instructional design has a purpose that both parties can enthusiastically appreciate. Therefore, when conditions are such that students are voluntary and highly motivated to learn at the outset, instructionally designed formats for learning may be considered ideal. In fact, one of the main reasons why some adults choose to learn something on their own rather than taking a course (college or otherwise) is that they consider the learning pace too slow (Penland, 1977).

Instructors of formal courses are concerned about motivation because they often face learners who are not voluntary or highly motivated. They also are concerned, in such situations, about *value, appeal, perseverance,* and *continuing motivation. Value* refers to the pride taken by learners in the knowledge gained or the skill acquired (Brophy, 1983). Do the learners think that what they learned was important, something that makes a difference in their lives? Has their attitude positively changed toward what they have learned as a result of the learning experience? *Appeal* is a word used by instructional design theorists to deal with those components of instruction that help the learner to want to continue to learn during instruction (Reigeluth, 1983). How stimulating is the learning process? Do learners have difficulty paying attention, staying interested, or being involved in the learning activity? *Perseverance* is continuing effort. How well do students maintain their involvement in the learning task when they become fatigued or have difficulties or distractions while learning? *Continuing motivation* refers to using or applying what has been learned outside the formal learning experience. Will the students use what they have learned outside the classroom? Will adults apply what they have learned in formal courses in their daily work? These motivational issues are vital concerns to educators and trainers as well as to society in general.

Although such instructional design theories as the Gagne–Briggs Theory and Elaboration Theory include motivational-strategy components, neither does so in a manner that would be considered comprehensive or systematic (Reigeluth, 1983). By remaining committed to being precise and empirically scientific, instructional design theories have not to date been able to sufficiently and consistently incorporate the kind of conceptual structures that can address the motivational issues just considered. Therefore, when managers or policymakers are evaluating an instructional design format for possible inclusion within their instructional system, it would be important to know to what extent value, appeal, perseverance, and continuing motivation are relevant and desirable within the total system, as well as to what extent the design format positively incorporates such variables. Despite these cautions, however, today's instructional design theorists and practitioners are making significant progress, and are developing a range of choices for selecting motivational strategies that might respond to these motivational issues. This evolution is occurring in (among other areas) the development of motivation models, and computer-based education.

MOTIVATION MODELS

In recent years, two motivation models for instruction have been developed: the ARCS Model of Motivation Design (Keller and Kopp, 1987), and the Time Continuum Model of Motivation (Wlodkowski, 1985). Both models attempt to achieve a similar goal: to synthesize many lines of research on enhancing learner motivation in order to integrate numerous instructional strategies. Although each of these models emphasizes a different approach to the planning process, as well as some important differences among particular strategies, both are serious attempts to make instruction more appealing. Each model postulates a major set of factors that influence motivation to learn, with each factor serving as a category for the inclusion of specific motivational strategies. In the ARCS Model, the four major factors are *attention, relevance, confidence,* and *satisfaction.* In the Time Continuum Model of Motivation, six major factors are identified: *attitude, need, stimulation, affect, competence,* and *reinforcement.* See Table 4.1 for an example of an instructional plan designed with the use of the Time Continuum Model of Motivation (Wlodkowski, 1985).

The instructional plan in Table 4.1 is for a staff developer who is conducting a four-hour training session with a small group of instructor trainees on how to use an overhead projector and make appropriate transparencies. The learning objectives are stated below.

By the end of training, all the instructor trainees will be able to:

1. Label the components of an overhead projector
2. Adjust an overhead projector
3. Design and make transparencies
4. Successfully use an overhead projector to give a fifteen-minute lecture

Although the plan does not designate specific amounts of time, it does synchronize each major motivation factor and related strategies according to a time phase—*beginning, concurrent,* and *ending.* The Motivational Purposes in the far left column have been established on the basis of an audience and task analysis (conditions and outcomes). The Motivational Strategies are the re-

Table 4.1. INSTRUCTIONAL PLAN DESIGNED WITH THE USE OF THE TIME CONTINUUM MODEL OF MOTIVATION

Motivational Purpose	Motivational Strategy	Learning Activity or Instructor Behavior
(Attitudes) To establish learner expectancy for success.	1a. Make the learning goals as clear as possible. 1b. Make the criteria of evaluation as clear as possible. 1c. Use models similar to the learners to demonstrate expected learning.	1. After explaining the value and purpose of the overhead projector, pass out a performance criteria checklist to each trainee for group use of this machine and show a fifteen-minute videotape in which a former trainee demonstrates exemplary utilization of the overhead projector. Explain the criteria during the showing of the tape.
(Needs) To satisfy and respect adult safety needs within the content and process of the instructional situation.	1. Reduce or remove components of the learning environment that lead to failure or fear.	1. Explain to trainees that they will have a chance to practice making transparencies and using the overhead projector and that you will be available to them as a consultant during these times.
(Stimulation) To maintain learner attention.	1. Provide variety in personal presentation style, methods of instruction, and learning materials.	1. Pass out a diagram of the projector among trainees. Have them label it as you point out its components and explain their function with an actual model of the projector.
To develop learner involvement	2. Make learner reaction and active participation an essential part of the learning process.	2a. Give each trainee an opportunity to adjust a "problem" projector, asking them to label each part they manipulate to solve the problem. 2b. After passing out the instructions for making write-on and burn-on transparencies to each trainee and demonstrating how to make each type, allow trainees to practice making their own under your supervision.
(Affect) To maintain an optimal emotional climate with the learning group.	1. Use cooperative goal structures to develop and maximize cohesiveness in the learning group.	1. Divide the six trainees into two triads. With assistance from the peers in their triad, each trainee is to develop a fifteen-minute presentation on any topic accompanied by appropriate use of the overhead projector as a visual aid. Each triad will receive one projector for practicing. The trainees are encouraged to use the performance criteria checklist

Table 4.1. (continued)

Motivational Purpose	Motivational Strategy	Learning Activity or Instructor Behavior
		passed out at the beginning of the training session to give feedback and guidance to members of their triad.
(Competence) To increase learner awareness of progress, mastery, and responsibility in learning in a manner that enhances the learner's confidence, self-determination, and intrinsic motivations.	1a. Whenever possible, use performance evaluation procedures to help the learner realize how to operationalize in daily living what has been learned. 1b. Provide consistent feedback to learners regarding their mastery, progress, and responsibility in learning.	1. Each trainee is videotaped and evaluated while making a fifteen-minute presentation using an overhead projector as a visual aid. Each person is evaluated by the entire group of trainees as well as the staff developer with the performance criteria checklist as the evaluation standard. Any trainee receiving less than 80 percent average score on the checklist will be requested to make another fifteen-minute videtaped persentation for evaluation by the staff developer.

Source: Adapted from Wlodkowski, 1985, pp. 264–265.

search-established instructional methods that have been selected from a pool of sixty-eight strategies to effectively achieve their related Motivational Purposes. The particular Learning Activities and Instructor Behaviors are what the instructor would do to implement the Motivational Strategies. The major factor of reinforcement has been left out of this plan because the competence-related strategies of performance evaluation and feedback provide a motivationally sound ending to the sequence.

To design this instructional plan, the instructor should follow these steps:

1. Clarify instructional objective(s) for the particular learner and learning situation.
2. Estimate the amount of time *desirable* for instruction.
3. Consider the inherent structure of the material, skill, or knowledge to be learned.
4. Review the motivational purposes (a pool of 19 motivational objectives) to select the appropriate related motivational strategies. Then develop the learning activities for these selected strategies so that they fit the structural and time parameters of the learning objectives and their related content.

When the entire plan has been designed, the following criterion must be met: *The sequence of instruction for the particular learning objective(s) includes significant positive motivational influence on the learners in each time phase (beginning, concurrent, and ending).*

The orientation of the Time Continuum Model of Motivation toward

54 Analysis and Assessment

learner motivation is to view it as an unstable potential. Thus, the learner's volition, perseverance, value, and continuing motivation for both the content and process of instruction are elements that can increase or decrease in strength throughout the instructional sequence. One of the main purposes of this model is to make the *development* of learner motivation an essential part of the design and, therefore, of the process of instruction. The model fits the actual process of instruction as it is usually conducted in learning environments. Sequenced activities leading to the achievement of particular instructional objectives form a holistic, patterned framework that is created and organized according to a time orientation, a situational viewpoint, and a set of motivation factors in order to continuously and positively influence learner motivation. See Figure 4.1.

Figure 4.1. *The Time Continuum Model of Motivation.*

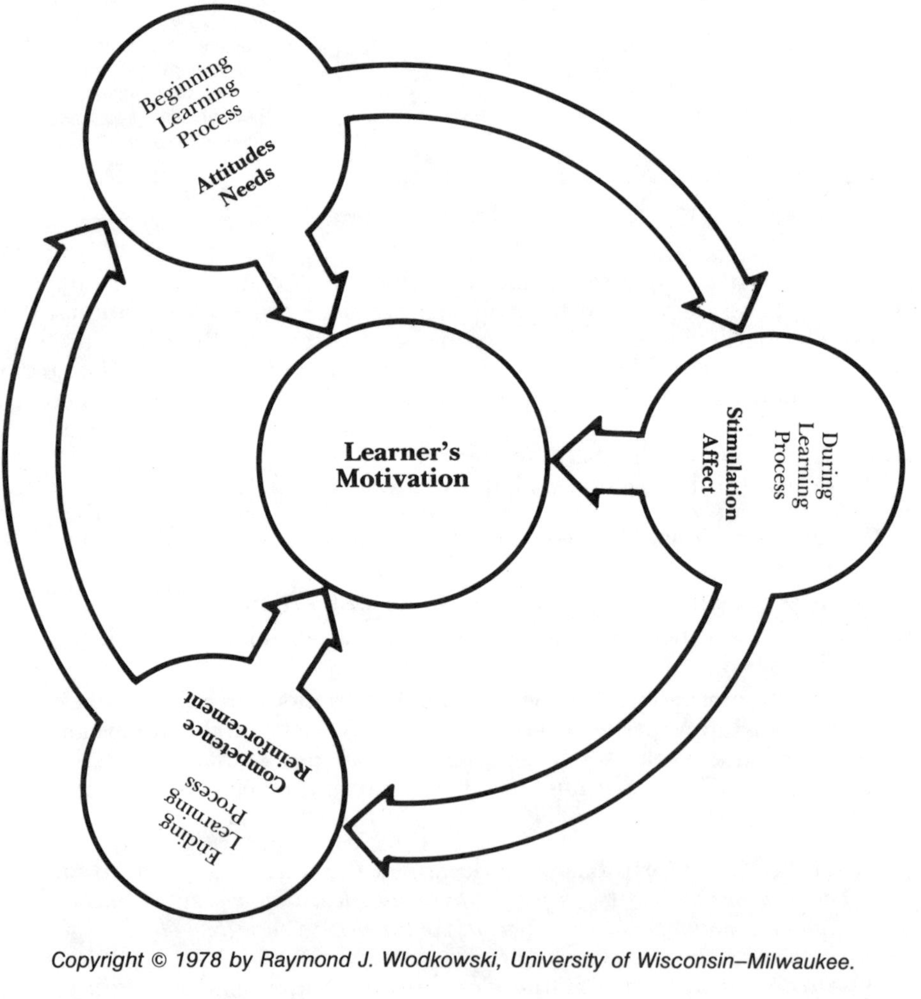

Beginning Learning Process — Attitudes, Needs

During Learning Process — Stimulation, Affect

Ending Learning Process — Competence, Reinforcement

Learner's Motivation

Copyright © 1978 by Raymond J. Wlodkowski, University of Wisconsin–Milwaukee.

Through memory, physiology, and situational perception, *needs and attitudes* influence the learner at the *beginning* of the learning sequence. These two factors seem to have the greatest motivational impact on the learner whenever that person starts a new learning process. "Do I need it?" and "What do I think of it?" are internal questions that immediately come to the minds of learners when they begin a learning task. These result in the formation of *motives*, or goals, which the learner wants to achieve through the learning experience. These needs and attitudes combine to interact with the *stimulation and the affective processes* that occur *during* the main body of the learning experience itself to further influence learner motivation.

Every learning sequence has a series of main activities (reading, problem solving, lectures, discussions, drills, etc.) to increase learning. Unless these activities are stimulating and/or affectively salient, there may be little motivational influence to sustain learner attention and involvement. The initiative provided by beginning attitudes and needs can wane. When the process of learning itself is stimulating and affectively salient, it maintains the learner's effort to continue learning. At the *ending* of the learning sequence, the *competence and the reinforcement* gained interact with the previous four major motivation factors to influence the learner's motivation at that moment, and for the future as well, resulting in new attitudes and needs.

Both the ARCS Model and the Time Continuum Model of Motivation offer many useful prescriptions to guide instructional designers. The ARCS Model has been adapted to microcomputer courseware design (Keller and Suzuki, 1987). These models also point out certain directions that instructional designers will have to pursue if their field is to evolve into a more holistic and useful science. More accurate audience analysis to identify such factors as learner attitude and confidence is important because these factors are necessary in formulating instructional methods (Keller and Kopp, 1987).

Motivational objectives will have to become an integral part of instructional outcomes as well. Learners' feelings of competence, value for what has been learned, and continuing motivation are instructional outcomes essential for pragmatic as well as scientific reasons. Just as there are standards for achievement, such as the number of correct responses, there need to be standards for motivation, such as the amount of time learners are *alert and paying attention* or *alert and involved* in the learning task (Wlodkowski, 1985). Such standards can serve as criteria for the quality of instruction for learners. What these models suggest is that instructional design as a theory and a process concretely integrates conditions, methods, and outcomes that are directly tied to learner motivation. If managers who contract for or create employee training using instructional design processes do not have some criteria by which to judge the motivational impact and value of this approach, they will have either abandoned their commitment to the quality of the learner's experience, or blindly cast their learners into a process where achievement is, at best, a vacuous indicator of instructional success.

MOTIVATION AND COMPUTER-BASED EDUCATION

The computer evokes many different reactions in the fields of education and training. To some it represents a technological solution to many of the problems facing higher education and training, such as declining budgets and the shortage of well-qualified instructors. To others, the computer represents a potential threat to traditional forms of education, a dehumanizing influence. Thus far, available evidence appears to support computer-based education as an innovation that has great potential to improve instruction and to expand the horizons of instructional design, especially in exploring and developing a stronger motivational orientation.

Kulik, Kulik, and Cohen (1980) conducted a meta-analysis of findings from fifty-nine independent studies of computer-based college teaching. They concluded that, in comparison with conventional instruction, computer-based instruction: (a) substantially reduced the amount of time needed for instruction; (b) produced slightly more favorable learner attitudes toward instruction and the subject matter; and (c) made small but significant contributions to course achievement. Comparable support for computer-based instruction has been obtained in other instructional contexts, including military education (Orlansky and String, 1981). It could be assumed that adult learners will generally find more efficient instruction appealing. But there are many other reasons why their attitude toward instruction and subject matter might be more favorable in computer-based instructional formats than in conventional instruction.

Computer-based instruction can allow self-pacing. People learn at different rates. To learn at one's own most efficient rate can reduce both the boredom and the tension of group-paced instruction. For drill and practice, the computer offers limitless patience and endurance. This can reduce learners' self-consciousness and potential embarrassment. Too, computers can encourage learners to have a strong sense of personal control and involvement in their learning by being immediately responsive, gathering information, determining solutions, and giving prompt feedback. Because of their graphics and animation, computers offer a myriad of possibilities for simulating real-life events in learning. This directly appeals to adult learners' desire for pragmatic effectiveness. Because computers can be easily programmed with game formats, which can include color and sound as well as animation, they often prove to be a good deal of fun for learners. It can readily be seen that there are many reasons beyond self-determination and competence that explain why computer-based instruction can positively influence adult learners' motivation.

At the same time that computer-based education offers numerous ways to develop learner motivation, it offers instructional designers a unique ability to empirically study various motivational influences on both singular and comparative bases (Lepper and Chabay, 1985). Because computers can be precisely programmed, they can consistently hold at the macro level constant significant independent variables as large as an overall instructional method, and at the micro level as small as a motivational embellishment. They can also be programmed to precisely compare different sequencing and/or synthesis of these variables.

Suppose one wanted to compare the relative merits of a basic drill-and-practice model for learning statistical concepts and a games approach. Here the instructional goals of the two methods are identical, but their instructional components are widely divergent. Use of the computer would permit direct comparisons of programs specifically designed to present entirely standardized instructional sequences in different formats. The computer allows instructional designers to empirically investigate the motivational influences of something as concretely obvious as differing educational materials, as well as something as delicately subtle as the timing of feedback.

At another level, computers have offered a laboratory for the initial development of a motivationally oriented theory of instructional design. Using an analysis of computer games as an inspiration, Malone (1981) suggests how a more comprehensive theory of instructional design might be developed, based on the three categories of *challenge, fantasy,* and *curiosity.*

Malone describes an environment as *challenging* when it provides goals whose attainment is uncertain. By manipulating characteristics of the educational goal—such as how personally meaningful it is to the learner, as well as by influencing the certainty of the learner's goal attainment—an instructional designer can to some extent prescribe the challenge, and therefore the pleasure, of an educational activity.

He describes a *fantasy*-inducing environment as one that evokes cognitive images of things not present to the senses or within the actual experience of the person involved. These images can be of physical objects (e.g., spears and apples) or of social situations (e.g., being the captain of a ship), and they may or may not be likely to occur in the learner's environment (e.g., apples vs. lions). By designing games in which the learner's progress toward some fantasy goal (e.g., a hidden kingdom) or avoidance of some fantasy catastrophe (e.g., a bottomless pit) depends on the learner's application of knowledge or skill, the fun of learning can be positively influenced.

Basing his approach to *curiosity* on the work of Piaget (1952) and Berlyne (1965), Malone describes environments that can evoke a learner's curiosity as those that provide an optimal level of informational complexity. They should be neither too complicated nor too simple with respect to the learner's existing knowledge. They should be novel and surprising, but not totally incomprehensible. An optimally complex environment is usually one wherein the learner knows enough to have expectations about what will happen, but where these expectations are sometimes unmet. By manipulating such variables as completeness or consistency in the information given in a learning activity, instructional designers can create puzzles, paradoxes, and mysteries that will engage the curiosity, and thus the involvement, of the learner.

Malone has provided a provocative, coherent framework that may be used as a checklist of heuristics to design more intrinsically motivating instruction. Like the primary colors, challenge, fantasy, and curiosity provide an endless array of possibile ways to blend—in this case, information to make instruction more stimulating.

Computer-based education has its motivational limitations, however. Computers lack the human qualities of feelings and conviction that can be so important when giving feedback or support. They do not remotely approach the sensitivity or flexibility that teachers can display. And, they cannot supply the reality of human interaction the way a good discussion or debate can do. Nevertheless, they *are* a boon to the empirical and creative aspects of instructional design. They can move this discipline toward greater scientific as well as aesthetic development. In terms of motivation, they can inform the entire realm of education and training. Where useful, they offer managers and developers of instruction one of the few teaching options that can be consistently evaluated, continuously refined, and creatively changed to the exclusive benefit of the adult learner.

LEARNER CONTROL

Most of the previous discussion of instructional design has dealt with those approaches that might be considered *external* instructional strategies to enhance learner motivation. There is yet another promising approach—one that helps learners to acquire and implement *internally* generated strategies for taking control and processing learning in a manner that can enhance their motivation to learn. Traditionally, instructional designers call this *learner control* (Merrill, 1979). However, educational psychologists have a similar orientation, *self-control of learning*, which has a growing, empirically established body of knowledge that may be informative to the discipline of instructional design (McCombs, 1984).

According to Merrill (1979), the concept of learner control refers, in its broadest sense, to the learner's freedom to take command of the selection and sequencing of:

1. The content to be learned (content control)
2. The rate at which the learner will learn (pace control)
3. The specific instructional strategy components the learner selects and the order in which they are used (display control)
4. The specific cognitive strategies the learner employs when interacting with the instruction (conscious cognition control)

Learner control is used in both Component Design Theory (Merrill, 1983) and the Elaboration Theory of Instruction (Reigeluth and Stein, 1983). Thus, these theories propose externally designed formats that include instructional components precisely adapted to learner selection and guidance. (See Chapter Five for a more complete description.) Although Reigeluth and Stein (1983) indicate that learner control as a metatheory shows great promise, the actual empirical research remains quite limited (Merrill, 1983).

Self-control of learning is a function of students' motivation, as well as of their possession of the skills and abilities to take personal responsibility for their own learning process by actively engaging appropriate metacognitive, cognitive, and affective learning strategies (McCombs, 1984). The metacognitive skills important in this regard include self-assessment evaluation, setting realistic self-standards, planning, self-correction, and self-rewards. Influential cognitive components include problem-solving and decision-making skills that can help students evaluate learning-task requirements against their cognitive self-knowledge. Affective skills contributing to motivation include goal setting, and deriving positive expectancies for success and personal control.

Unlike learner control, self-control of learning is not specifically related to any instructional design theory or model. However, an examination of the overall skill patterns found in self-control of learning indicates that a person thoroughly trained in this approach would theoretically be an ideal student for taking command of the learner control component in an instructionally designed program that includes it. The competencies that make up self-control of learning appear optimally transferable to learner control formats. They also theoretically dovetail with the important factor of self-determination in motivating adult learners.

Evaluation data obtained to date from the implementation of a training program that included many of the skill components identified as part of self-control of learning indicate that this type of training contributes to both higher course performance and to greater feelings of competency (McCombs, 1984). Further research is needed in several areas, including the long-range impact of this type of training and its differential effectiveness with other learning formats, such as computer-based instruction.

CONCLUSION

At this time, the potential of instructional design theory and processes to be effective, positive influences on adult learner motivation appears to be in early developmental stages but with a promising future. When adults are initially motivated, confident, and seeking efficient learning of specific knowledge or skills, instructionally designed formats may be ideal and should be fully considered. If the type of learner or subject matter varies from this description, managers and administrators who consider adopting an instructional design process should be careful and rigorous in appraising how motivational benefits are incorporated in the instruction.

REFERENCES

Baldwin, A. L. 1967. *Theories of child development.* New York: Wiley.

Bandura, A. 1977. *Social learning theory.* Englewood Cliffs, NJ: Prentice–Hall.

Berlyne, D. E. 1965. *Structure and direction in thinking.* New York: Wiley.

Brookfield, S. D. 1986. *Understanding and facilitating adult learning.* San Francisco: Jossey–Bass.

Brophy, J. 1983. Conceptualizing student motivation. *Educational Psychologist* 18(3): 200–215.

Carp, A., R. Peterson, and P. Roelfs. 1974. Adult learning interests and experiences. In K. P. Cross, J. R. Valley et al., *Planning non-traditional programs: An analysis of the issues for postsecondary education.* San Francisco: Jossey–Bass.

de Charms, R. 1968. *Personal causation: The internal affective determinants of behavior.* New York: Academic Press.

Deci, E. L., and R. M. Ryan. 1985. *Intrinsic motivation and self-determination in human behavior.* New York: Plenum.

Keller, J. M., and T. W. Kopp. 1987. Application of the ARCS model of motivational design. In C. M. Reigeluth (ed.), *Instructional theories in action: Lessons illustrating selected theories and models.* New York: Erlbaum.

Keller, J. M., and K. Suzuki. 1987. Use of the ARCS model in courseware design. In D. H. Jonassen (ed.), *Instructional Designs for Computer Courseware.* Hillsdale, NJ: Erlbaum.

Knox, A. B. 1977. *Adult development and learning: A handbook on individual growth and competence in the adult years.* San Francisco: Jossey–Bass.

Kulik, J. A., C. C. Kulik, and P. A. Cohen. 1980. Effectiveness of computer-based college teaching: A meta-analysis of findings. *Review of Educational Research* 50: 525–544.

Lepper, M. R., and R. W. Chabay. 1985. Intrinsic motivation and instruction: Conflicting views on the role of motivational processes in computer-based education. *Educational Psychologist* 20: 217–230.

Levin, T., and R. Long. 1981. *Effective instruction*. Alexandria, VA: Association for Supervision and Curriculum Development.

McClelland, D. C. 1985. *Human motivation*. Glenview, IL: Scott, Foresman.

McCombs, B. L. 1984. Processes and skills underlying continuing intrinsic motivation to learn: Toward a definition of motivational skills training intervention. *Educational Psychologist* 19: 199–218.

Maehr, M. L. 1976. Continuing motivation: An analysis of a seldom considered educational outcome. *Review of Educational Research* 46(3): 443–462.

Malone, T. W. 1981. Toward a theory of intrinsically motivating instruction. *Cognitive Science* 4: 333–369.

Merrill, M. D. 1979. *Learning-controlled instructional strategies: An empirical investigation*. Final report on NSF Grant No. SED 76-01650.

———1983. Component display theory. In C. M. Reigeluth (ed.), *Instructional design theories and models: An overview of their current status*. Hillsdale, NJ: Erlbaum.

Orlansky, J., and J. String. 1981. Computer-based instruction for military training. *Defense Management Journal*, 2d Quarter, 46–54.

Penland, P. 1977. *Individual self-planned learning in America*. Washington, DC: Office of Education, U.S. Department of Health, Education and Welfare.

———1979. Self-initiated learning. *Adult Education* 29(3): 170–179.

Piaget, J. 1952. *The origins of intelligence in children*. New York: International Universities Press.

Reigeluth, C. M. (ed.) 1983. *Instructional design theories and models: An overview of the current status*. Hillsdale, NJ: Erlbaum.

Reigeluth, C. M., and F. S. Stein. 1983. The elaboration theory of instruction. In C. M. Reigeluth (ed.), *Instructional design theories and models: An overview of the current status*. Hillsdale, NJ: Erlbaum.

Smith, R. M. 1982. *Learning how to learn*. Chicago: Follett.

Tough, A. 1979. *The adult's learning projects* (2d ed.). Austin, TX: Learning Concepts.

Van Patten, J., C. Chao, and C. M. Reigeluth. 1986. A review of strategies for sequencing and synthesizing information. *Review of Educational Research* 56: 437–471.

Walberg, H. J., and M. Uguroglu. 1980. Motivation and educational productivity: Theories, results, and implications. In L. J. Fyans, Jr. (ed.), *Achievement motivation: Recent trends in theory and research*. New York: Plenum, 1980.

Weiner, B. 1980. *Human motivation*. New York: Holt, Rinehart and Winston.

Wlodkowski, R. J. 1985. *Enhancing adult motivation to learn*. San Francisco: Jossey–Bass.

SECTION II

Design and Implementation

CHAPTER FIVE

Instructional Design and the New Teaching Technologies

Kerry A. Johnson

It is clear that new communication technologies—particularly computer technologies—hold great promise for education. It is equally clear, however, that the use of these technologies for instruction requires a careful reconceptualization of (a) the structure and sequence of instructional information; (b) the presentation and representation of learning materials; and (c) the roles of teachers and students.

In the broadest sense, at least three major themes should guide decisions about using technology in teaching. The first theme involves the concept of instructional design and its potential applications. The second involves the intrinsic, dynamic nature of the media themselves, including their level of acceptance among educators. The third theme involves the manner in which specific technologies are integrated into traditional educational practices: The ultimate goal in using technology for teaching and learning should be to enhance what we already do well, and allow us to explore approaches we have never been able to consider.

As the role of technology becomes more central in a given instructional situation, predicting learner questions, identifying instructional paths, and anticipating learning outcomes become much more crucial. In a teacher-controlled learning environment, strategy changes can take place readily. In contrast, in a technology-facilitated learning environment, teacher and student needs and behaviors must be anticipated as much as possible to provide the completeness, reality, and challenge characteristic of the best instruction.

INSTRUCTIONAL DESIGN: BASIC APPLICATIONS

Excellent instructors, involved with traditional content and a straightforward goal of transferring the content to the student, probably do not need to consciously fret over instructional design decisions. They naturally apply good design principles. They understand the structure of the knowledge; they order that knowledge based on hierarchies of prerequisite information, and they then monitor the reception of that knowledge by the learners, providing guidance and feedback along the way.

Exceptional instructors also recognize the importance of balance between what is provided for the student and what the student should independently and responsibly seek. They match complexity of content with student ability. They loop back to earlier topics, providing bridges between new learning and previous learning. They match examples to student interest. They involve. They engage. They motivate. They create a single, exciting environment containing content, learner, and instructor in a dynamic, organic blend.

In contrast with instructor-led learning, which relies in part on the instructor's personal style, technology-based learning proceeds under conditions which call for clear analytic processes in order to create effective, efficient materials. As we have seen in earlier chapters, many instructional design theories exist, and while much more research is required to clearly understand how precise applications can create successful materials, enough good work has been done for us to proceed comfortably.

Elaboration Theory (ET) (Reigeluth and Stein, 1983) and Component Design Theory (CDT) (Merrill, 1987) are among several useful, direct responses to the special requirements of designing for technology-based instruction—in particular for computer-based instruction (CBI) and its extension, interactive video (CBIV). While each theory is certainly useful in other, more traditional instructional contexts, their combined use in the areas of CBI and CBIV is almost imperative.

Elaboration Theory

Elaboration Theory is based on the notion that instruction should begin with a special kind of overview—one that teaches a few general, simple, fundamental, concrete concepts, and then proceeds progressively to more complex, detailed, abstract ideas that elaborate on the initial concept. ET focuses on subject-matter organization issues and on the way in which individuals are most likely to organize that subject matter into their own cognitive structures. As a result, selection, sequencing, synthesizing, and summarizing of the content are the principle decision issues for designers using this theory.

Three major learning theories or approaches form the basis for ET. The first is the concept of prerequisites and learning hierarchies, as developed by Gagne and Briggs (1974). They argue that there is structural order to any information to be learned, and that this structural order needs to be explicit in the establishment of any learning environment. The second major antecedent concept is that of procedural prerequisites. Procedural prerequisites derive from task analysis, or an understanding of how the knowledge to be gained will be applied in a direct way to some procedure, typically a workplace procedure. Third, the concepts of spiral curricula (Bruner, 1966) or web learning (Norman, 1973) lead to ET by suggesting the importance of building connections between each new concept and those that precede it, gradually constructing a complete treatment of a given subject area.

Each of the antecedent instructional theories contributes to one or more of the seven components of the Elaboration Theory:

1. *An Elaborative Sequence.* An elaborative sequence is created as an overall organizational element of the instruction. It is the most "macro" design approach. It is a simple-to-complex sequence, but of a very special type: It epitomizes, rather than summarizes, the major idea of the instruction. An elaborative sequence takes a broad, general, concrete concept that represents the major ideas to be presented, and builds on that concept throughout the instruction—gradually adding detail, counterconcepts, and abstraction.

2. *A Learning-Prerequisite Sequence.* This sequence is created to deal with lesson-level organization. Each principle or concept to be learned has a unique set of defining attributes, or characteristics. These are the critical components of the idea that must be understood before new learning in relation to that idea can take place. A learning-prerequisite sequence, therefore, depends upon the structure of the content to be learned.

3. *A Summarizer.* It is important to systematically review material throughout a lesson, to prevent forgetting. The summarizer need only be a concise statement recapitulating the major concepts or principles. For complex lessons, or in dealing with complex concepts or principles, it may be necessary to provide internal lesson summaries. For simpler ideas, a single summarizer at the end of a lesson might suffice.

4. *A Synthesizer.* A synthesizer relates learning of a particular subject to a broader body of related, previously learned concepts or principles. It provides a means for the student to tie new learning to previously learned ideas by identifying conceptual links.

5. *An Analogy.* Analogies are useful learning devices because they help tie new learning vividly and concretely to familiar ideas. They allow the learner to bring knowledge from one content area to bear on learning in a new content area; but, even more importantly, they do so by creating strong images of the new material in the terms of known concepts or experiences.

6. *A Cognitive Strategy Activator.* Cognitive strategies are generic, or basic, learning skills. Cognitive strategy activators are simply devices embedded in the lessons that focus the student on a particular strategy. For example, visual cues such as diagrams, or models, can be used to teach many concepts more clearly than can verbal descriptions. Calling on students to use their visual cognitive strategies provides them with alternative means of considering the same phenomena.

7. *Learner Control.* This is a particularly important element of Elaboration Theory for computer-based instruction. In many independent study formats,

such as print-based instruction or video-based instruction, learners have a clear sense of where they are in the material. This is generally not the case in CBI, however, unless there is a conscious effort to build a clear control system into the materials. This control system should include learner control of content, rate of learning, cognitive strategies, and order of learning.

This quick overview of Elaboration Theory is intended to provide a general grasp of the major components of the theory. Reigeluth and Stein (1983) provide much more discussion of examples and applications of the theory. The significance of Elaboration Theory to an instructional design problem is that it provides a working set of hypotheses for macro design, for the organization of large bodies of concepts or principles. Micro design—the design of lesson-level materials, or instruction on single ideas—can be accomplished using Merrill's Component Design Theory.

Component Design Theory

Merrill (1987) argues that the present capabilities of computer-based instruction systems allow students more direct access to experiences and knowledge. In addition, the use of CBI changes the function of the teacher, from acting as a mere deliverer of information to doing what the teacher can do best—tutoring, advising, or providing subject-matter expertise.

Merrill bases his Component Design Theory (CDT) on one fundamental assumption and four basic principles. The assumption is that there are different categories of learning, or learning outcomes—that is, that learning tasks can be categorized and that the accomplishment of those tasks can be measured. Related to that assumption, the first principle argues that it is important to create cognitive structures consistent with learning outcomes. It presupposes a direct relationship between what must be done with the concepts to be learned, and the intrinsic structure of those concepts. The second principle is that Elaboration Theory is the desired macro-design approach; that while CDT guides the order of lesson-level instruction, ET guides course design. The third principle is that the learner needs to be carefully and deliberately guided through the instruction, but that as the learning progresses he or she should assume greater control over the guidance. And, finally, the learner needs ample opportunity to practice using new concepts and skills in a dynamic, responsive, monitored environment.

When applied, therefore, CDT is concerned with the way learning goals are defined and stated, with how content is represented and organized, and with the transactions that the student engages in with the system. It is the transactions between student and system that provide learner control, suggest learning strategies, and give guidance—because they solicit and monitor student responses to the learning materials. If instruction is truly interactive, the relative frequency and complexity of these transactions will be high, and an outline of them will provide a clear view of the activities of instruction, as well as of the nature and organization of the content.

INSTRUCTIONAL TECHNOLOGY AND INNOVATION

Technological innovations typically take as much as fifteen years to be fully accepted by a broad class of users. However, within the first five years after its introduction a new technology as useful as interactive video can enjoy the support of at least the innovators and activists, representing about 15 percent of the total target-user group. This is in fact the present state of receptivity of interactive video technology in industry and education.

The importance of interactive video as a technology for training and education is that it combines the power of the computer to control, manage, and organize information with the power of video to represent visual data. The difficulty for designers and other users of the technology is that there is no analogous predecessor—and the possibilities of the new medium stretch the designers' imaginations.

In a talk some years ago at WGBH, Boston, Harry Lasker proposed that the significance of interactive video was actually that it is a new form of software—what he referred to as *image-enhanced software* (see Figure 5.1). In essence, to conceptualize this medium, one has to think about an entirely new structure for organizing and accessing information. Starting from a core of visual images, one works outward, through various levels and forms of meaning, to arrive finally at the social or cultural context of the message itself.

The foundation of image-enhanced software is video—used for motivational purposes, for appeal, and to ensure visual identification. Structured around the video is the first level of computer controls that enable the user to move around in the materials and to find the way back again. The next level is the content itself, organized around some learning theory such as those discussed above, and stored in conceptual hierarchies. These layers of meaning form the raw material of the messages.

Both the images and the environment are ultimately organized into a "hyper-environment," a term that refers to a set of interrelated data bases that allow for maximum exchange of information between components of a system. These data bases might include text and visuals drawn from mythology, or a dictionary of quotes and illustrations of famous scientists, or a complete in-

Figure 5.1. *Image-enhanced software.*

1. Videos
   Appeal/Identification

2. User Control
   Communication
   Navigation

3. Image Dimension
   Layers of Message
   Answer Analysis

4. Hyper-environment
   Data Bases

5. Perspective
   Viewing Mode
   Conceptual Level

6. Social Structure

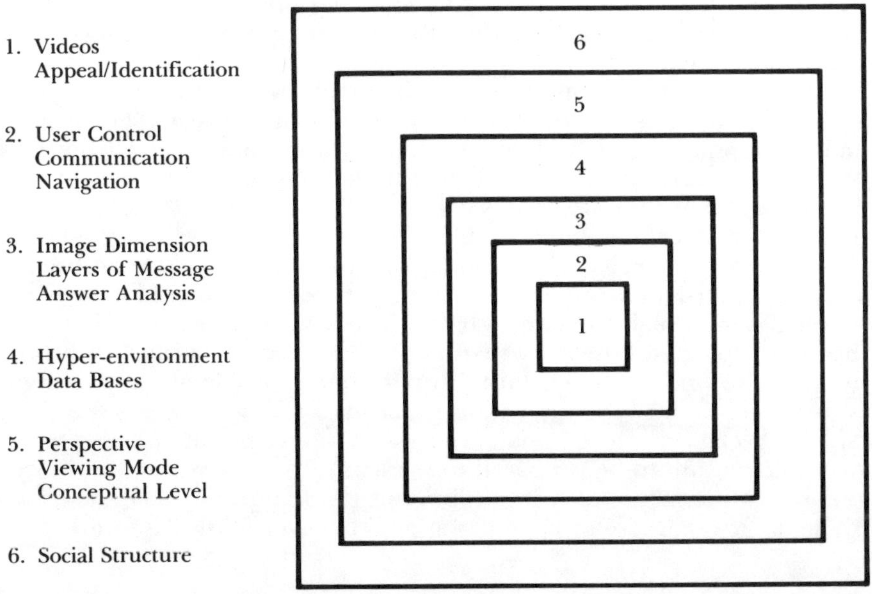

teractive encyclopedia of poets and poetry. This is the most obvious level at which the user interacts with the system. These interactions between user and system in turn provide a means to examine the learning materials from varied perspectives, or different conceptual levels. Finally, the entire system is embedded in particular social or cultural structures in the same way that any training system is embedded in the culture of a corporation or a profession. The system assumes the standards, the look, the feel of the host structure. It is the total effect, the interactive levels of meaning and expression, that constitutes image-enhanced software—and, in particular, interactive video.

USES OF TECHNOLOGY FOR TEACHING

Given that interactive video and computer-based instruction, or image-enhanced software, are complex, flexible, dynamic, engaging media, and that they have a place in education and training, how do we determine what that place is? How do we envision where they fit? One thing is clear—they must fit into existing instructional settings. Instructors' roles may change, but they will not disappear.

Figure 5.2 is an attempt to organize the uses of technology for teaching. It is a multidimensional matrix of applications of technology, such as CBI and CBIV. The *horizontal* dimension is the level of student independence (or, to use Merrill's term "learner control"). Independence depends in large part on the degree to which the student chooses his or her own learning activities, or is directed to them by the will of the instructor or the group. A typical unit of analysis for this dimension, therefore, might be group size, which varies from class to individual.

The *vertical* dimension portrays a rough taxonomy of cognitive activities, ranging from straight reception of presented information at the top to the more active, involving analysis and evaluation of information at the bottom. A third dimension, one that sweeps *diagonally* across the plane from upper left to lower right of the matrix, suggests an increasing size of instructional unit from an activity within a lesson, to whole lessons, to entire courses. It is like an overlay that encompasses the other two dimensions or ignores them, as the case may be.

Examination of a few sample cells of the matrix will suggest ways in which it can be used and possibly modified to meet individual needs. For instance, at the level of practice and application within a classroom setting, CBI or CBIV could be used in an instructor-led format to demonstrate variations on a particular concept that the class works collectively to discuss, solve, or compare. Drill and practice, or annotated problem-solving activities, might guide a discussion that asks students to apply concepts to a new situation. The instructor—using a computer and a projection system, for example—could have control of sample data or visuals to share with the class. A math instructor, for instance, might choose to extend the presentation of the solution to a calculus problem by stepping the students as a group through similar problems, annotating the steps in the solution as the discussion proceeds.

At a more elaborate level, small groups of students might be asked to work on case studies, and to be prepared to present information back to the class. In a more traditional use of case studies, this would typically take the form of analyzing large quantities of print materials. However, if the case studies were

Figure 5.2. *Uses of technology for teaching.*

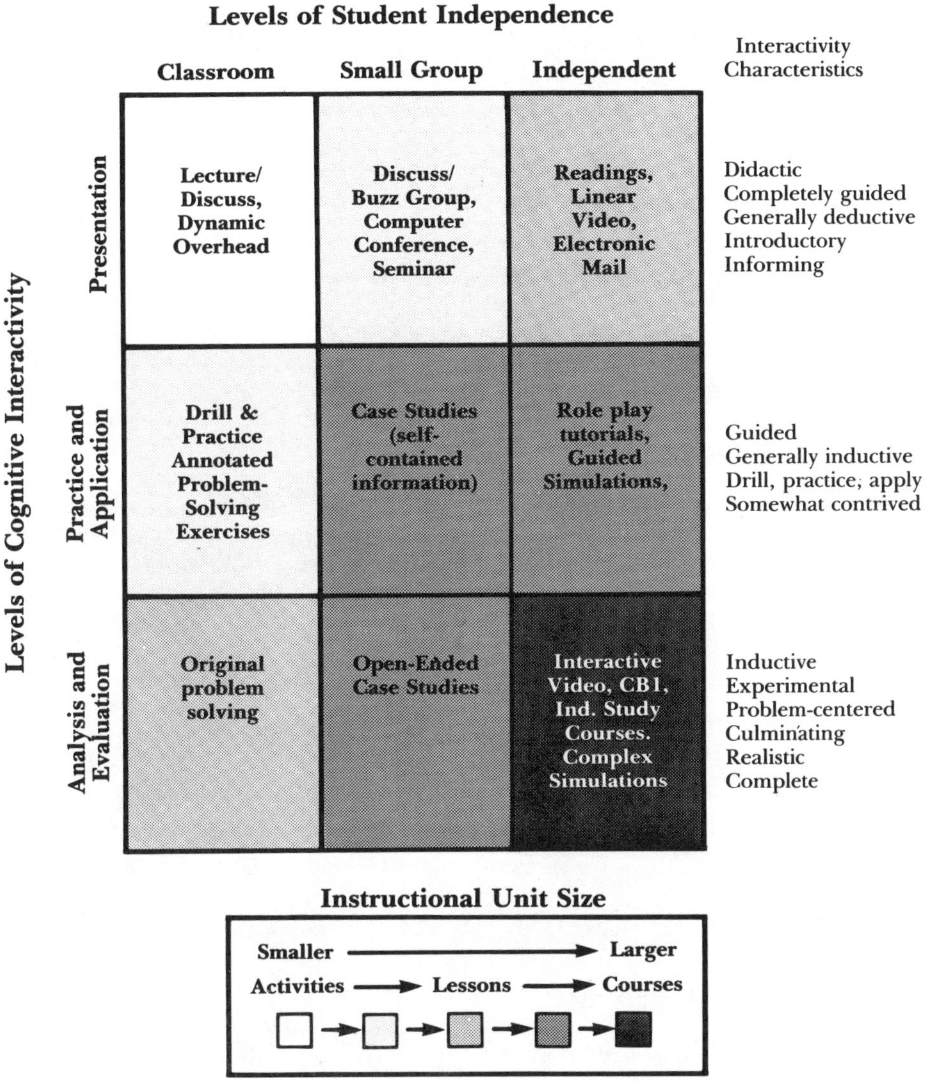

Levels of Student Independence

	Classroom	Small Group	Independent	Interactivity Characteristics
Presentation	Lecture/ Discuss, Dynamic Overhead	Discuss/ Buzz Group, Computer Conference, Seminar	Readings, Linear Video, Electronic Mail	Didactic Completely guided Generally deductive Introductory Informing
Practice and Application	Drill & Practice Annotated Problem-Solving Exercises	Case Studies (self-contained information)	Role play tutorials, Guided Simulations,	Guided Generally inductive Drill, practice, apply Somewhat contrived
Analysis and Evaluation	Original problem solving	Open-Ended Case Studies	Interactive Video, CBI, Ind. Study Courses. Complex Simulations	Inductive Experimental Problem-centered Culminating Realistic Complete

(Levels of Cognitive Interactivity)

Instructional Unit Size

Smaller ⟶ Larger
Activities ⟶ Lessons ⟶ Courses

presented in a computer-based format, they could be designed to be much more interactive and open-ended than typical paper-based case studies are. At the level of practice and application, they might be self-contained, with all relevant information provided through the system. At the analysis and evaluation level, however, the instructor (through the computer system) might require the students to create or find new information outside of the computer-based system, information that called on a greater synthesis of knowledge from other learning experiences.

At the most elaborate level, the student might be asked to work independently on a totally self-contained course. The course, delivered technologically (e.g., with interactive video), would present information, probe understanding of that information, and provide opportunities to apply and evaluate that information in new situations. It would be characterized by a careful elaboration of concepts from the key concept to analogous concepts from other fields. It would also be characterized by a careful arrangement of transactions that would challenge and engage the student, and that would provide constructive guidance and feedback to the student. Finally, it would provide information on student progress to the instructor.

CONCLUSION

The design of instruction for technology-based instructional systems is more complicated than the design of traditional lecture-lab instruction because the instruction itself must anticipate student behaviors and understandings. As a result, the design process must be more analytic and deliberate than corresponding design processes for traditional instruction. Recent improvements in instructional design theory, combined with an increased understanding of the characteristics of the available technologies, are leading us to make more sensible use of those technologies for teaching. In the final analysis, given an understanding of the desired learning outcomes, we are now able to predict with reasonable accuracy a set of successful instructional approaches.

REFERENCES

Briggs, L. J. (ed.), 1977. *Instructional design: Principles and applications.* Englewood Cliffs, NJ: Educational Technology Press.

Bruner, J. S. 1966. *Toward a theory of instruction.* New York: W. W. Norton and Company.

Davis, A. B. 1986. *Managing technological innovation.* San Francisco: Jossey-Bass.

Dick, W., and Carey, L. 1978. *The systematic design of instruction.* Glenview, Illinois: Scott Foreman.

Gagne, R. M., and L. J. Briggs. 1974. *Principles of instructional design* (2d ed.). New York: Holt, Rinehart & Winston.

Gropper, G. L. 1974. *Instructional strategies.* Englewood Cliffs, NJ: Educational Technology Publications.

Knox, A. B. 1986. *Helping adults learn.* San Francisco: Jossey-Bass.

Lasker, H. 1985. Informal discussion, WGBH Interactive Video Conference. Boston: November.

Merrill, M. D. 1987. The new component design theory: Instructional design for courseware authoring. *Instructional Science* 16:19–34.

Messick, S., and Associates. 1978. *Individuality and learning.* San Francisco: Jossey-Bass.

Niemi, J. A., and Gooler, D. D. (ed.) 1987. *Technologies for learning outside the classroom.* San Francisco: Jossey-Bass.

Reigeluth, C. M. (ed.), 1983. *Instructional design theories and models: An overview of their current status.* Hillside, NJ: Erlbaum.

Reigeluth, C. M., and F. S. Stein. 1983. The elaboration theory of instruction. In C. M. Reigeluth (ed.), *Instructional design theories and models.* Hillsdale, NJ: Erlbaum.

Resnick, L. B. 1977. Task analysis in instructional design: Some cases from mathematics. In D. Klahr (ed.), *Cognition and instruction.* Hillsdale, NJ: Erlbaum.

Richard, R. 1986. *The theoretical and conceptual bases of instructional design.* New York: Nichols.

Solomon, G. 1981. *Interaction of media, cognition, and learning.* San Francisco: Jossey-Bass.

CHAPTER SIX

Power and Potential
The University and Instructional Design

Lin J. Foa

In our universities and colleges, more than in any other environment, instructional design displays the many facets that have made it an exciting and controversial concept. Academics—teaching faculty, administrators, researchers—have yet to decide whether instructional design represents more of a threat or an opportunity to higher education. Does it offer a powerful tool to help solve the universities' newly emergent identity crises and rapidly multiplying external pressures, or is it simply another expensive fad that will have little effect on the future of postsecondary education?

Regardless of the fact that these questions are still unanswered, instructional design exists in our universities and colleges both as an academic discipline and in varied functional roles. As an academic discipline, instructional design frequently is housed in education schools. Having had the education schools as a home has been useful for the development of applied theory, but has undoubtedly been a detriment in developing relationships with the other, more "traditionally academic," departments of the university—because of the disrespect that education schools, deservedly or not, often engender. As a consequence, instructional design has too frequently been considered a subject perhaps useful for elementary-school teachers, but having as little relevance to liberal arts and sciences professors as, say, the "new math."

The frequent reliance on technology or nonprint media to achieve the goals of instructional design has also resulted in the field's often being referred to as "Educational Technology" or "Instructional Media"—on the surface still further removed from the interests or activities of traditional faculty in philosophy, history, or physics. Nevertheless, in 1986 more than eighty ID degree programs, the majority at the master's or doctoral levels, were offered under a variety of names, and the discipline shows every sign of continuing its rapid growth (*College Blue Book*, 1987).

More immediately significant, however, is the field's functional strength. In its functions as a support service to individual faculty, as a development unit that creates courses and whole curricula, and as an outreach activity that brings government and corporate contracts and dollars to the campus, instructional design displays the potential to become a powerful contributor to a university's success. In this chapter, each of these functions will be explored and analyzed in terms of both the controversies they have prompted and the opportunities they provide. These opportunities, important as they are to individual students and faculty members, are even more vital to university and college administrators and decision makers.

To date, theories and processes of instructional design have been relatively little recognized as management tools in higher education. Yet they offer a powerful means of responding to the issues that are prompting educational institutions worldwide to reexamine their very reasons for being.

GATHERING PRESSURES FOR CHANGE

On a specific level, university and college administrators face enormous changes and unrelenting new pressures:

- New populations of learners, newly armed with raised consumer consciousness
- Changing knowledge structures
- Demands from students, employers, and communities for applied learning
- A changing faculty, many of whom choose to teach part-time while they engage in other professional endeavors, but all of whom are being pushed to improve their teaching skills
- Proliferating off-campus sites where courses are offered, with a resulting need for cost-effective and comparable curriculum design
- Demands from state and federal governments, funding agencies, and parents for greater assessment and accountability
- The need to create external linkages with the corporate, military, and nonprofit sectors

Is it any wonder that the turnover rate for senior administrators and presidents is unprecedented? Whether those in positions of leadership will be able to respond appropriately and successfully is of course unknown, but they have an effective, and as yet underutilized, ally for their efforts. To demonstrate the potential assistance in decision making and management practice that instructional design can offer, it will be useful to analyze its application to each of the changes and pressures listed above. Following that, the chapter will conclude by examining three remaining questions that face our universities.

Final answers to these questions are not yet available, but instructional design may well provide direction and impetus to those seeking imaginative solutions.

The New Learners

Advocates of nontraditional education in the mid-1970s focused mainly on the rapidly enlarging adult populations on the nation's campuses (e.g., Cross, 1976). Certainly these older students have begun to change our ideas of the traditional college student, but, as was suggested in Chapter Three, universities should be adapting to several other populations as well—all with new and diverse learning needs. In these past few years, there have been well-publicized calls, particularly on the federal level, to return to earlier configurations of the university—to move back to more aristocratic concept of liberal learning devoted to the classics, reserved for the few who had the time and money to afford it. There may in fact be a need for this type of education, but it is going to satisfy only a small proportion of our population, and only at a particular time in their lives. If the universities choose this path, other institutions will spring up to satisfy the need for more immediately practical postsecondary education for the larger and more diverse population. Moreover, whether by accident or design, most universities have already become too dependent on the economic benefits of new students to retreat to a classical concept of higher education. Instead, they must continue to seek new institutional paradigms to deal with the needs of new populations.

Instructional design, with its focus on the learner, and its insistence on carefully defining the learner and his or her specific needs, can help them to do just that. By taking learners "where they are," by understanding learner needs, by meaningfully structuring content, and (as discussed in Chapter Four) by building in the motivational factors to explore and persevere, instructional designers can ensure that the proper foundations in any subject are understood before students move on to more abstract and difficult concepts. The architectural analogy used in earlier chapters is apt here when one thinks of the strict requirement for strong and practical foundations to provide the underpinnings for aboveground activity *or* creativity. Similarly, by using technology to enable students to proceed at their own pace through the early skill-building stages of a subject, faculty members are left with the time to help students develop more deeply the understandings and insights into interrelationships that are the possession of an educated person.

Thus, an instructional design team might work with faculty members in the English department to develop computer-based courses in writing and reading skills that could be pursued independently or in a classroom situation. This self-paced study frees instructors from the stultifying repetitiveness of teaching (for example) proper paragraph structure over and over again, and encourages them to concentrate on providing the strong motivation and support that epitomizes the best student-teacher relationships. Such a structure also ensures faculty that, once students have satisfactorily completed the prerequisites, they are indeed prepared for further study, whether they are young, non-native speakers of English, or older, displaced homemakers, or traditional 18- to 22-year-olds.

Instructional design, particularly in conjunction with technology, provides a means of offering higher education to the masses, but the resultant increased structure and standardization does not imply a lessening of quality. The new learners often are unable to participate, and may be uninterested in the traditional four-year, full-time campus experience wherein classroom learning often takes second place to growing up. Thus, they may have little patience with courses that do not achieve their purpose efficiently and effectively.

How many of us have taken courses, even in highly regarded institutions, that turned out to be irrelevant, ill-prepared, and useless? Today's students, often taking only one or two courses at a time, and usually paying for them themselves on a course-by-course basis, simply won't tolerate a lack of organization and purpose. They know they can vote with their feet, and do. Administrators who seek to serve these students successfully might well want to contemplate the effect that needs assessments, the development of clear objectives and built-in motivators, and the accurate and publicized measurement of outcomes would have on the majority of courses they schedule.

Changing Knowledge Structures

Besides a rapidly changing population of students, today's educators and policymakers face an even more pervasive change that is already having a definite effect on the structure of our universities and colleges. As discussed in Chapter Three, the nature of *knowledge itself* is changing—at such an accelerating rate that it is commonly said that what an engineer knows upon graduation today will be totally outdated in five years. This calls into serious question our traditional view of education as the process of a faculty expert pouring information into a receptive student's open mind.

When the faculty-as-authority model was developed, it seemed possible for an individual to know a good deal of what there was to know about a given subject. The cliché of yellowed lecture notes reused *ad nauseum* could develop because the presentation of a subject didn't change radically from year to year. Today, our knowledge—including both facts and understanding—is changing so rapidly, and is becoming so intertwined dynamically with other fields that one person cannot hope or claim to know most of the information worth knowing about *any* given subject. Rather, the knowledge that is of use today is structural understanding and the application of skills—the conceptual and practical systems that allow us to find and plug in new facts and behaviors appropriately, as needed. These "cognitive systems" enable us to function interactively, attentive to the dynamic nature of knowledge and experiential activity.

The protest could arise that this might be true of biotechnology, or any of the other high-tech fields emerging today, but that it is hardly a requirement of history. Yet, as our understanding of the narrowness of many of our earlier disciplines increases, we come to realize that much of what we accepted as fact is no longer accurate if, for example, viewed from a non-Western perspective. We have also learned there is little purpose in memorizing great masses of information that quickly become outdated or that are readily available from a computer. As a result, we are increasingly faced with the need to structure interdisciplinary institutes and programs that respond to new demands, and to view our material from more global perspectives. If our society is not to succumb totally to the forces of entropy, these changes mean that we are also clearly in need of people well trained in both analysis *and* synthesis.

The New Liberal Arts Program, begun by the Sloan Foundation in 1982, provides a good example of this renewed emphasis on interdisciplinary education, but also points to one of the real dangers facing faculty and administrators trying to cope with changing knowledge needs. The Sloan Foundation hopes to emphasize the importance of quantitative reasoning, and an understanding of technology, to all students. To reach this goal, they award grants to selected liberal arts colleges and universities to design interdisciplinary courses and intructional materials, promote lecture series, and fund special faculty development efforts.

Significant revitalization of traditional courses in such fields as history, literature, and mathematics has already occurred in several institutions. Yet, too often, the impetus for change has come from only one or a few individuals—and some of their best work may disappear as they move on to other things. Administrators can formalize and generalize these new insights using the instructional design process (whether via the written word, faculty development workshops, or computers or other technology), thus ensuring that a stronger foundation for more lasting and widespread change could be produced.

Applied Learning

Many critics of higher education decry the current emphasis on applied learning—and, indeed, on the whole of thought concerning career education and contracting with industry or the government to deliver on-site programs. Yet students, employers, and community leaders have expressed their unrelenting need for an education that draws from sound theoretical principles and puts them to work for the common good.

Ernest Lynton, one of the chief spokespersons for this position, says "Universities must recognize that the effective attainment of their scholarly mission calls for a complex and interactive process with their constituencies that goes beyond carrying out basic research. There is no question that such research continues to be important, yet by itself it has limited societal value and impact. Such scholarly work needs to be part of a variety of interrelated activities that link the research efforts to their eventual applications and that produce a two-way flow of continuous feedback and adaptation" (Lynton and Elman, 1987).

Applied learning occurs today in some classrooms, and the most effective faculty have learned intuitively to make bridges between theory and practical application—a skill they were never taught in graduate school. These "relevant" faculty members constantly show students how their studies in English composition or environmental science can help them in their daily and professional lives. How many other faculty members would like to do something similar, but simply don't know how? Instructional design offers faculty members and researchers the skills to discover and build-in those connections explicitly and effectively.

The instructional design team can work with faculty subject-matter experts, as well as external contracting agencies, to design applications of learning skills and theories directly to the task at hand—whether it be business management or historic preservation. As a consequence, a kind of sea change occurs, wherein faculty start thinking in terms of how their fields and their assignments can integrate theory and practice. Nor should we think of applied learning as only that which is immediately recompensable, or a skill that is immediately needed in the outside world. Rather, in more general terms, applied learning can be considered to be that which the student *needs* to know, for some individual and self-recognized purpose.

Significant agreement exists that it is only when students do recognize a personal need to know something that they will actively learn it (e.g., Butler, 1985). The instructional designer aims to make sure that the needs that will supply the motivation are clearly presented and accepted by the student. Traditionally, of course, the pressure of the need to get good grades has driven many students, but that has resulted in a passivity and inability to learn independently that troubles both faculty and employers. As one recourse, many colleges and universities are discovering that actually combining education and work creates an environment highly conducive to learning. This discovery has produced more and more interest in co-op programs and internships, and more and more employers who are willing to provide learning opportunities at the work place.

Applied learning, when properly designed, can also lead to what might be termed the "applied university." The leaders of such institutions recognize not only that they have an important task in educating people, but also that education must be enmeshed in our lives—leading to the much-discussed and hoped-for lifelong learning. Moreover, these educational institutions understand their responsibility to the communities and states that support them, as well as to the less-well-developed populations of the world struggling to catch up. As Lynton and Elman (1987) point out:

> A wide variety of private enterprises, as well as public agencies and organizations, now find themselves having to cope with the implications of new technologies and new knowledge. Almost all of them require assistance in this process. The opportunity for university involvement ranges from basic and applied research to technical assistance, policy analysis, and—last but certainly not least—a great deal of continuous updating of individual skills and understanding.

Two successful examples of this broader "applied university" concept can be seen at Syracuse University and at the University of Georgia. During the late 1960s and early 1970s, an Instructional Communications program at Syracuse was split into two entities—the Center for Instructional Development, a centrally administered faculty development, service, and consulting center; and the Instructional Design, Development, and Evaluation (IDDE) program that offers masters' and doctoral degrees and does significant external contract work. One of the largest of these contracts is a ten-year program of assistance provided to the government of Indonesia. Working with USAID, the World Bank, UNESCO, and others, Syracuse's IDDE program has been instrumental in developing centers, academic programs, production facilities, and faculty development programs in Indonesia (Doughty, 1987).

An interesting footnote to these contractual undertakings is that few American universities or government units have been so open to developing such large-scale coordinated instructional programs, perhaps feeling they were unnecessary. Yet it is foreseeable that, in a few years, the sophistication and efficacy of our educational systems may trail behind those of "less-developed" countries.

At the University of Georgia's Department of Instructional Technology, an ongoing project to promote adult literacy has been very successful. Instructional designers from the university, Dr. John Henry Martin, and IBM software designers developed PALS (Principle of the Alphabet Literacy System). PALS is a computer-based interactive videodisc program using a comic-book format designed to teach adults who read at or below the fifth-grade level.

Thus, whether involved with international development or national literacy projects, instructional design departments are often in the forefront of the movement toward more direct applications of research. Applied learning enables universities and colleges to respond to the new responsibilities they are facing, and (as we shall see later in this chapter) also enables them to develop new funding sources that serve more traditional goals as well.

Faculty Development and Part-Time Faculty

As the size of continuing education programs increases, and as faculty in fields such as business and computer science are more drawn to industry, the use of part-time faculty has burgeoned in many institutions. In response, faculty development programs, once rare, are now becoming more commonplace on our campuses—and they are increasingly aimed at permanent, full-time faculty as well. One of the major outcomes of instructional design theory and process has been the creation and acceptance of facilities such as Syracuse University's Instructional Development Center. Available for use by any faculty person on campus, it (like most such centers) offers help in course design, materials development, and evaluation methods.

However, such centers have far more potential at colleges and universities nationwide than is currently being realized. The growing body of faculty development research could be combined with instructional design theory and techniques, to create at every institution way stations for revitalizing older faculty and helping the many new faculty that will be required in the next several decades. People preparing to teach in our colleges are the only professionals who receive absolutely no training in the practice of their profession. Just as we wouldn't think of letting an unpracticed surgeon operate on our bodies, no matter how much anatomy he or she might know, so should we be leery of letting an unpracticed professor operate on our minds.

Moreover, these instructional development centers can, and should, be structured as vehicles for transferring research results to faculty in many disciplines. It has been noted, particularly by administrators in continuing education, that practitioners are rarely cognizant of research on adult learning styles. If this is the case for a new and relatively self-conscious field, how much more so for those who teach undergraduates?

Instructional design theory and processes have drawn on research in cognitive science to predict, for example, that certain types of materials can best be learned when visually presented, and other types by verbal review; that presentation of an overview at the beginning of any teaching session helps retention; and that students' attention spans can only be sustained in any given activity for a certain number of minutes. If these concepts are known, yet not broadcast and practiced in the universities, perhaps there is merit to the criticisms leveled by some of the recent national reports on higher education. Before they are directed to do so by their boards or state governing agencies, might it not make sense for university administrators to urge faculty to use the tools that instructional design makes available? If the use of these resources is appropriately rewarded, all faculty could be encouraged to take visible steps toward improving their teaching.

Off-Campus Sites and Program Comparability

Our colleges and universities are drawing ever larger nets around potential student populations, and more and more are establishing off-campus centers. These proliferating and sometimes remote sites require campus leaders to weigh the value of instructional design centers in ensuring comparability of course offerings. There are two ways in which an instructional design unit can accomplish this, depending upon whether the course will be faculty-taught or offered for independent study.

If an instructional design team is asked to develop a course that will be taught simultaneously at a variety of sites, they can build the development of faculty guides into their approach. Faculty guides, with specific syllabus outlines, reading and reference lists, and suggestions for class discussion and assignments, will help any given faculty member move through the syllabus in such a way that all significant material is comparably covered, but so that considerable room is also left for individual faculty to insert their own variations on the theme. This is the procedure used for courses developed at The University of Maryland University College.

University College serves adult students at more than 300 sites on military bases around the world, and at civilian sites in Maryland, enabling students to earn University of Maryland residential credit regardless of their location. A course must be not only equivalent to the same course offered in College Park, but what is taught overseas must also give the student comparable preparation for the next course in the sequence, wherever it might be taken. Thus, the instructional design unit, in this case called the Center for Instructional Development and Evaluation, works with faculty subject-matter experts to develop courses that can be taught worldwide. The course might be a basic English composition or calculus course taught in traditional "stand-up" classroom style, or it might be part of the Open University program.

Open University courses, based on the British Open University system, are developed using a full instructional design process. The courses, which allow students to learn independently, rely on well-developed student and faculty guides. Unlike lower-level courses that may be single-discipline based and develop lower-level learning skills, the Open University courses are interdisciplinary, requiring seriously motivated students who are capable of rigorous and significant reading and writing. These courses may focus on such topics as "Risk," viewed from its sociological, psychological, literary, and economic perspectives; or "Life in and Around Chesapeake Bay," which covers everything from literary and musical re-creations of life on the Chesapeake to environmental studies of marine culture. Having these courses designed, reviewed, evaluated, and revised by professional course designers working closely with faculty subject-matter experts ensures that Maryland students will be provided a top-quality learning experience.

The courses, while initially more expensive to produce, can be replicated again and again at many sites, thus ultimately proving to be cost-effective. Cost-effectiveness is a serious concern for university administrators when it comes to curriculum planning, and obviously the traditional and most easily accountable costs result from a faculty member developing and teaching a single course. Replicable courses developed by instructional design teams may seem inordinately expensive by comparison, but only if they are viewed in terms of initial cost.

By way of example, consider *Sesame Street*. This children's television show, which arguably has had a bigger influence on young children's learning than anything the schools have ever done, was one of the most expensive television shows ever produced. Yet, it now costs only one cent per viewer hour, making it one of the least expensive learning methods available (Perelman, 1986). College and university administrators need to learn to measure costs in new ways, and to think creatively about how development costs for particular courses can be amortized, and how collaborative funding arrangements can be developed.

Clearly, it would be foolish to use a thoroughgoing instructional design process on a course that enrolled ten people once each year. However, just as clearly, the $8,000–$10,000 that it costs to fully develop a standard three-credit course can be quickly recovered if it is delivered to 1,000 students at ten different sites each year for three years. Decision makers need to develop long-range planning and curricular accountability strategies with their faculty, and with deans who will allow them to know which courses require and/or will benefit from some or all of the instructional design process.

Once such a process is developed and is an accepted alternative to traditional course development by an individual instructor, there are subsidiary benefits. Faculty are given new opportunities to stretch themselves, to work with colleagues in other departments, to develop new techniques and materials that may influence their traditional teaching, and to create courses that will enable them to extend their expertise to students who may be geographically or temporally distant. (e.g., with telecourses).

Accountability and Assessment

Accountability and assessment are two concepts that may well become the touchstones of education in the late twentieth century. Astute policy makers and administrators in higher education have begun to perceive that simply providing entrance and exit exams to their students will neither satisfy the critics nor provide positive benefits to students.

Accountability can be defined in both internal and external terms. *Internal* accountability refers to the self-conscious integrity of the educational systems that an institution develops—usually visible mainly to faculty and students. *External* accountability can then be defined as the outcomes that an institution may be required to produce (the quantifiable and public evidence) that are visible to governing boards, state and federal funding agencies, etc.—proving that their graduates learned and succeeded as a result of their enrollment.

Internal accountability, the interdependent integrity of the courses, advising systems, curricular requirements, and faculty assignments all can be fostered by using the instructional design process. The needs-assessment process that is developed in detailed fashion by instructional designers (discussed in

Chapter Two) has been applied mainly in military and corporate settings to date, but could prove of great value to universities in this era of shrinking resources.

Major corporations frequently hire an instructional design team to figure out what skills and concepts are required by their senior management to deal with changing technology. Similarly, deans or academic affairs vice-presidents could take advantage of the experts often residing on their own campuses, or bring in outside consultants, to assess the areas that the institution's curricula should address. A clear-eyed review and evaluation of the courses and programs currently being offered frequently highlights areas of needed improvement, unseen gaps, and courses that are irrelevant or unmatched in quality to the mission of the university or college. By virtue of their independence from any specific discipline, instructional designers can offer objective evaluations based on factual evidence and logical analysis, a useful scythe for an administrator trying to cut through encrusted departmental politics.

Internal accountability, once developed, will allow university leaders to respond more positively and constructively to the pressures for external accountability. Many colleges and universities are already being asked to justify to state boards of higher education the quality of their instruction. The federal government's quest for proven return on its financial investment via its loan and aid programs is being matched by heightened consumer awareness among both parents and students alike. No longer cloistered from criticism, universities and colleges are being asked to prove their worth, and to identify exactly what it is they are asking people to buy at such a high price.

By virtue of their adherence to objectively analytic needs assessments and evaluations, instructional designers can readily provide administrators with substantial quantitative results, whether it be for a particular course or an entire curriculum. Furthermore, if administrators make it possible for instructional designers to work with curriculum committees and faculty councils to design a course or curriculum from the beginning, rather than letting it grow topsy-turvy, the initial data bases crucial to any kind of ultimate assessment of results for external audiences will already be built into the process.

To be sure, much has been written about this whole question of assessment and accountability in higher education circles. There is considerable backlash against the idea, particularly from traditional academics. In a recent essay, David M. Grossman (1987) said, "To the extent that technology and distance learning compromise professionalism and subvert the role of faculty, then no standard measure of quality will have any meaning." But what we should be upholding here is not some idealistic and anachronistic vision of who and what faculty are supposed to be, but rather the idea that student learning is what counts, whether it is done at the end of the log or on a distant computer or in a lecture room seating 300.

In this consumer-oriented age, and particularly with so many adult students paying for their own educations for very specific purposes, it does not seem at all unreasonable that people should seek to make sure they are getting their money's worth. Enmeshing the accountability issue with seemingly irrelevant questions of faculty rights and our inability to measure learning accurately does not advance student learning. Instead, more progress can be made if we can all acknowledge that, while it is difficult to measure learning, delivered by either new or old means, there is little to be lost and much to be gained by trying—if we are open and open-minded about the process.

External Linkages

Openness, responsiveness, and accountability also are important factors in the contracting process, with either the government or private industry. When external dollars are spent to design and deliver educational packages, universities must be prepared to plan effectively, meet deadlines efficiently, and accurately evaluate the success of programs—particularly if they hope to be awarded future contracts. This nimbleness and clear communication of results has not always characterized universities' efforts in the past. But today, more and more educational institutions are relying on outside funding for support of not only their research programs but their educational programs. Thus the capability to develop, deliver, and evaluate innovative and effective courses and materials in an efficient manner will be ever more important, or else universities will find the external funders turning elsewhere for services.

At The University of Maryland's University College, several projects illustrate this need for fast and effective response to industry and government needs, as well as demonstrating the range of subject matter that instructional design units are called upon to develop. Several years ago the nuclear power industry recognized the need to upgrade the education of power-plant operators. These employees worked unusual and irregular shifts; they were located miles from population centers; and they needed to be available at any time in case of problems—circumstances hardly conducive to their being enrolled in a traditional university program.

Using the Plato system and working closely with the university's College Park Nuclear Science department, the Center for Instructional Development and Evaluation (CIDE) developed a full nuclear science degree program. These courses, complete with supporting general education requirements, can be completed via computer by students on site at nuclear facilities around the country. Scheduled visits by touring faculty and advisors support the program, but by and large students take classes and tests, communicate with their peers and their instructors, and are evaluated—all with the aid of their computers.

In another instance, CIDE developed emergency medical training via interactive videodisc for the Navy Health Services Command. The immediacy, interactivity, and drama of these training videos allow the students to experience a lifelike simulation of an emergency, without either patients or students being jeopardized if the wrong answer or treatment is chosen. Similarly, a recent project involved creating video-based training programs for government workers, on ethics—a subject much in the national consciousness. Actors portray realistic situations with all the attendant emotions that might confront government civil servants, and the videos make their points dramatically and unforgettably.

These few examples demonstrate a range of learning projects that universities can provide for their surrounding constituents locally, nationally, and/or internationally. Outreach efforts like these allow an enormous amount of new information about "real world" practice, new technologies, and cross-fertilization of expertise to be gained. The instructional design unit thus serves as an "R & D" (research and development) unit for the whole university, bringing new skills, ideas, and dollars back for further university development.

Unfortunately, the work of an instructional design unit too often will be more widely known and appreciated outside the institution, because such efforts provide excellent public-relations material for annual reports and presentations to state legislators. Relatively less effort on all sides has been placed on internal communication, so that traditional faculty members, while mildly curious, too often regard the instructional design units on their campus as exotic and impenetrable "black holes." It is perhaps time for both the instructional design units and university administrators to take what has been learned about applied learning, faculty development, accountability, and external relationships, and attempt to redirect some of these lessons inward.

CONCLUSION

The potential for instructional design as a management and leadership tool in the universities is significant. Besides the issues discussed in this chapter, a new set of questions will become increasingly pressing in the next decades as universities and colleges seek to determine their place in our rapidly changing society. Instructional design theory and practice can help in formulating the varied answers to these questions, but the responses will require extensive collaboration among administrators, faculty, and practitioners of this newly emerging discipline.

An antecedent question that college and university leaders must face is whether, and how, they will distinguish between education and training, and how that distinction will be reflected in their missions and practice. Myriad definitions and emotional responses for both terms exist, and the enormous increase in "careerism" has been both praised and bemoaned on every campus. In the interests of moving forward with constructive and clear-cut agendas, it may now be important for educators to take a stand on whether their institutions want to separate the two, or whether they want to create a more seamless and proactive blend in their curricular structure and course content.

Adjunct to this question is the recently (if recurrently) raised issue of skills versus content. It is argued that we have forsaken knowledge for skills and are graduating facile but empty-headed students. Again, this is a decision that university policy makers should face, rather than letting it be decided by nonaction. Instructional design processes can clarify the relevant options and suggest alternative and all-encompassing ways that courses might be structured.

Finally, tomorrow's faculty and administrators are going to be faced with decisions about how effective distance delivery of higher education can be, and how much traditional role modeling by the faculty can be integrated into these new systems. There is no doubt that distance delivery will be an important part of higher education in the next century. How traditional colleges and universities will structure themselves to meet this eventuality is a question they should consider *now*.

REFERENCES

Butler, F. C. 1985. The teaching/learning process: A unified interactive model (Part One). *Educational Technology* September, pp. 9–17.

Case, R., and C. Bereiter. 1984. From behaviorism to cognitive development: Steps in the evolution of instructional design. *Instructional Science* 13: 141–158.

The college blue book [21st ed.]: *Degrees offered by college and subject. 1987.* New York: Macmillan.

Conrad, C. F., and A. M. Pratt. 1985. Designing for quality. *Journal of Higher Education.* 56(6): 601–622.

Cross, P. K. 1976. *Accent on learning.* San Francisco: Jossey-Bass.

Diamond, R. M. and R. R. Sudweeks. 1980. A comprehensive approach to course evaluation. *Journal of Instructional Development* 4(1): 28–34.

Doughty, Philip. 1987. Private Correspondence. May 15.

Grasha, Anthony F. Learning styles. *Improving College and University Teaching* 32 (1): 46–53.

Grossman, D. M. 1987. Hidden perils: Instructional media and higher education. *NUCEA Occasional Paper 5.*

Hannafin, M. J. 1986. The status and future of research in instructional design and technology. *Journal of Instructional Development* 8 (3): 24–30.

Lynton, E. A., and S. E. Elman. 1987. *New priorities for the university,* San Francisco: Jossey-Bass.

Perelman, L. J. 1986. Learning our lesson. *The Futurist* March-April. pp. 13–16.

Reeves, T. C. 1986 Research and evaluation models for the study of interactive video. *Journal of Computer-Based Instruction* 13 (4): 102–106.

Sweeney, J. J., and C. M. Reigeluth. 1984. The lecture and instructional design: A contradiction in terms? *Educational Technology* August pp. 7–12.

Wildman, T. M., and J. K. Burton. 1981. Integrating learning theory with instructional design. *Journal of Instructional Development* 4 (3): 5–12.

CHAPTER SEVEN

Instructional Design
A Template for Change

Janet Whitaker
Joyce K. Elsner

The principles and processes of instructional design have been evolving for several decades. Until recently known to only the few who pioneered this strange new discipline, those principles and processes employed by instructional designers suddenly are showing up in larger educational contexts, with the practitioners often totally unaware of their source.

In this chapter we present a case study wherein instructional design began as an isolated function and, almost unnoticed, grew to influence the curriculum and planning mechanisms of a large and complex system. In a multi-campus institution, instructional design became in one sense a template for change, and in another a catalyst that still remains largely unrecognized—but whose impacts can definitely be demonstrated. The case study serves to illustrate that the basic tenets of instructional design, applicable in diverse situations, can become generic tools for any organization that wishes to retain currency and relevance in this changing world.

HISTORICAL PERSPECTIVE

The Maricopa Community Colleges are seven (soon to be nine) separately accredited community colleges, organized as one district and charged with serving the 9,266 square miles of Maricopa County in central Arizona. Created as a community college district in 1963, the system grew to five colleges by 1978. During that year, two more were added.

The District Support Services Center, as it was then known, employed two full-time instructional designers who were available to college faculty and staff as resources for solving educational problems. These designers were available on a first-come, first-serve basis for major instructional program development or revisions. Although they were consistently busy, few in the organization were aware of these available services, and therefore few took advantage of the expertise.

One of the colleges created in 1978 was a noncampus institution charged both with serving all off-campus locations of the existing institutions, and with developing new clientele for the system. The other sibling colleges did not greet this organizational change with much enthusiasm. They expressed concern that the new institution would jeopardize the credibility of their programs, threaten the transferability of district-wide courses to the nearby university, and generally undermine all the "excellence" that had been built into the system since 1963. To ensure that disaster was not levied on all instructional programs, improved procedures were called for to protect the integrity of the system as a whole.

The University Becomes Involved

The nearby university played an active role in the process. For years, the university accepted transfer students' credits, the assumption being that the community college district had a "district course bank." That is, that while individual system colleges might differ in the specific certificate and degree programs offered, the individual courses developed by the system colleges were the same for all institutions. Once a new course was approved, it was to be placed in the district course bank, and all member colleges could have access to it. Thus, when this new noncampus college was created, it too would be using the same courses as the other existing colleges. There should have been no question as to the transferability of such courses, as the university had agreed to accept them.

With the ensuing debate, internal and external, about the new college, the university began to look more closely at the courses being accepted from system institutions. They were somewhat shocked at what they found, and finally came to the district curriculum committee, indicating that they had discovered some interesting discrepancies from college to college. Courses had similar course prefixes and numbers, but in some instances the title had been modified; or the description changed somewhat; or the credit given, or periods scheduled, varied. Finally, they asked, "Are you *one* district course bank or seven separate course banks? We will deal with you either way; just let us know how you want to be treated."

The district curriculum committee decided to remain one district course bank, and initiated the "six common elements" project. They agreed that there could be no variation in the following course elements: prefix, number, title, description, prerequisites, and credits/periods. More important, the committee also recognized that there was major curricular work to be done, and that specialized personnel would probably be needed to get the course bank in order.

The Vice Chancellor for Educational Development was the person responsible for the curriculum processes of the district. The two designers on his staff became active in suggesting strategies to implement this major effort. The need for more instructional designers was soon obvious to the Vice Chancellor, but budget realities would not allow the immediate employment of additional personnel, nor would more centralized staff necessarily be welcomed by the colleges in this quasi-decentralized system. Instead, the district office, in conjunction with the member colleges, developed a strategy for identifying faculty members who could be provided reassigned time to serve as instructional designers on each college campus. Of equal importance, the funds for the instructional design effort would be budgeted by the district office each year and allocated to the individual colleges for use as they saw fit.

There is a certain irony in that the only college at the time that had budgeted for a full-time instructional designer was the noncampus college. Knowing that alternative (technology-based) course delivery would be controversial in the best of environments, the noncampus college developers planned from the beginning to include instructional design as a key element to ensure the success of their curriculum processes and to ward off hostility from sibling colleges.

State Board Initiatives

At about the same time, the State Board for the Arizona Community Colleges was becoming concerned about standards for curriculum processing at the state level. All courses from the ten system college districts were processed from local governing boards to the state board for final ratification and eligibility for state support. While not dissatisfied with the current approval procedures, the State Board acknowledged that some freshening might be in order. Moreover, strengthening the development of occupational education programs would ensure that system colleges would be in a good position to continue to receive federal vocational dollars. A study to improve the entire curriculum approval process was authorized.

Meanwhile, the "six common elements" project began slowly—but then continually gained speed. Full-time faculty from the Maricopa district colleges were identified and trained, and began the process of identifying disparities among the existing courses offered at the seven colleges. The curriculum processes currently in place were analyzed and restructured, and the faculty designers produced a curriculum manual that specified the instructional design roles and responsibilities for everyone involved in the procedure. For the next few years, old curricula were revised while new curricula were developed in response to identified needs. Slowly, the function of instructional design was woven into the fabric of each college, and the system as a whole.

As often happens, the State Board initiative was slightly behind the steps being taken by the district. When it came time to identify a leader for their process of "examination and enhancement of the curriculum," they selected the person who had provided the leadership within the Maricopa system. As the other community colleges in the state became involved in the process of development, the model that emerged was very much like what the Maricopa district had put in place only months earlier. The language and processes of instructional design were now installed in the State Board procedures as well.

CURRENT STATUS

At each of the seven accredited colleges and within each of the two educational centers (extensions of full-service colleges expected to become separate institutions), instructional designers continue to play a key role in the curriculum development and evaluation process. In some cases, the designers are faculty members with reassigned time. One institution that has few full-time faculty employs a number of part-time designers to facilitate the processes.

The current role of the instructional designers at the district office is now evolving into something quite different from what it was in 1978. Because the colleges are taking the lead in instructional design from the curriculum perspective, the district designers are evolving into specialists, or resource people, for the applications of new technologies within the colleges.

Over the past few years, the instructional designers have developed a new district entity, the Center for Instructional Technology (C-IT). Pronounced "See It," the center features a wide variety of computers and other telecommunications equipment not only available for experimentation, but requiring that such experimentation be structured according to the principles of good instructional design. That is, the equipment is not there for its own sake, but is placed in an environment where instructional strategies can be explored within the context of sound learning methodologies.

Curriculum Development Today

We have now moved into an era of accountability to students, employers, and postsecondary institutions that requires a more systematic and consistent design of educational programs in community colleges. We have found that excellence in, and quality control of, the entire educational enterprise can be approached by applying instructional design principles. As a result, the Maricopa Community Colleges have incorporated instructional design in their development of curriculum at all levels and in a variety of ways.

The first step in developing a new course or program of study is the needs assessment—conducted by the project initiator, who may be a faculty or staff member of the college, or a community member requesting the program, in cooperation with the district staff in the Office of Educational Development. Developers must consider such factors as employment projections in the community, salaries expected for graduates, and "fit" within the mission and resources of the institution. Many sources of information are consulted, including economic development studies, federal and state publications on occupational areas, and informal surveys of, and discussions with, both local employers and faculty who are familiar with the field of study.

If the needs assessment demonstrates an actual need for the course or program, the design effort begins. In the case of occupational course/program development, an advisory committee is convened. This committee consists of faculty in the discipline(s), staff, representatives of the community who work in the content field, and an instructional designer. The instructional designer assigned might be a faculty member trained in instructional design principles, or a professional instructional designer under contract for the project—the difference being a result of the human resources available at a given institution.

The advisory committee reviews the curriculum as it is being developed in light of "real-world" needs for student skills and knowledge. In the past, a curriculum developed without this examination was in danger of being non-responsive to community needs in terms of content included or not included, scheduling strategies, breadth and depth of skill outcomes, and datedness of equipment used in the community in various employment settings. Advisory committees are the key to avoiding these errors in designing appropriate curricula for the local environment.

Preliminary work done by the faculty, staff, and designer before the first advisory committee meeting might include an examination of existing courses in the college, faculty available for teaching in the field, and/or retraining and renewal needs for faculty. This information provides a starting point from which the advisory committee, particularly community representatives unfamiliar with community college procedures, can begin the design process.

One of the first tasks of the advisory committee is to recommend subject matter experts (SMEs) to work with the designer. These SMEs include faculty, and at least one person from the community. The task of the SMEs is to develop the required curriculum components.

In the case of course design, the required components include the six common elements used in all courses in the district (course prefix, number, title, credits/periods, description, prerequisites), course competencies and objectives, and the content outline. New degree programs require a program needs statement, program description, program competencies, course listings, and a prerequisite flow chart.

The instructional designer works with the SMEs to ensure that all these components are present and that the structure developed provides an instructionally sound "map" for faculty and students. The components must be logically integrated and reflective of each other. The number of credits (translated to time spent in learning) must reach the intended learning outcomes and remain within the guidelines of lower-division instruction. If the course is designed for distance delivery, special adapations must be included. The design proposed should also fit within the resources available at the delivery college.

The design team also must consider instructional material availability, the equipment needed for delivery of the program, and the faculty abilities necessary for teaching the course or program. These issues have budget implications not generally within the purview of the design team, but that need to be shared with other college staff.

Once the draft components are developed, the advisory committee as a whole reviews and comments on them. It identifies omissions, discusses structural inconsistencies, and reviews competency statements for attainability and accuracy. Any necessary adjustments are made, and the curriculum is submitted for the complete approval process through the college, faculty instructional councils, District committees, and the District Governing Board. Any deficiencies identified during the approval process may be corrected by the instructional design team before it continues to the next approval step.

The one area that still needs to be strengthened in this process is the formal summative evaluation of the curriculum. Currently, data concerning enrollment patterns are collected and analyzed. Annual review of the curriculum takes place in the advisory committee forum. Data are not routinely collected, however, on student performance after course or program completion, except in the form of grades. Assessment of learning outcomes by course and by program would be helpful in revising the curriculum, placing students in jobs, and demonstrating the transferability of courses to the university.

Strategic Planning

Although not initially foreseen, the application of instructional design strategies has affected many planning efforts undertaken by colleges. Instructional design has provided a common way of thinking about missions and goals. Strategic planning is thus the newest system-wide venture employing the theories and techniques of instructional design.

Strategic planning formulates mission statements, assumptions, issues, goals, objectives, and approaches to organizational development. Because of our successful application of instructional design in the curriculum development process, we are already comfortable with using the same techniques to look at our entire organization. Multilevel staff involvement, community advisory committees, examination of the desired outcomes, development of implementation strategies, resource need identification, and evaluation of the outcomes are all part of instructional design. Employing these instructional design processes fosters more cohesive strategic planning.

Special Projects and Innovation

Instructional design strategies are often also employed in a variety of ways as models to encourage, guide, and structure special projects and innovative activity in the colleges. The framework of a special project usually includes a needs statement, goals and objectives, an action plan, and an evaluation strategy. Instructional designers, skilled in applying these processes and often used as sounding boards for new-project development, may be enlisted as project team members or may initiate projects themselves. Instructional design skills are seen as valuable qualities in staff seeking to explore new and possibly high-risk ventures because the step-by-step process seems to lead to higher completion and success rates.

General Education Revisions

In the early 1980s, the district felt a need to reexamine its general education requirements for the three degrees its colleges offered: the associate of arts, the associate of applied sciences, and the associate of general studies. A subcommittee was formed to study the various reports being issued nationwide, and to study various models—those existing and those emerging—around the country. Not surprisingly, a number of persons chosen for that analysis role were faculty already trained in instructional design processes.

It took quite a long time to develop, and then to process, revisions to the general education requirements through this multicollege system and the governing board. An interesting sidelight was that, soon after, the nearby university felt it too should examine its general education requirements. To enable their study committee to benefit from our experience, members from our subcommittee were appointed to serve with the university staff. Two members of the original Maricopa District subcommittee continue to participate on the university's general education committee, serving as resources and developing appropriate articulation so that students who transfer do not have to repeat learning.

The university process is nearing completion, and much has been accomplished. Differences exist at present, but they are being resolved in positive ways that could not have been anticipated. We share a commitment to instructional design principles as efficient and effective tools. There is little question in our minds that this spirit of collegiality that exists between a two-year and a four-year institution is due in no small part to that commitment.

CONCLUSION

Since 1980, the influence of instructional design methodology has been pervasive, though perhaps not always recognized specifically. What was a process originally acknowledged as a tool for curriculum development and evaluation has become a process useful for addressing other concerns of a changing organization. The movement to this methodology over a period of years has not only affected the quality of the curriculum developed; it has also influenced the planning processes of the system and, thus, the changes that have occurred.

What has been interesting to note is that over this time period, the skills associated with instructional design have moved from the cognitive level of awareness to an almost visceral application of the strategies. The strategies of instructional design are so much a part of the fabric of the organization that they are hardly recognized as separate tools any longer. Individual staff use the tools so automatically in so many of their work applications that it is almost an autonomic response—thus the reference to "visceral" knowledge.

It would be wonderful to be able to say that this was all planned, and that the Vice Chancellor for Educational Development knew that this would be the outcome. However, we fear it would be stretching the truth a bit. In reality, we had the opportunity to match a pressing crisis (potential university rejection of all community college courses) with an existing resource (instructional design theory and processes in place in the system)—and produced a result that, our apprehensions notwithstanding, improved the system overall.

CHAPTER EIGHT

Instructional Design for Distance Learning

Jocelyn Calvert

Distance learning has a history in correspondence programs, radio schools of the air, career training advertised on matchbook covers, and the 1960s experiments that telecast the professor to the overflow lecture hall next door. But as a global phenomenon, distance learning rose to prominence in the seventies and skyrocketed in the eighties. While the old programs were second-best alternatives for the disadvantaged who could not attend classes, the new distance education accepts no such premise. Distance learning may have challenges, but they are merely different in kind from those of classroom learning, and no more numerous.

The first enterprise that attracted international attention was the Open University of the United Kingdom. The British ability to set a style for export was manifest in professionally printed units that were a far cry from mimeographed course notes. What was more impressive, these were only a part of multimedia instructional packages that included national television and radio broadcasts; elaborate home experiment kits that today may include a robot; regular regional tutorials; and residential schools on university campuses. Also impressive was public demand. From teachers upgrading, to degrees in the early years, to business managers today, the Open University has served a substantial market (McIntosh et al., 1980).

The Open University model employs faculty members to participate in course development teams and to preside over course statistics instead of to pace at the front of lecture amphitheaters. Instructional designers, editors, media specialists, and educational technologists may participate in course teams as contributing members, not as quasi-clerical assistants. Indeed, the spectacle of university teaching designed by a team generated years of debate in the Open University periodical *Teaching at a Distance* (e.g., Drake, 1979; Riley, 1981; Tight, 1985).

Educators were impressed, and the model was adopted in several countries. Examples include Everyman's University in Israel; Allama Iqbal Open University in Pakistan; Athabasca University in Canada; and Sukhothai Thammathirat Open University in Thailand. A variation integrated distance learning with a parallel campus-based alternative, resulting in the dual-mode institution (Jevons, 1986), with Deakin University in Australia and Universiti Sains Malaysia as leading examples. Other new institutions reviewed the cost of supporting full faculties, and opted for academics as adjuncts or on contract. Such institutions ensure academic standards by enlisting faculty of other institutions to advise on programs and policy, write courses, and tutor students. Examples of this model include the Open Learning Institute in Canada; Universitas Terbuka in Indonesia; and Indira Gandhi National Open University in India (Rumble and Harry, 1982; Holmberg, 1986; Shale, 1987).

Natural consequences to this expansion and enhancement of distance learning were the revitalization of marginal programs in traditional institutions; a worldwide network of distance educators supported by regional organizations and the International Council for Distance Education; and the formation of collaborative associations among institutions—exemplified by the International University Consortium and the National Technological University in the United States (see also Mugridge, 1983; McClean, 1986; Konrad and Small, 1986). Dedicated periodicals in Europe, Australia, North America, and Asia have progressed from description to analysis and research (Calvert, 1986a). The natural outcome of this traffic is collaboration in development and delivery, both regional and international. Certainly, the Commonwealth Open University Network project is the most ambitious, setting the goal of distributing educational opportunities throughout the Commonwealth via the distance learning programs and materials of its educational institutions.

THE CHALLENGES FOR INSTRUCTIONAL DESIGN

For the purposes of this chapter, I will risk oversimplification by defining *distance education* simply as *formal instruction delivered mainly to remote locations and/or asynchronously* (see also Keegan, 1980; Thompson, 1986). Its widespread appeal around the world, in both rich and poor countries with concentrated and scattered populations, suggests that it is useful for more than one reason. Distance learning can help meet national needs when:

1. Traditional institutions can accommodate only a fraction of qualified applicants.

2. Population concentrations will not support local delivery of programs.
3. The target audience is not free to participate in traditionally delivered programs.
4. A program must be delivered to a dispersed audience.
5. There are not sufficient experts available to teach face-to-face the number of prospective learners.

These circumstances have special implications for instructional design. First, distance learning tampers with a central feature of traditional formal learning by omitting or substantially reducing the frequency of the regular meeting-in-class of teacher and learners. Besides serving as a venue for the transmission of knowledge, classes provide an occasion to clarify expectations, correct misconceptions and errors, share perceptions through informal contacts, and simply pace study. Effective distance learning programs will take account of these functions and find ways of ensuring that communication needs are met.

Second, the range of possible learners in distance programs suggests that instructional designers should possess, and be able to employ effectively, a collection of strategies. Learners may be children who cannot attend school; recent school-leavers who have been unable to obtain a place in traditional programs; or adults with the full range of educational backgrounds and a variety of reasons for studying. Designers of distance learning programs must define clearly the target audience (age, educational background, personal circumstances, reasons for studying) and take account of what is already known about such student populations. Furthermore, some distance learning programs, through flexibility of place and time, are accessible to a much broader audience than a classroom counterpart. The challenge in that case is to design instruction that meets the diverse learning needs of a student population that is more heterogeneous and far larger than usual.

Third, when the goal is to teach these larger numbers of students than the classroom can accommodate, the usual forms of feedback and assessment may be impractical. Economies of scale require reducing or eliminating labor-intensive activities. These may include time not only for instruction but also for answering individuals' questions and marking their work. The instructional design must find ways of ensuring educational quality while meeting the need for mass education.

Fourth, physical and temporal distance mean isolation, and under conditions of isolation motivation may be more difficult to sustain. Student attrition has been a continuing concern of distance educators. As was emphasized in Chapter Four, effective instruction must find ways to help ensure that students do not simply drift away.

INSTRUCTIONAL DESIGN STRATEGIES: EXTENSION OR TRANSFORMATION

Distance learning programs can be characterized by the extent to which they derive from extension or correspondence modes (Calvert, 1986a). The extension mode occurs when the designer visualizes the *class*, and considers how to extend the classroom to other places and times. The resulting instructional program will mimic in many ways the campus classroom experience, and attempt to compensate for lost features and cues. If, instead, the designer visualizes the *student*, and considers how to provide classroom-style instruction to students who don't attend class, the instructional program will transform classroom lectures and discussion into individualized learning materials. Programs do not necessarily exemplify strictly one model or the other, but the distinction is useful for understanding the design issues that distance education confronts.

The *extension* philosophy that traditionally saw itinerant instructors leading classes in regional communities was clearly translated to a distance learning mode in the University of Waterloo program (Leslie, 1979). Instructors were enlisted to tape the lectures they normally would deliver in class, and to supply a set of hand-printed blackboard notes to accompany the lectures. Tapes and notes were reproduced and sent to students, who followed the same study schedules as their classroom counterparts. The type of in-class commentary that normally would accompany the setting and return of assignments and midterm examinations was also taped for distance students, and this constituted the primary teacher–student communication during the course of study. Clearly, in this model, whether or not students ever encountered classmates, they were taught as part of a lecture class. What they missed were contact with fellow students, the opportunity to put questions directly to the instructor for immediate reply, and easy access to campus facilities such as the library. This impoverished cousin-of-the-campus-class has been remarkably successful, both in generating faculty support (310 courses were offered in 1987–88; *Canadian Distance Education Directory*, 1987) and attracting students (approximately 20,000 course enrollments across Canada).

While the Waterloo model provides a classroom extension that does not depend on time and place, the more common application of the extension model uses some form of communication technology to convene remote classes, usually at a set of fixed locations. Audio teleconferencing systems using telephone lines, exemplified by the University of Wisconsin network (Parker and Monson, 1980), may be augmented by equipment that approximates what is commonly available in the classroom. Those who use the blackboard can write on an electronic blackboard, their words and sketches transmitted to screens in the receiving sites. The overhead projector is replaced by a computer that allows simultaneous voice-and-data transmission, the data (notes or diagrams) either loaded in advance or written directly to a screen (Bates, 1984). In another method for extending the classroom, live television broadcasts via satellite can take the best instructors from top universities to other institutions, and to corporations (*National Technological University Bulletin*, 1987). Live television may also include a phone-in option for student questions and comments (Catchpole and MacGregor, 1984).

The prototype for the instructional *transformation* model is correspondence study, the traditional mode of distance learning in North America. Instructors prepared notes that included an outline of the course, reading assignments, some commentary, and assignments to be submitted for marking. A mimeograph machine (eventually supplanted by a photocopier) reproduced the notes for students, who normally were permitted to take only a small number of correspondence courses for credit. The important point about these courses is that, whatever their format, they seldom attempted to mimic the style of the classroom lecture or seminar—although unfortunately this often meant a lack of guidance rather than a redesign of presentation. Not only were students isolated from fellow students, instructors, and campus facilities, but often they were presented with a sketchy outline of the program of study.

The simple correspondence course raised its aspirations with the establishment of new institutions without classrooms whose faculty members were challenged to teach students throughout the country without bringing them to campus. At the British Open University, a generous budget enabled faculty and technical teams to spend three years developing multimedia courses and to produce them lavishly. Over the years, the Open University, and more recently, institutions funded by the Annenberg/CPB Project in the United States, have been at the forefront of experimentation with new methods and technologies for distance learning, and their examples have helped others to extend the range of possibilities. As models of higher instructional quality became available, standards for others rose and, as production technologies became widely available, production values improved. Of course, many institutions still do not have access to sophisticated delivery media, but it is significant that print materials are the core of courses in almost all distance teaching institutions. Exceptions are most likely when print production and paper itself are luxuries, or when the size of the audience and available facilities make radio or television delivery economical options.

In their pure forms, the extension and transformation models contrast with one another in several ways. First, the extension strategy, by treating the class *as* a class, retains the sense of the group. In so doing, it may also retain the inflexibility of campus-based instruction by requiring students to attend at a particular place and at regular times. In contrast, the transformation strategy tends to isolate the individual, while adding flexibility to student schedules by reducing or eliminating time-and-place restrictions. Second, extension courses are relatively easy and fast to mount, because teachers continue to perform as they normally do in the classroom; thus development costs are relatively low. Creating a course for the transformed system is, by comparison, slow and costly (Sparkes, 1984). Third, delivery costs under both strategies will vary with choice of media, but here also differences exist. Delivery costs of extension courses increase directly as a function of the number of groups and offerings, because the performance must be remounted for each. With transformation, in contrast, economies of scale are possible. Materials once developed can be delivered to any number of students at the cost of reproduction and/or transmission. Finally, by trying to emulate the classroom ideal, extension models by definition are doomed to be second best. Transforming the instruction, at its best, can redefine effective teaching.

As time passes, however, the distinction between extension and transformation strategies blurs. When an institution holds optional tutorials or establishes residential schools, it is adding elements of the extension model. Extension programs, including those of some members of the International University Consortium based at The University of Maryland, may use distance learning packages but add a classroom component. As we move further into the age of computer and satellite communications, teleconferencing and electronic mail reduce isolation, allowing asynchronous conversations that have some of the flavor of the class meeting. It is not farfetched to suggest that the distance learning phenomenon will profoundly affect the future design and delivery of much of the teaching at the postsecondary level. Already, Universitas Terbuka is the largest educational publisher in Indonesia, and students at some universities in Canada, Australia, and the United States are opting for a mix of campus and distance study, even in the same semester.

INSTRUCTIONAL DESIGN IN THEORY

Thompson (1986), struggling with diverse definitions of distance education, drew parallels with adult education, and distinguished between distance education as practice and as an area of study. Analyzing the role of instructional design in distance education requires attention both to the literature on models and methods of distance education, and to institutional practices.

With reference to the literature on practical implementation, it is difficult to trace the origins of "how to" manuals for distance education. Rowntree (1986) claimed roots in programmed learning, but his guide for writers of distance learning materials is a smorgasbord of helpful hints with almost no acknowledgments. Jenkins (1985), writing in the same encouraging spirit, but for editors rather than writers, provided but a few references, and these only to books she had found useful. Both authors, in any case, assume a fairly rudimentary print-based system and little technical support. Neither encourages a critical look at assumptions and methods, or special consideration of disparate target populations. In a more academic treatment of "media, methods, and learning materials," Kaye (1981) elaborated the philosophy guiding such commonsense approaches. Citing Schramm's (1972) observation that students learn well from good instructors and materials, whatever the medium, he prescribed as a goal a clear, unambiguous, and interesting presentation—not the application of a theoretically based formula.

Until recently, the academic literature on distance learning has been largely descriptive rather than analytical or research-based (Coldeway, 1982; Moore, 1985). New institutions and programs were eager to announce their inception, but not yet settled enough to be reflective. Ljosa (1980) commented that distance education research occurred in three contexts: large distance teaching institutions with specialized research units; scattered individuals with a special interest in the subject; and specially funded projects. Research addressing instructional design in distance education is confined to the last two.

Two specially funded projects that focused on aspects of instructional design were rooted in the behaviorist tradition. The first, in Sweden, assessed the effects on dropout rates of such variables as assignment turnaround time and telephone contact (Baath, Flinck, and Wangdahl, 1975–77). The second, Project REDEAL, was an undertaking of Athabasca University in Canada that investigated the "motivation and management of the distance learner" (see Coldeway, 1982, for an overview). The studies in this project tested the effects of various interventions on student persistence in courses. Among these were immediate test feedback (Coldway and Spencer, 1982), paced instruction (Crawford, 1980), optional seminars (Peruniak, 1984), and contact between institution and student (Peruniak, 1983). These projects generally supported (if not as dramatically as the researchers hoped) the hypothesis that dropout rates are reduced by motivating variables such as timely feedback and, particularly, reward.

Another collection of research literature relevant to instructional design in distance education derives from a cognitive orientation. In this case, the research is more qualitative and focuses on the ways that students use distance learning materials. Assessments have been made of how students plan their study of distance learning materials (Dodds and Lawrence, 1983), how they actually *use* the materials (Clyde et al., 1983), and how they evaluate the usefulness of course components (Duchastel, 1983). A general conclusion that can be drawn from this type of research is that students use materials in almost as many different ways as there are students. Others have identified cognitive styles that may affect students' approaches to study materials and their success in distance learning programs (e.g., Cropley and Kahl, 1983; Thompson, 1984).

Adult learning concepts have not received the widespread research attention that we might expect, given the predominantly adult nature of the distance learning population. The greatest attention has been given to the notion of learner autonomy. Moore (1986) advised attention to the self-directed learner in distance education, and others have tried to introduce flexibility and choice into courses. Fales and Burge (1984) used computer communications to keep options open, and Taylor and Kaye (1986) deliberately introduced choice in study emphasis and sequence. The latter reported anxiety among students in a credit course who assumed that there was a "best" choice for them to divine. The conflict between choice and the concrete goals of many distance learners is perhaps more apparent to practitioners than to theoreticians.

Finally, the concept of interaction has received periodic attention, sometimes challenging the heartfelt biases of committed educators. While there isn't yet a cohesive body of literature, it deserves attention as an important theme for instructional design. Daniel and Marquis (1979) explored the balance between independence and interaction, and Daniel (1983) reconsidered the subject in the context of new technologies. Garrison (1985) recommended that we abandon "the restrictive view that interaction is mediated person-to-person communication" (p. 238), and criticized tutor–student telephone contact as extravagant. Garrison then severely qualified his broader statement, however, by arguing that computer-based instruction is the only technology that can simulate interaction. Baath (1982) compared student reactions to tutor comments and computer-generated comments on assignments, and found that they preferred the latter. Holmberg et al. (1982) compared responses to correspondence texts written in an impersonal academic style and in a more personal interactive style that they referred to as "guided didactic conversation"; surprisingly, the latter was not dramatically more effective. And in an analytical review, Bates (1986) considered the differences between two uses of computers in distance education—for presentation of preprogrammed learning materials and for communications—and concluded that the latter use "offers a more appropriate, humanistic and pragmatic route for future development."

INSTRUCTIONAL DESIGNERS IN DISTANCE LEARNING PROGRAMS

Distance education, according to Smith et al. (1984), has provided one of the most significant inroads for instructional design into university teaching. It is not difficult to see how this has occurred. Instructors have experience teaching in the classroom and normally do not avail themselves of assistance in that area even if it is offered. In contrast, they are unlikely to claim similar expertise in distance teaching, particularly if it involves technologies with which they are unfamiliar. Furthermore, distance teaching in most of its forms creates a public record of instruction (Shaw and Taylor, 1984). What is acceptable today in the classroom is not necessarily acceptable as a permanent document of teaching skill.

The solution embodied in the course team approach so effectively employed by the British Open University has much of the print dialogue on course development. Shaw and Taylor (1984) even predicted the eventual demise of distance education in institutions that do not provide sufficient input for technical experts—including instructional designers. However, few institutions that teach at a distance can contemplate the expense of the type of course production mounted as a matter of course by the Open University. Most institutions with distance learning programs are fortunate if they can afford to provide minimal editing of text and advice when requested, on matters pertaining to instructional design (Kelly, 1987).

Issues of power and status also limit the influence of instructional designers on the design of materials. Seaborne and Zuckernick (1986) surveyed the practices of a sample of Canadian universities that teach at a distance, and identified three levels of involvement of a central distance teaching unit in the design of courses. In their analysis, institutions differ in the extent to which they prescribe instructional standards or offer helpful hints. They introduced the expression "author sensitive" as a euphemism for deference to the subject matter expert (SME) (the faculty member) and attributed variations in the SME's degree of influence to institutional commitment to excellence in distance learning programs. A survey of institutions with distance teaching experience would undoubtedly also reveal that faculty members' perceived need for design assistance, personally and in the institution, declines as they gain practice.

A limitation on innovation in course design arises from the working conditions of instructional designers in most educational institutions. Kerr (1983) noted the tendency of instructional designers to solve design problems with the solutions they had used on their most recent projects. This is not surprising if they work in environments where they have responsibilities on several projects, and where the system makes some activities easier to implement than others. Furthermore, one easy way to assist a course writer is to supply examples of methods that have worked well in the past, which is another way of perpetuating a style. An appropriate expression here is "system sensitive" as a euphemism for deference to the habits of the organization.

BROADER INFLUENCES ON INSTRUCTIONAL DESIGN

System sensitivity is not, in fact, an ailment to be overcome or ignored; on the contrary, it is essential for survival in a distance teaching system. Instructional designers may (and should) have continuing influence on such structural elements as the statement of learning objectives, and the degree of correspondence among practice tests and graded assignments. However, their options in other aspects of design may be severely constrained by factors that have little to do directly with helping students to learn. Leaving out factors over which we have little control, like population size and geography, we can still identify groups and practices that influence design decisions.

The highest level of influence on instructional design may come from government. Most of the distance teaching institutions in the world are public institutions, and their establishment has often included stated assumptions about how they would teach. In Canada, the province of British Columbia established an educational television network, the Knowledge Network, with the expectation that public educational institutions, as well as community groups, would broadcast elements of courses. At a time when funds were tight and a great deal of course development was under way, institutions were strongly encouraged to engage in television programming. As frequently occurs, the resulting demand for air time soon exceeded supply, despite the irony that television broadcasts are not necessarily a central element of distance instruction. However, the Knowledge Network continues to provide daily advertisements for the distance learning programs of the province.

Distance teaching organizations and institutions also influence instructional design through their own structures. My own organization, for example, began with a course design unit that spent considerable time in its first year of meetings on the development of a house style. But the effect of the house style guide was minor compared with the establishment of print production, audio production, and graphics units that provided services on demand (Bottomley, 1986; Timmers and Mugridge, 1986). We became an institution that taught by means of printed units, fairly lavishly illustrated (though not in color), with supplementary audio cassettes in a substantial minority of courses. Other media, like video or computers, required an often futile search for funds.

Publishing companies increasingly are affecting design decisions. Now that they have converted to electronic publishing, they have discovered that they can do an end run around the used-book market by publishing frequent new editions of textbooks. This is most effective, they've found, if they introduce the new edition with as little warning as possible. Most distance learning courses are designed to have a four- or five-year life. The effect of sudden new editions on institutions that cannot afford to stockpile several years' supply of textbooks is electrifying. People who should be contributing to new course projects or tutoring students find themselves assessing the extent of revision required and, in the happiest case, changing a few page references. Nevertheless, when good ones are available, commercial textbooks are irresistible when compared with the time and effort that would be required to create their equivalent as part of course development. Consequently, designers are experimenting with ways to make basic course materials independent of specific texts, while assuming assignment of one or another comprehensive text.

The availability of different media to students has always been a factor in the design of courses, and institutions have varied in their approaches. Some have chosen to teach using only those media that are accessible to the vast majority of the public. Others have undertaken to supply equipment. Still others choose sophisticated media and open their programs only to those who can receive them. Yet (in developed countries) even institutions that have universal mandates have seen a vast change in what media access can be expected among the general public. Ten years ago we could assume that students could play audio cassettes. Now we can assume that all but a few can easily play video cassettes and receive video broadcasts; and in some programs we can assume access to one of two types of microcomputer. Not only that, but public and private institutions in small communities (schools, hospitals, community colleges, businesses) can be enlisted to host programs requiring satellite downlinks and audio conferencing. These advances are increasing the disparity between the poorest countries and the rest of the world in educational opportunities. The challenge for distance educators, as the technologies become cheaper and more portable, will be to determine how they can help expand opportunities in circumstances where a country's foreign-exchange difficulties preclude replacement of an institution's single IBM typewriter ball.

TRENDS AND NEW CHALLENGES

Where distance learning is concerned, life for the instructional designer is assuming a pattern of continuous change, and most of the changes involve the use of technology. Expanded delivery options mean that those articles on appropriate uses of media, formerly read out of curiosity or as a diversion from one's own hidebound system of delivery, become required reading (see Bates, 1984, for the most comprehensive guide). Technologies for delivery that only recently were out of the question must be reconsidered. And you no longer decide whether to deliver a course by audio cassette, video cassette, print, or audio conference—but *how much, if any, of each* of the options to incorporate.

Another change for instructional designers involves course development. Ten years ago, subject matter experts wrote courses by hand and sent them to be typed and retyped and, eventually, in deluxe systems, typeset. Or, they took a cassette recorder home and recorded their lectures (sometimes, we thought, while they were in the bath). Nowadays, the print portions of courses are word processed, often by the writer, and transmitted electronically for editing and typesetting. This situation provides wonderful opportunities for guidance before the writing starts. Timmers (1986) reported the advantages in time and clarity gained by establishing computer templates for course structures, and by reviewing and editing a course using electronic communications among the course team. As different media are demystified, we can expect more than the audio cassette to be prepared, at least in draft, by the subject expert. The challenge will be to provide design guidance across the range of media, with the understanding that the subject matter expert will become an adviser to media developments that in the past were considered the territory of experts.

A third development, the breakdown of institutional boundaries, challenges our biases about making courses relevant to our local students. Writers in the past (Rowntree, 1986; Kaye, 1981) have been skeptical about the feasibility of importing courses from other countries or regions. In spite of obstacles, but often with difficulty, institutions around the world have recognized the value of acquiring courses rather than developing them anew. Examples are the International University Consortium, which imported courses from the Open University for distribution in North America; and Open College of the University of East Asia, Macao, which imported courses from several universities, including Massey in New Zealand and the Open Learning Institute in Canada.

Electronic publishing and *telecommunications* promise to change the parochial nature of education. *Electronic publishing* makes it possible to transmit a course from one institution to another anywhere in the world. That done, the receiving institution can make the changes necessary to tailor the course to its own system (Calvert, 1986b). The rationales for rejecting courses developed elsewhere will succumb to the opportunity to modify courses that approach a good fit. Such agreements between institutions have begun. Widespread application awaits only the development of conventions for price and copyright. *Telecommunications,* however, provide a different option (except where they are transferring course materials). Using satellite and computer links, it is possible to engage students, individually or in groups, around the world. The implication of *both* these developments is in the first case that courses and programs should be designed to allow for adaptation to local conditions, and in the second case to address examples from the world rather than the region.

THE ROLE FOR INSTRUCTIONAL DESIGN IN A CHANGING ENVIRONMENT

Drawing a summary of conclusions about the situation, observers have noted distance learning has led to the institutionalization of technical expertise for instructional design of materials and delivery strategies. This result stems in part from early recognition that the situation and character of distance learning audiences pose special challenges to meet communication needs. Two traditional approaches to design, emulating face-to-face classroom practice (extension strategy) and elaborating individualized correspondence study (transformation strategy), are breaking down as new communications technologies become widely available.

However, although instructional design is nominally entrenched in distance learning systems, it stands on shaky footings. The academic and practical literature of distance education design is scanty and, although posing important questions, has provided little guidance or conceptual support for practice. Also, while instructional designers typically are a part of distance teaching units, circumstances conspire to limit their role as advocates for sound practice and innovation. Further, the rigidly defined structures and services of the larger institution or educational system constrain choices—particularly choices of media.

Trends suggest important new roles for instructional designers, coupled with greater potential threat to their place in distance learning systems. The ability to develop media—from print to video to computer communications—is descending from the realm of experts to the everyday world of the academic and other lay people. The danger is that instructors may come to feel as little need of advice and guidance in developing multimedia packages as they typically do where their classroom teaching is concerned. Yet this broader range of options makes informed decisions about appropriate uses of media even more important. And the breakdown of institutional boundaries, through course sharing and international delivery, means that the course that may be developed within a parochial context should be adaptable to the challenges of different institutional systems, and even of cultural contexts. Individual subject-matter faculty may not be able to bring this broader perspective to their course development.

Our challenge is to ensure sound teaching practices in this evolving environment of increasing complexity where no one's dogma is impervious to argument. This will require unprecedented cooperation and a common sense of purpose among academics, instructional designers, and administrators. Academics who have been accustomed to autonomy and isolation in their teaching will have the opportunity to try new mixes of media and methods for presenting their subjects. Instructional designers will derive applications for distance education from the current theory and knowledge of relevant disciplines, and they will be advocates for system flexibility to enable innovation. Administrators will be active participants in the process, encouraging exploration—but with a critical eye to ensure that new methods are not only educationally sound but economically defensible.

REFERENCES

Baath, J. A. 1982. Experimental research on computer-assisted distance education. In J. S. Daniel, M. A. Stroud, and J. R. Thompson (eds.), *Learning at a distance: A world perspective*. Edmonton, Alberta: Athabasca University/International Council for Correspondence Education, pp. 303–305.

Baath, J., R. Flinck, and A. Wangdahl. 1975–77. Pedagogical Reports 1, 2, 4, 5, 8, 9, 10. Lund: University of Lund. For description and review, see P. Northcott, B. Hamilton, A. Inglis, M. Kelly, and K. Livingston. 1981. Pedagogical reports: The Lund studies in correspondence education. *Distance Education* 2: 110–123.

Bates, A. W. (ed.) 1984. *The role of technology in distance education*. Beckenham, Kent: Croom Helm.

Bates, T. 1986. Computer assisted learning or communications: Which way for information technology in distance education? *Journal of Distance Education* I: 41–58.

Bottomley, J. 1986. Production, storage and distribution. In I. Mugridge and D. Kaufman (eds.), *Distance education in Canada*. London: Croom Helm, pp. 50–59.

Calvert, J. 1986a. Research in Canadian distance education. In I. Mugridge and D. Kaufman (eds.), *Distance education in Canada*. London: Croom Helm, pp. 94–110.

———. 1986b. Facilitating transfer of distance courses. *Open Learning* 1: 34–37.

Canadian distance education directory. 1987. Ottawa: Association of Universities and Colleges of Canada.

Catchpole, M. J., and A. A. MacGregor. 1984. British Columbia's Knowledge Network: Macro and micro perspectives on the use of television in educational delivery. In L. Parker (ed.), *Teleconferencing and electronic communication III*. Madison, WI: University of Wisconsin—Extension.

Clyde, A., H. Crowther, W. Patching, I. Putt, and R. Store. 1983. How students use distance teaching materials: An institutional study. *Distance Education* 4: 4–26.

Coldeway, D. O. 1982. Recent research in distance learning. In J. S. Daniel, M. A. Stroud, and J. R. Thompson (eds.), *Learning at a distance: A world perspective*. Edmonton, Alberta: Athabasca University/International Council for Correspondence Education, pp. 29–37.

Crawford, G. 1980. Student completion rates under three different pacing conditions. REDEAL Technical Report No. 11 Athabasca University.

Cropley, A. J., and T. N. Kahl. 1983. Distance education and distance learning: Some psychological considerations. *Distance Education* 4: 27–39.

Daniel, J. S. 1983. Independence and interaction in distance education: New technologies for home study. *Programmed Learning and Educational Technology* 20: 155–160.

———, and C. Marquis. 1979. Independence and interaction: getting the mixture right. *Teaching at a Distance* 15: 29–44.

Dodds, A. E., and J. A. Lawrence. 1983. Heuristics for planning university study at a distance. *Distance Education* 4: 40–52.

Drake, M. 1979. The curse of the course team. *Teaching at a Distance* 16: 50–53.

Duchastel, P. C. 1983. Independent study strategies: reactions to study guide components. *Programmed Learning and Educational Technology* 20: 122–125.

Fales, A. W., and E. J. Burge. 1984. Self-direction by design: Self-directed learning in distance course design. *Canadian Journal of University Continuing Education* X: 68–78.

Garrison, D. R. 1985. Three generations of technological innovations in distance education. *Distance Education* 6: 235–241.

Holmberg, B., R. Schuemer, and A. Obermeier. 1982. Zur Effizienz des gelenkten didaktischen Gespräches. Ziff Project 2.6. Hagen: Fernuniversität.

Holmberg, B. 1986. *Growth and structure of distance education.* London: Croom Helm.

Jenkins, J. 1985. *Course development: a manual for editors of distance-teaching materials.* Cambridge: International Extension College.

Jevons, F. 1986. Dual mode institutions—the way forward. *Open Campus* 12: 4–9.

Kaye, A. 1981. Media, materials and learning methods. In A. Kaye and G. Rumble (eds.) *Distance teaching for higher and adult education,* pp. 48–69.

Keegan, D. 1980. On defining distance education. *Distance Education* 1: 13–36.

Kelly, M. E. 1987. Course teams and instructional design in Australian distance education: A reply to Shaw and Taylor. *Distance Education* 8: 106–120.

Kerr, S. T. 1983. Inside the black box: Making design decisions for instruction. *British Journal of Educational Technology* 14: 45–58.

Konrad, A., and J. M. Small. 1986. Consortia in Canadian distance education. In I. Mugridge and D. Kaufman (eds.), *Distance education in Canada.* London: Croom Helm, pp. 111–120.

Leslie, J. D. 1979. The University of Waterloo model for distance education. *Canadian Journal of University Continuing Education* VI: 33–41.

Ljosa, E. (1980) Some thoughts on the state of research in distance education. *Distance Education* 1: 99–102.

McClean, P. 1986. Universities combine to teach women's studies. *Open Learning* 1: 29–33.

McIntosh, N. E., A. Woodley, and V. Morrison. 1980. Student demand and progress at the Open University—the first eight years. *Distance Education* 1: 37–60.

Marland, P., W. Patching, I. Putt, and R. Store. 1984. Learning from distance-teaching materials: A study of students' mediating responses. *Distance Education* 5: 215–236.

Moore, M. G. 1985. Some observations on current research in distance education. *Epistolodidaktika* 1: 35–62.

———. 1986. Self-directed learning and distance education. *Journal of Distance Education* I: 7–24.

Mugridge, I. 1983. Consortia in distance education: Some Canadian ventures. *Open Campus* 8: 22–29.

National Technological University Bulletin. IV. 1987. Fort Collins, CO: National Technological University.

Parker, L. A., and M. K. Monson. 1980. *Teletechniques: An instructional model for interactive teleconferencing.* Englewood Cliffs, NJ: Educational Technology Publications.

Peruniak, G. S. 1983. Interactive perspectives in distance education: A case study. *Distance Education* 4: 63–79.

———. 1984. The seminar as an instructional strategy in distance education. *British Journal of Educational Technology* 15: 107–124.

Riley, J. 1981. Course team alternatives. *Teaching at a Distance* 19: 69–71.

Rowntree, D. 1986. *Teaching through self-instruction.* London: Kogan Page.

Rumble, G., and K. Harry (eds.) 1982. *The distance teaching universities.* London: Croom Helm.

Schramm, W. 1972. What the research says. In W. Schramm (ed.), *Quality in Instructional Television.* Honolulu: University Press of Hawaii, pp. 44–79.

Seaborne, K., and A. Zuckernick. 1986. Course design and development. In I. Mugridge and D. Kaufman (eds.), *Distance education in Canada.* London: Croom Helm, pp. 37–49.

Shale, D. 1987. Innovation in international higher education: The open universities. *Journal of Distance Education* XII: 7–26.

Shaw, B., and J. C. Taylor. 1984. Instructional design, distance education and academic tradition. *Distance Education* 5: 277–285.

Smith, W. A. S., J. S. Daniel, and B. L. Snowdon. 1984. University distance education in Canada. *Canadian Journal of Higher Education* XIV: 75–81.

Sparkes, J. 1984. Pedagogic differences between media. In A. W. Bates (ed.), *The role of technology in distance education.* Beckenham, Kent: Croom Helm, pp. 207–222.

Taylor, E. and A. Kaye. 1986. Andragogy by design? Control and self-direction in the design of an Open University course. *Programmed Learning and Educational Technology* 23: 62–69.

Thompson, G. 1984. The cognitive style of field-dependence as an explanatory construct in distance education dropout. *Distance Education* 5: 286–293.

———. 1986. I'll know it when I see it: What is distance education? *Canadian Journal of University Continuing Education* XII: 83–91.

Tight, M. 1985. Do we really need course teams? *Teaching at a Distance* 23: 48–50.

Timmers, S. 1986. Microcomputers in course development. *Programmed Learning and Educational Technology* 23: 15–23.

———, and I. Mugridge. 1986. The Open Learning Institute: Recent innovations. In C. Osborne (ed.), *International yearbook of educational and instructional technology 1986/87.* London and New York: Kogan Page/Nichols.

CHAPTER NINE

Instructional Design in Interactive Video Development
A British Perspective

Angus Doulton

The National Interactive Video Centre (NIVC) was established in September 1984 to act as an independent focal point for everyone involved in interactive video in Britain. At the time, interactive video was just beginning to appear in the UK, and was seen almost exclusively as a tool for skills training in large industrial concerns. As organizations of all types began to discover more uses of interactive video, it quickly became clear that interactive video would have to make heavy demands on many different aspects of instructional design, on pedagogic theory generally, and on the steadily growing practice of varied educational technologies, if it was to be at all effective in meeting the needs of industry and education in the United Kingdom (U.K).

The situation outlined in Figure 9.1 is perhaps more volatile than that in the United States. Few British organizations have a long history of development of instructional design techniques, and links between industry and education in this field are rarer than they might be. Figure 9.1 shows the networks of the different groups of people who began to use the NIVC as we started our work.

The first part of this chapter will summarize some of the important and

Figure 9.1. *Groups of people involved with the National Interactive Video Centre.*

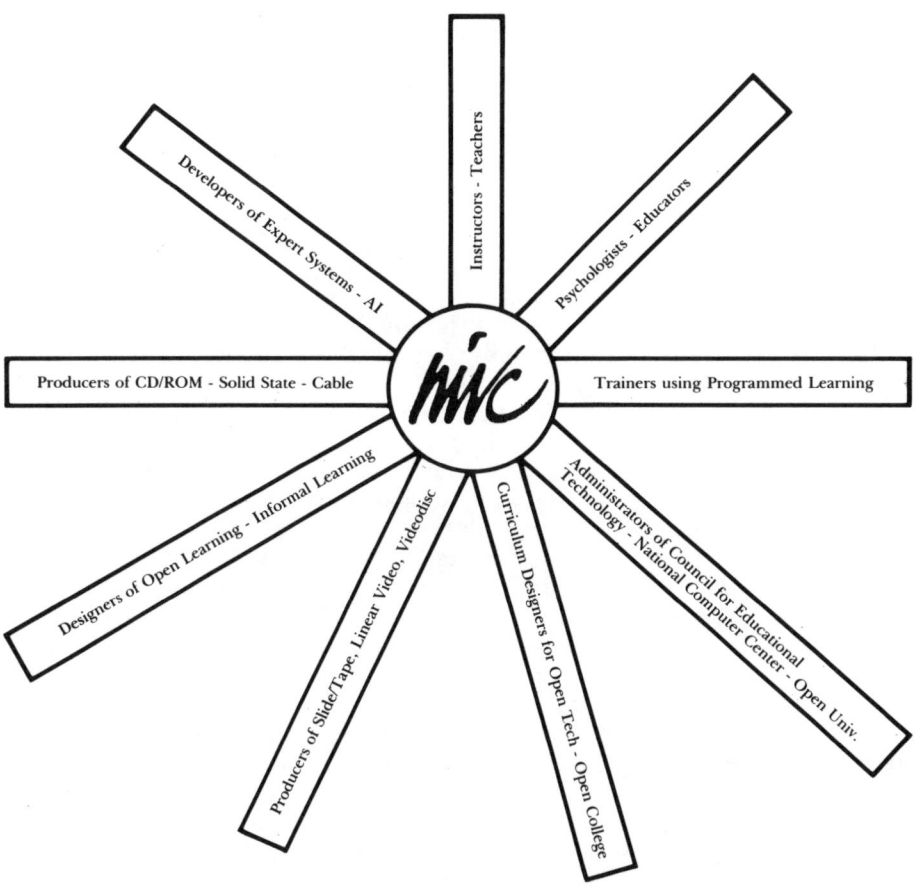

relevant historical developments in education and training in the U.K., and how instructional design and interactive video systems began to be used. Next some present-day user needs and problems will be described, along with some slowly emerging solutions. A series of "Guideline Questions" are included for organizations considering the use of interactive technologies. The short end section emphasizes the overriding importance of increased international cooperation in meeting future demands, and examines the prospects for success.

SIGNIFICANT DEVELOPMENTS IN OPEN LEARNING AND DISTANCE DELIVERY IN THE U.K.

Since the mid-1960s, the provision of open learning has grown steadily throughout the U.K. As this has taken place, courseware providers have looked for increasingly powerful delivery systems, and have frequently broken new ground in doing so. In its early days, for instance, many of the Open University's student texts set new standards in the design of print materials for learning. Interactive video is increasingly seen as a powerful tool in the open learning context.

Total acceptance of this new medium is still relatively distant, however. NIVC staff often are asked to speak all over Britain, and frequently this involves being expected, on short notice, to transport a fair amount of hardware to university lecture theaters. The challenge can be extensive, especially if the hosts have elected (as the New University, Ulster, Belfast did) to furnish the auditorium with a display of antique teaching machines.

Over the last two decades in Britain programmed learning in varied forms, and a fair amount of computer-based training (CBT) and computer-assisted learning (CAL), have foundered on the twin rocks of practitioners' skepticism and the costs of creating the materials. Delivery system costs are often seen as relatively insignificant. The wildly different figures given by different organizations as a cost per hour for creating materials are one sign of the struggle to come to terms with the problem.

Rightly or wrongly, another significant factor in the cautious approach to all these innovations has been that they have been seen as technology-led. Both educators and trainers have, over these years, had broad concerns that their students' needs should be met by technology only where and if this would be an appropriate and cost-effective solution.

This deeply entrenched skepticism began to be modified first by the establishment of the Open University (OU) and then, following that institution's U.K. and international success, by a number of government initiatives aimed at expanding and developing open and distance learning strategies. Significantly, these strategies were initiated not by the education system but by the Manpower Services Commission (MSC), the leading agency of the U.K. government's Department of Employment. In 1979 the MSC established its Open Tech division, which was intended to broaden links between industry and distance education establishments—and to increase the provision of open learning courseware. (Unlike most design units in the United States, Open Learning Centres in Britain frequently combine both courseware development and delivery.)

As a direct result of the Open Tech initiative, a growing number of large industrial organizations have begun to develop their own open learning centers with, for example, Jaguar and Austin Rover leading the way among motor manufacturers. Jaguar's Coventry plant houses a fully equipped center now capable of delivering over 400 courses—both work-related and not—to employees. Austin Rover's Haseley Manor Training Centre has established satellite centers in each of its main plants in the U.K. However, as the benefits of open learning have become apparent, the questions have remained. In one form or another, nearly all of these concern the issue of how anyone can, on the one hand, create sufficient courses of adequate quality to meet the demands that open learning strategies create, and, on the other, sufficiently change educational organizations to allow those strategies to achieve optimum results.

Open College

In 1987 a further MSC initiative—the Open College—was announced. The Open College is designed to offer noncredit education and training (as distinct from the academic degrees that the Open University offers) by whatever broadcast medium is suitable to the whole of the U.K.

Enter the Computer (Sometimes Bearing Gifts)

Running almost parallel with the early developments in open learning were the first signs of more serious development of both computer-based training and computer-assisted learning.

As occurred in the United States, computer-based training began to be introduced to British companies as a means of meeting urgent training needs in large organizations with widely dispersed staffs. British Telecom, Lucas, and the Ministry of Defense were early users of systems largely imported from the United States that relied on American theories of instructional design. WICAT, MENTOR, and TICCIT were among the first comprehensive systems adopted in the U.K. The high costs of doing so—despite some clearly identified cost benefits—deterred many potential users.

Computer-assisted learning took a different route. CAL could not be seriously introduced in schools before the advent of microcomputers. Their use in the schools, following a major initiative by the government's Department of Trade and Industry in 1980, got off to a rather halting start, due partly to a lack of suitable educational software and partly to a teaching strategy initially aimed at producing computer programmers rather than computer-literate users. Two major initiatives, the Microelectronics Education Programme in England and the Microelectronics Development Programme in Scotland, began to attack this situation by producing curricular materials. Their efforts were extended by individuals working in a variety of subject areas. The work of Margaret Cox at Chelsea (now King's) College addressed microcomputing in math and science. Daniel Chandler working in English, and Jon Nichol in History, were two of the early exponents of microcomputing in arts subjects.

In 1987 the Department of Education and Science funded a major new initiative that established the Microelectronics Education Support Unit. This unit was charged with developing the use of microcomputing in schools and, in particular, its implementation in all curricular areas.

From Television to Video

Television and, subsequently, video have an established record of successful implementation both in education and all forms of corporate communication in the U.K. BBC Education began broadcasting educational television almost as soon as it began transmission, and has a long and proud tradition of sending programs to all parts of the world. The formation of a range of independent television companies served, among other things, to broaden the educational output, and this has always been greatly increased by radio transmissions. "English by Radio" is only one of the programs known throughout the world.

From its inception, the Open University designed a considerable proportion of its courses for broadcast TV. Today the BBC/OU production unit in Milton Keynes combines the efforts of an impressive range of skilled technicians, courseware designers, and subject experts. In the early days of the OU, a major problem for students was the ungodly hours of transmission. While the arrival of time-lapse VCRs in the 1980s was not specifically designed to allow OU students some sleep, it clearly had a major effect both in the university world and in the schools. Teachers rejoiced in their ability to free the use of broadcast material from the constraints previously imposed by trying to match transmission times to classroom schedules.

VCR

The VCR also allowed considerable development in the use of video for all kinds of corporate communication. As both internal company messages and training films were developed, TV producers and designers—many of whom had been trained on the job by the BBC—began to form companies to meet growing client requirements.

Summary

This truncated history outlines the steps leading to the energetic development of interactive video in the UK since the mid-1960s, and illustrates that it has become increasingly difficult to separate the medium from the message. More flexible learning strategies demand more sophisticated delivery. Equally, more powerful media encourage educational experimentation. However, it would be wrong to assume that they are all part of a concerted pattern. Rather, the opposite has been the case. Developments in each of the areas discussed have occurred almost independently of each other, and there has been little consensus about design principles. Laurillard (1987) of the OU, Lewis (1985) of the National Extension College in Open Learning, and Rothwell (1985) of the National Computing Centre all have published useful work on various aspects of the design debate.

Interactive video, with its foundations in all the media mentioned so far, as well as its dependence on instructional design theory and process, arrived in the U.K. precisely when it might either solve everyone's problems or (more probably) compound the confusion in the field.

THE PRESENT SITUATION
Interactive Video in the U.K.

In 1984 a handful of large corporations, including Lloyds Bank, British Telecom, and IBM, began seriously to create interactive video. Each firm chose a different route into the new technology, but each faced similar questions. It was not, for instance, immediately apparent whether they were involved primarily in a computing activity or a video activity. Nor was it clear whether any of the commercial companies that had in the past specialized in supplying video to large corporate users could be particularly helpful in providing interactive video.

Throughout 1985 and 1986, a steadily growing number of corporations began to discuss and use interactive video. As part of her work with the National Interactive Video Centre, Claire Bayard-White identified a pattern of rapid and significant development. However, her instructive corporate case studies also begin to identify a set of common problems listed below—largely stemming from an unfamiliarity with effective instructional design.

Organizations need considerable help in carrying out more than a cursory study to identify whether their training objectives will meet their company objectives. Few organizations conduct a detailed training-needs analysis before beginning their work. Many try to develop their own theory of instructional design during their project, with the result that even the most basic issues, for instance about the use of multiple-choice items, are unnecessarily reconsidered.

The problems are compounded as large corporate users respond to the lack of sufficient expertise in the marketplace by establishing their own in-house design and production units. Typically, they will employ a number of educators as courseware designers, as well as a growing number of computer and video experts. Also typically, their learning experiences in project management, and particularly in meshing the courseware division with the rest of the organization, will be painful. Along the way, these large corporate endeavors risk developing an inward-looking and narrow division that is likely to produce programs in which the basic instructional principles are repeated across a range of topics, regardless of either the subject matter or the students' needs.

To be sure, some of the organizations that have determinedly forced themselves along this route are now, two years later, creating very satisfactory interactive video and, as Bayard-White's survey shows, commissioning increasing amounts of it. But what is now needed is a concerted effort to ensure that new organizations, beginning to assess these techniques for the first time, do not all have to go through the same two-year assault course—where the winners reach the end bruised, gasping, and unsure whether it was all worth it, while the losers drop rapidly from sight.

New Technology in Instructional Design

At the National Interactive Video Centre we see well over a thousand potential industrial users of new learning technologies in a year. A common observation is that only a small number of them have seriously considered how new technologies can help them, while even fewer have analyzed what they need to do along the lines of the basic construct shown in Figure 9.2.

In this context, the overriding need for more commonly accepted theories of instructional design becomes increasingly apparent. Personal computers now allow an increasing range of companies to access relatively cheap delivery systems, and so spread their training widely across the organization. In turn, this should give rise to a rapidly increasing demand for courseware as managers become aware of training potential that has simply been unavailable to them before. How is this courseware to be created? How are the creators to set for themselves worthwhile quality standards? The problems split between organizational and pedagogic concerns, and are of equal concern to the manager or administrator and to the instructional designer.

In summary, the need for developing instructional design theory fully capable of supporting widespread interactive video development nearly all rises from industry, which is as interested in management improvement and attitudinal change as it is in basic skills training. Although instructional design techniques often are applied at the skills level, corporate users have been quite skeptical about their effectiveness in management development. Rightly or wrongly, they have tended to see the traditional instructional design process

Figure 9.2. *Interactive technology in the learning/training process.*

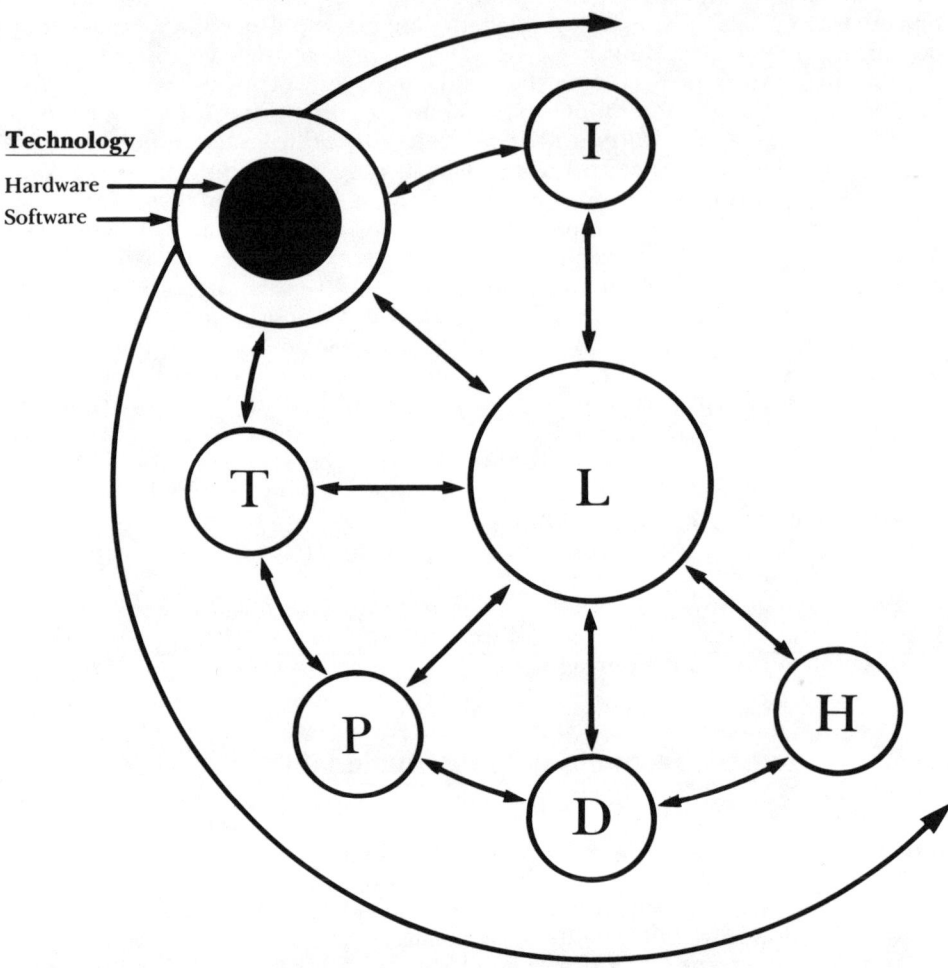

L = Learner.	The Learner, not the technology, is in the middle.
Around the learner are a variety of inputs that help (or hinder) any learning process.	
I = Information.	Note the videodisc's ability to deliver a large quantity of it very accurately
T = Teacher/Trainer.	Question: How challenging would their role be if freed of the task of delivering information?
P = Practical Activity.	Question: How can courseware designers best relate videodisc material to interactions with print, experimental work, hands-on experience, etc.?
D = Discussion.	Consider the machine's ability to stimulate discussions among small groups of learners.
H = Home.	Question: Where will modular courses be delivered in future?

as a relatively rigid way of imposing some sort of order on a confusing scene, where what is needed is something much more adaptable. Older methods of instructional design have been found lacking in all the crucial affective areas where the key requirements are motivation and learner involvement.

Not surprisingly, interactive video has been seen to have great potential to solve these problems—because it can so easily support an extremely wide range of instructional strategies, and also because interactive video producers come from a wide range of creative backgrounds. During the past few years we have seen gaming theory, simulation, a gamut of dramatic techniques, the beginnings of computer management of learning, and self-study disciplines all being applied—sometimes consciously and sometimes more intuitively— to the creation of interactive video. British production companies have steadily adopted such techniques and, as they have done so, a number of crucial demands for instructional design improvements have emerged.

Indeed, an organization that begins to find interactive video useful is likely to start wanting more of it, more quickly, more cheaply, more effectively. The blocks to progress now lie mainly on the pedagogic side. For example, designers in the U.K. need better ways of identifying the target audience and producing a sharp audience profile quickly. Behind this is a need for strategies that enable designers to capture detailed subject knowledge rapidly and accurately, and (then) to have a more precise tool for selecting the correct medium of instruction. In the U.K. now, there is considerable debate about just how far the techniques of artificial intelligence can help or hinder these processes.

But perhaps overriding these considerations is the need for a wide-ranging drive on facilitating a variety of learning styles. In the past, most forms of instructional design in Britain have been seen as likely to produce rigid patterns of learning with completely closed approaches to instruction. The traditional instructional design process has not therefore been seen to be very effective for those involved in open learning. As open learning developed, it increased the need for more flexible, attractive, and compelling learning strategies that could be harnessed to produce desired results.

Instructional Design Solutions in Interactive Video

Many of the early British interactive video projects set themselves extremely generalized objectives for correspondingly broad target audiences. It was quite common to see projects "to train all levels of management" in very generalized areas. Equally commonly, most levels of management would be assumed to have no previous knowledge of any kind! The resulting programs were judged to be relatively ineffective, and for a time we watched interactive video suffering criticism for what would clearly have been design faults in any medium.

As the large corporate users began to come to terms with the complexity of their training objectives, the need for more rigorous training in needs analysis procedures implacably arose. Companies found that they simply could not commission successful IV without taking considerable care over their needs and tasks analysis. In a sense, interactive video development began to create a fresh demand for instructional design! At one of the meetings held at the Centre, a leading trainer remarked, "Interactive video would be worth it just because it makes you think so hard about what you're doing."

The IV in Schools Project

At a very early stage, interactive video was seen as a potentially important tool for education in the schools. As educators began to explore this potential, the proposition that they might well be able to make a major contribution to the whole question of what kind of learning styles could be supported and developed around IV was advanced. In 1984 the Department of Trade and Industry launched a major project with one million pounds (approximately 1.6 million dollars) funding to design and create videodiscs in different areas of education.

While many of the outcomes of the Interactive Video in Schools project are naturally concerned with practice in schools, it is already clear that the work on learning styles could provide many of the fresh approaches needed in the training world. The eight different discs already created cover teacher training as well as wide sections of the school curriculum, including such subjects as geography and elementary science. This diversity automatically suggests widely differing learning and teaching styles. It is very much to be hoped that this work can be developed more broadly in the near future, and that the lessons learned can be transmitted throughout the interactive video profession.

And so the drive toward a seamless integration of education and technology has begun. What seems to be needed in many areas are instructional programs that closely engage the student, achieve positive outcomes, and yet are structured so transparently that the underlying design process only becomes apparent quite a long way through the course. Interactive video would seem to have the potential to deliver such courses, provided that it is carefully underpinned by flexible instructional design theory. Achieving the right relationships between students, tutors, subject matter, and technology will require nothing less.

GUIDELINE QUESTIONS

For organizations considering the use of interactive technologies, Claire Bayard-White of the NIVC has developed the following questions, slightly modified and abbreviated for the purposes of this book, but essential to consider before undertaking any such project.* A preliminary tactical question is:

How do you get prospective corporate, school, or other users to ask themselves such questions at the beginning of, rather than half way through, the process?

Background

Defining the client organization

- Who are you as an organization, what do you do, and what are your organizational aims?
- How large is your organization and your staff? What is the financial turnover? How is your organization structured?

First Steps

Why interactive video?

- Why are you choosing IV? Were other methods considered? Were current methods analyzed?

*Adapted from Bayard-White, 1986.

- How was the decision to use IV arrived at? Was a feasibility study undertaken?
- What key issues or potential pitfalls surfaced in the process of deciding to use IV?

Budget/Resources

- What percentage of your total organizational budget is spent on all training (not only training that has used IV)?
- If you are considering a training package that will be marketed, what percentage of your total organizational budget is spent on advertising/promotion?
- What percentage of total staff undertake training?
- Within what kinds of structure does training occur, e.g., decentralized, centralized, or a combination of both?
- How long, how often, and in what areas are staff trained? What percentage of staff resources are dedicated to providing overall training/promotion/marketing?
- What percentage of staff resources will be dedicated to the production and implementation of the IV program?
- What outside resources can be called upon to produce the IV program and why?
- Having made the decision to use IV, on what basis will you decide to use or not use an outside production company?
- What percentage of your total training or promotional budget will be allocated to the IV program?
- Will there be a formal contract between the commissioning agent and the production company specifying:
  —project management and individual responsibilities
  —duration of complete project, timetables, and sign-off points for the major phases of the project
  —method of payment; for instance, a phased payment where 10 or 20 percent of payment is retained until a satisfactory end-product is received
  —the criteria for acceptance of a program
  —conditions for terminating a contract
  —licensing agreements
  —copyright ownership and intellectual property
  —the level of confidentiality
  —other key areas outlined in the case study questions, e.g., responsibility for and ownership of documentation, hardware installation, etc.?

Preproduction

Needs analysis/aims/objectives

- What specific needs have been identified?
- Have any skills or task analyses been done?

116 Design and Implementation

- What specific objectives need to be met, e.g., what are the trainees/learners/potential customers expected to be able to do or to have gained at the end of the program?
- Who is the program intended for? What is their age, experience, educational background?

Learning/training strategies

- What learning/training strategies will be adopted, e.g.:
  —What kinds of learner responses are incorporated?
  —How much control does the learner/user have over the way through the program? Is this predetermined, or do users decide on "what and when"?
- Who will decide on the approach to adopt? Why and how? Will trainers/learners/trainees be consulted?
- Cost?
- Key issues/pitfalls?

Design/treatment

- Who will produce the initial
  —flowchart?
  —storyboard?
  —script?
- Cost?
- Key issues/pitfalls?

Delivery system

- What hardware/systems configuration will be chosen to deliver the program?
- Why?
- Cost?
- Key issue/pitfalls?

Production

Visual/audio material

- Length of program?
- How much moving footage?
- How many stills?
- Will you shoot "new" or use existing materials?
- Are there any problems with copyright?
- Will you use actors/real people?
- Voice-over/presenter?
- Computer graphics?
- Animation?
- Teletext?
- Will you use a production house? Which one and why?

Programming

- Is the control/training program encoded directly on the disc/tape, or is it held elsewhere? Why?
- What programming/authoring language/system will be used? Who will choose the system? What are its advantages/disadvantages? Given what you want to accomplish, can you, for instance, fully implement your preferred learning and teaching strategies?
- Who will undertake the authoring task, and what previous experience do they have?
- How long will this take? At what stage will it be undertaken?
- Cost?
- Key issues/pitfalls?

Hard-copy textual materials/accompanying documentation

- Will the IV courseware be self-sufficient, or will there be accompanying documentation? What sort?
- If so, why/why not?
- How was this material produced? By whom? Cost?
- Key issues/pitfalls?

Postproduction/Editing

Assembly

- When will the structure of the program be determined?
- How and where will editing be carried out, e.g., will an offline editing studio be used in the initial stages?
- Key issues/pitfalls?

Replication

- Disc pressing, tape duplication
  —Where?
  —How long?
  —Cost?
  —Key issues/pitfalls?

Project management

- What liaison will there be? To what degree will consultation/collaboration take place between the senior management of the commissioning organization and the production organization?
- Who will act as the client/production company liaison?
- Who will be responsible for financial administration?
- Will one or more people be responsible for final decisions?
- How much time should these activities take?
- During the course of production, will there be any negotiations with unions?
- Key issues/pitfalls?

118 Design and Implementation

- Will the program's use be directed/supported by someone other than the user, e.g., a trainer, salesperson, teacher, etc.?
  —Why?
- How will learner achievement be measured?
- Is mastery of the program content necessary for course completion or important for career purposes?

Evaluation

Comparisons

- Will evaluation of any form be undertaken once the program is implemented?
  —Will you make any comparisons between IV and other existing training/learning or point-of-sale methods? If so, what form will this take, and who will undertake the task?

Implementation

Testing and use

- Will the intended user/trainees be involved in the development, decision-making, or production process of the program?
  —Who?
  —How?
  —At what stage?
  —Why?
- Key issues/pitfalls?
- Will there be a test of the program before full implementation?
  —What form?
  —At what stage?
- Who is responsible for obtaining and installing the delivery system(s)?
- Key issues/pitfalls?
- Who will be responsible for introducing the system or program to its intended users in the organization?
- What form will this take, e.g., formal/informal introduction?
- Pitfalls?
- In what environment is the trainer/learner/potential customer expected to use the program, e.g., Where: on the job, shopfloor, separate training center? When: predetermined times or flexible hours? Why?
- Pitfalls?

Quantitative Benefits

- Will you forecast any quantitative cost benefits at the start of the project, e.g.:

—that training will be completed in less time
  —that better job performance will be an outcome of the program and therefore likely to save in cost
  —that sales will increase as a result of using IV?
- If so, how will you determine whether or not these forecasts are borne out in experience?

Qualitative Benefits

- Do you foresee any qualitative benefits?
  —Are you using IV for something that hasn't previously been possible using conventional methods? (A new activity may not be subject to quantitative comparisons, but qualitatively important, e.g., in terms of expanding organizational expertise.)
  —Will the production of the program help produce positive changes in training/learning/selling practices or procedures in the organization or company?
  —Will trainers/trainees/users enjoy using the program? Will the IV use improve motivation? Why/why not? How will you determine this?

TOWARD INTERNATIONAL COOPERATION

Once individual institutions, and even individual nations, have the process organized and can answer all the questions adequately, they still need to take one more step to be truly effective. They need to begin international collaborations. The need for international cooperation is quite simple: The job is too big to be done by any one country. Increasingly, forward-looking industrialists who wish to gain access to powerful but expensive new technologies are acknowledging that the solution is to share projects across countries.

Of course the concept of sharing expertise and materials across international boundaries is not an easy one. No two organizations, let alone countries, have the same approaches to either training or education. Cultural difficulties are bound to arise. However, the attempt *must* be made. Already, members of the IVIS team are in contact with their counterparts in Europe. An increasing number of American instructional design experts are visiting Europe to lecture and share experiences. Cooperative ventures are emerging. The question for the future, then, is whether we can reach some kind of global consensus that would allow us all to develop these systems effectively while retaining the individual cultural differences and approaches that are so vital to all.

REFERENCES

Bayard-White, C. 1986. "Interactive Video: Case Studies and Directory." London: National Interactive Video Center, internal report.

Laurillard, D. (ed.). 1987. *Interactive media.* Chichester: Ellis Horwood Ltd.

Lewis, R., et al. 1985. *An introduction to computer-based training.* Milton Keynes: Open University Press.

Rothwell, J. (ed.). 1985. *CBT library module 4 interactive video.* Manchester: National Computing Centre.

CHAPTER TEN

Building an Instructional Design Organization

Richard M. Lent

Instructional design and the instructional design process have been explained in earlier chapters. The roles and tasks of instructional designers have also been described, as have the varied applications of the design process. But what is the nature of the organizational unit in which all these activities and people reside? How is such an entity structured, staffed, and managed? How can you maximize the benefits and productivity of such an organization? And the basic question: When does it make sense to create your own instructional design unit at all, as opposed to buying the products and services of "outside" contractors?

WHAT IS AN INSTRUCTIONAL DESIGN ORGANIZATION?

An instructional design organization can take many different forms across various business and institutional settings. It can be defined as either a provider of services (training) or of products (materials). It can be at line or staff levels in the larger organization. It can function as a profit center. It can measure its outcomes in numbers of students, in productivity improvements, in dollars, or in employee morale. It can be of any size, encompassing a wide range of functions and specialists.

In short, the nature of an instructional design organization is difficult to classify. It can have many things in common with such different organizational units as an academic department, a public relations unit, a market research group, a publications office. However, what will always distinguish the unit is the primary purpose or function it was established to fulfill.

An instructional design organization can be defined as any organization whose purpose is to design, develop, and produce materials and activities intended to address a learning or performance requirement of a given audience. This definition emphasizes several critical characteristics of such an organization through the presence and absence of certain key terms.

- The definition focuses on "a learning or performance requirement" to distinguish it from marketing, communication, entertainment, and "pure" research organizations that encompass many similar characteristics, but which are fundamentally different in success factors and management requirements.
- The characteristic that it "produces materials" can be taken very broadly to include any medium to any stage of completion. The instructional development organization may do more management of production than actual production, but in the end it is accountable for the final deliverable.
- The stipulation that these units "design, develop, and produce materials or activities" is also intended to point out that instructional design organizations differ in focus from the more general category of training organizations or academic programs. The focus of these latter organizations is as much on the actual delivery of instruction as it is on the preparation of materials from which the training is to be delivered.
- A "given audience" emphasizes the targeted nature of instructional design activities. Mass communication is not the point here. Instructional designers address the needs of specific populations and the specific conditions under which they can be expected to access and use the materials that the instructional designer produces.

This definition, then, identifies a finite role for an instructional design unit. This unit benefits the parent organization by crafting materials and programs which, when implemented, will improve the performance of individuals. The instructional design unit is held accountable first and foremost for the quality and cost-effectiveness of the materials produced, and second for the impact that those materials have on the performance of the individuals in the target population. Research, analysis, and evaluation—activities also usually associated with the purpose of an instructional design organization—are omitted from this definition because the emphasis here is on the applied nature of the organization.

The remainder of this chapter examines how an organization so defined should be staffed and should function. Similar issues arise whether the parent organization or purchaser of the instructional design services is a business or a public institution, such as a university. Regardless of setting, it is assumed that the instructional design unit consists of senior and junior professionals across the disciplines of project management, instructional design and development, writing, graphics, media production, and evaluation. But before considering how to establish such an instructional design unit, we should find out when it makes more sense for a business or university to develop in-house instructional design capabilities rather than buying these functions from outside sources.

WHEN IS AN INSTRUCTIONAL DESIGN UNIT NECESSARY?

One of the most critical decisions any corporation, university, or government agency makes with respect to instructional design is whether or not to do its own instructional design work or to hire specialists. The importance of this decision is seldom recognized. Instead, the organization proceeds by default to do its own instructional design work on an ad hoc basis, using people whose primary value to the organization has little to do with the design of instruction or the fulfillment of learning/performance needs. Because this ad hoc approach is the most common way in which instructional design needs are addressed, we will consider its advantages and limitations first before examining the costs and benefits of using professional instructional design resources.

The Ad Hoc Approach to Addressing Instructional Design Needs

Most typically, individuals and organizations, when confronting the need to create some instruction, design it themselves. Thus the academician, engineer, or other subject-matter expert, whose specialization is to be the content of the instructional material, becomes both the designer of the instruction and the purveyor of its content. Often, this one-man/woman band also becomes the primary deliverer of the instruction.

The benefit of this approach is that it puts in charge of instructing others the individuals most familiar with the subject. This also means that the organization does not have to commit additional resources, beyond the subject-matter expert's time, to creating the materials.

A major drawback to the ad hoc approach is that it uses typically scarce and expensive resources (the subject-matter experts) to do something that they are typically *not* expert at: the design and production of instructional materials (Lent, 1986). The instructional design and development task becomes a high-risk endeavor for the subject-matter experts, in that they typically understand their material from a technical—not a learning—viewpoint. Furthermore, instructional materials development is typically not a formal part of most subject-matter experts' jobs, and they receive little recognition or reward for their contributions on such efforts. As has been pointed out, university faculty are hired and rewarded for their research and writing. They are rarely rewarded for their teaching effectiveness—and almost never for the quality of their instructional designs or materials.

In business, the picture is seldom any better. Training is often designed and led by someone who is a subject expert, not a teacher. Business typically defines the solution to a personal training need in terms of technology transfer or information dissemination. This leads inexorably to classroom lectures by the subject-matter expert because this is the archetypal information transfer technology—someone who knows tells someone who doesn't.

Even where a business has an established training organization, it frequently is staffed by people whose original value was subject-matter expertise. (They may have lost some of that original value as they devoted their efforts to training.) The training organization, meanwhile, is frequently judged for its dissemination function, for "getting the word out." The training organization is seldom measured or valued on its ability to "make the work stick." In this environment, the training organization may represent little in the way of instructional design or subject-matter expertise, but exists instead as a simple training delivery medium.

All of this is not to say that very good instruction cannot be designed and delivered by subject experts. Great experts/designers/deliverers like Socrates, Galbraith, Drucker, and Sagan come to mind. However, such renaissance individuals are rare. A more reliably cost-effective way of obtaining materials and programs to address specific instructional needs is to obtain professional instructional design assistance. The question, then, is whether to buy such services from an outside source or to build an internal instructional design unit to supply them.

BENEFITS OF HAVING YOUR OWN INSTRUCTIONAL DESIGN CAPABILITY

There are six main advantages to establishing a permanent, internal instructional design organization. The advantages are interrelated and emphasize the return to the host organization. A few of the advantages also reflect the benefits of professional instructional design support and could be achieved by using outside resources as well.

Dedicated Resources

For many businesses, government agencies, or universities, the ability to produce effective instructional programs on a fixed schedule and/or on short notice can be critical to the overall achievement of the organization's strategies and objectives. Nowhere is this more apparent than in a competitive, rapidly changing marketplace like the computer industry, where a company's success depends heavily on getting new products to market quickly, and ensuring that the company's sales and service staff are prepared to support the new product. An internal instructional design unit can begin designing the training support materials while the product is still in development and can coordinate the final production and "roll-out" of the training to correspond with the product's roll-out. In less commercial settings, a dedicated instructional design organization can also help an organization to respond more quickly to the changing needs of its clientele, or to ensure that existing training programs are being revised and updated as needed to maintain their utility.

Efficient Use of Scarce Resources

An internal instructional design organization can also help the host organization make better use of scarce subject-matter resources. Good instructional designers know how to extract the necessary information from subject experts while minimizing the demands upon the experts' time.

Control of Proprietary Information

In business and government settings, proprietary information often means the competitive difference. An internal design unit can manage such information more carefully and effectively. It can also help the host organization to implement key strategic moves quickly and efficiently when such moves require the retraining of large numbers of employees.

Quality Control

Internal design groups can facilitate tighter control of the quality and consistency of training programs. They can institute standards and systems that ensure consistency of instructional approach and delivery. They are also better able to place each program within the context of the parent organization's overall training and reward structure.

Organizational Effectiveness

Owning your own instructional design unit also means that it can help the parent organization to implement its various strategic initiatives for growth and change. Specifically, the instructional design organization's goals, priorities, and measures of success can be defined so that its efforts will be congruent with those of the larger organization. The design unit can shape both its programmatic emphasis and the content and language of individual courses to help introduce such cultural interventions as improved service. And, perhaps most important, an internal unit can develop strong, effective relationships across all areas of the parent organization's management structure, thereby fostering the effective implementation and integration of performance improvement programs.

Specialized Programs and Services

Finally, an internal instructional design group is likely to have one or more specific benefits unique to its charter and relationship to the parent organization. For example, this could mean the ability to develop highly specialized training programs on subjects where the parent organization itself may be the only source of specific subject matter expertise (as is the case with many high-technology industries). Owning your own instructional design capability could also mean the ability to develop a number of highly similar training programs more efficiently than anyone else could, particularly if such programs are likely to be needed on short notice in connection with a new-product introduction. Finally, many "in-house" instructional design organizations have been able to set themselves up as profit centers, reselling their courses and services to external clients to generate a net contribution of new dollars back to the parent organization. For example, Digital Equipment Corporation's Educational Services and The University of Maryland's Center for Instructional Development and Evaluation both provide significant financial returns in addition to fulfilling their internal charter.

In addition to these benefits, a number of liabilities are associated with maintaining an internal instructional design capability. These include the difficulties of establishing and maintaining what is a highly specialized function, and of keeping the instructional design unit productive, creative, and motivated in an environment where the only career ladder leads up and out of the training function. There are also questions of cost-effectiveness in light of high fixed expenses for what is typically viewed as a support function.

BENEFITS OF BUYING INSTRUCTIONAL DESIGN SERVICES FROM OUTSIDE SOURCES

Sooner or later most organizations, even those owning their own instructional design capability, will also buy some instructional design services from independent contractors. Some organizations forego any substantial internal investment and buy almost all of their services from outside sources. In general, the advantages of using outside resources have to do with flexibility, speed, and quality control.

Buying Just What Is Required

First, outside instructional design resources can be purchased only as needed. Projects can be planned and managed to fit the specific circumstances per the old project manager's saying: "Good, fast, or cheap, pick two." No ongoing overhead need be considered. And projects can be staffed to produce video tapes on one project and computer-based training on another, without concern for the effective use of existing staff (whose skills might be in workshop design).

Quality and Creativity

Second, going to external instructional design agencies provides an opportunity to select only the best and most creative specialists for a given job. Outside consultants also bring a fresh and original perspective to a problem, and they have often had experiences with other organizations that can be brought to bear on the new project.

Efficiency and Focus

Third and finally, the use of external resources means that they are clearly focused as a project team. They function outside local political issues and are completely focused on the task at hand. Furthermore, external contractors are usually managed by the job, not the clock, and they will devote themselves to whatever schedule is necessary to meet the deadlines.

A number of liabilities also are associated with the use of external instructional design resources. First and most basic, it is extremely difficult to choose good contractors. Many training companies, for example, claim to have instructional design expertise. What they actually offer, however, is a group of people who have a particular approach that they apply to all education and training problems. A second drawback is that where they lack skills and experience they may need to use the client's time and money to pay for their own learning curve. Finally, there is the risk of a lack of continuity from project to project, leading to potential inconsistencies and inefficiencies in the design and delivery of what should be a family of related programs.

Comparing the Costs of Each Approach

One area in which there is surprisingly little difference between owning your own and buying outside services is costs. When viewed at the level of the individual project or person–day of time, the cost of an external contractor is quite similar to that of a comparable internal resource. This comparison assumes that the cost of the internal resource also takes into consideration a portion of the overhead and benefit expenses appropriate to that resource, meaning that the salaries used for comparison are "loaded" with these extra costs. Moving from the project or individual level of cost comparisons, however, there is a meaningful financial differential between buying or building instructional development resources. It is a question of the financial risk inherent in investing in an internal capability and then not being able to apply it so as to receive the appropriate return on the investment. Outside of mistakenly buying the wrong contractor, this type of risk does not apply to a decision to use external contractors. On the other hand, there is never any economy of scale in working with external contractors.

Summary

In short, there are no simple answers as to when to choose to use outside contractors as opposed to building an internal capability. The best option may be to do both. Like a balanced investment program that includes both stocks and bonds, building an internal capability while also planning on the use of external resources for a certain percentage of projects enables the training investor to obtain many of the benefits of each approach while minimizing the risks.

HOW IS AN INSTRUCTIONAL DESIGN ORGANIZATION STRUCTURED, STAFFED, AND MANAGED?

Once the decision to create and maintain an internal instructional design unit is made, a number of fundamental decisions about structure, staffing, and management will determine the unit's overall efficiency and effectiveness in achieving its desired outcomes. The focus here is on strategic organizational issues that set the direction for the instructional design group's performance. More tactical issues, such as the skills required of an instructional designer, and desirable approaches to project management and performance appraisal, are addressed in the next chapter.

Structure

Planning for an instructional design unit should begin with answers to four questions. These questions help to define the essential nature of the new entity, and provide a basis for the organizational and management decisions to come.

Who Are the Unit's Clients?

Fundamental to planning any organization is an understanding of the clients whose needs that organization is intended to fulfill. For an instructional design unit, the clients may be other organizations within the parent organization, or the parent organization's external customers in its chosen market. An instructional design unit may also have a mixture of both internal and external clients.

This question can be more difficult to answer than it seems. It leads to consideration of organizational accountability for client satisfaction. It also raises the issue of whether the funder of the design unit is different from the entity receiving the benefit of its services. Not surprisingly, the best arrangement is usually to have the service provider (in this case, the instructional design unit) directly accountable to its client, and for its client to be the funder of the service provider's activities—to have, in other words, a client–provider relationship. Any difficulties or confusion that arise in defining this relationship typically reflect the parent organization's reluctance to grant sufficient accountability to the instructional design unit to manage its own success.

Will the Unit's Primary Value Be Judged in Terms of Services or Products?

This second question deals with what the client is actually buying. Instructional design units can provide two very different "goods." They can provide their clients with consulting services on how to solve a given performance improvement requirement. Or, they can provide the "solution" to the given requirement, e.g., a course. In the latter case, what the instructional design unit provides its clients is a finished product of its services. In the former case, the client buys the services directly. Whether the design unit is intended to provid services or products will have a major impact on its structure and staffing. It also determines whether the unit's business model will emphasize billing rates and applied time goals, or project size and production efficiencies.

Is It to Be a Cost Center or Profit Center?

A closely related "business model" question has to do with how the unit's financial performance is to be evaluated. Instructional design units can function as cost centers in which they are evaluated on their ability to apply their given resources effectively and efficiently. The measure of financial performance is its ability to satisfy its clients' needs while meeting the budget. On the other hand, the unit could function as a profit center whose performance is judged on its ability to satisfy clients and to generate a profit.

Where Should the Unit Be Placed Within the Parent Organization?

This final question should be considered even if it seems to be a foregone conclusion. The placement of the instructional design unit within the parent organization can have a marked influence on the unit's success. For example, if the design unit is to be an internal change agent, to fundamentally affect the operation of the entire parent organization, then the unit should be highly placed within the management hierarchy with an appropriate power base, visibility, and influence. On the other hand, if the design unit's primary clients are external, it should be closely associated with that part of the organization that has primary responsibility for sales and service to external clients.

A third option for organizational placement is also conceivable. If the instructional design unit is seen primarily as a research and design function for an internal client, then it might be located in a less visible position within the parent organization. This is like setting up a planned "skunkworks," where the key to the unit's success with its client is that it have sufficient freedom to experiment and make mistakes.

To summarize: The instructional design organization should be placed within the parent organization to be as close to its main client base as possible. It must have direct access to the parent organization's key decision makers, and sufficient authority to carry out its mission effectively.

Organization and Management

Another level of decisions in planning an instructional design unit involves its internal organization and management. The tradeoffs between project- versus nonproject-driven organizations, and functional versus matrix organization models, are considered first. The discussion concludes with a review of key personnel management challenges.

Project- Versus Nonproject-Driven Organizations

Howard Kerzner (1984) has done an excellent job of clarifying the management issues of project- and nonproject-driven organizations. His distinctions help clarify the management issues internal to the organization of the instructional design unit, as well as clarifying how the management and organization of that unit must match the management environment of the parent organization.

To begin with, Kerzner classifies all organizations as either project- or nonproject-driven. Project-driven organizations treat each project as a separate cost center with an individual profit-and-loss statement. The overall financial performance of the organization is determined by summing the individual project statements. Management attention focuses on project performance, and the organization is structured, and individuals rewarded, accordingly.

In the nonproject-driven organization, financial performance and management attention are focused along functional or vertical lines. Projects are viewed as supporting the parent organization's product or functional lines. Resources and priorities are allocated by revenue-producing line activities rather than by project.

Project- and Nonproject-Driven Instructional Design Units

Looking at the internal organization of the instructional design unit relative to its primary value to its clients, one can see that it can operate as a nonproject-driven organization if its primary value is in the provision of various *services* to its clients. The unit might consist of several functional areas or cost centers representing the various types of expertise to be sold, such as instructional design, media production, and so on. The basic unit of management is the hours or days of a particular expertise to be "sold" to the client. If, however, the instructional design unit is providing completed solutions or products to its clients, then it will make more sense to structure it as a project-driven organization, because it is the project that is the basic unit for managing costs and returns. It is the project and its outcomes, not the days of expertise, that is of value to the client.

Instructional Design Units in the Environment of a Project- or Nonproject-Driven Parent Organization

The organization and management of an instructional design unit must also take into account the management environment of the parent organization. A project-driven parent organization provides a much more successful environment for a project-driven instructional design unit. A nonproject-driven design unit, however, could successfully provide its services within either a project- or nonproject-driven parent organization.

A number of the challenges facing a project-driven unit and project management within a nonproject-driven organization have been specified by Kerzner (1984 p. 36):

- Projects may be few and far between.
- Not all projects may have the same project management requirements, and therefore they cannot be managed identically.
- Executives do not have sufficient time to manage projects themselves, yet refuse to delegate authority.
- Projects tend to be delayed because approvals most often follow the vertical chain of command. As a result, project work stays too long in functional departments.
- Because project staffing is on a "local" basis, only a portion of the organization understands project management and sees the system in action.
- There exists heavy dependence upon subcontractors and outside agencies for project management expertise.

While Kerzner was not addressing project management in the context of an instructional design unit's relationship to its parent organization, all the challenges he has identified are relevant. In general, then, the project- or nonproject-driven nature of the instructional design unit should be in agreement with that of its parent organization. But, as many sectors of American business have discovered, a project-driven organization has much to recommend it. The challenge of adopting a project-driven approach is in having an organizational model that supports it.

Functional Versus Matrix Organization Models

For much of this century, the dominant organizational model in Western businesses and institutions has been the "traditional" management structure or pure functional organization pictured in Figure 10.1. As organizations be-

Figure 10.1. *Traditional management structure.*

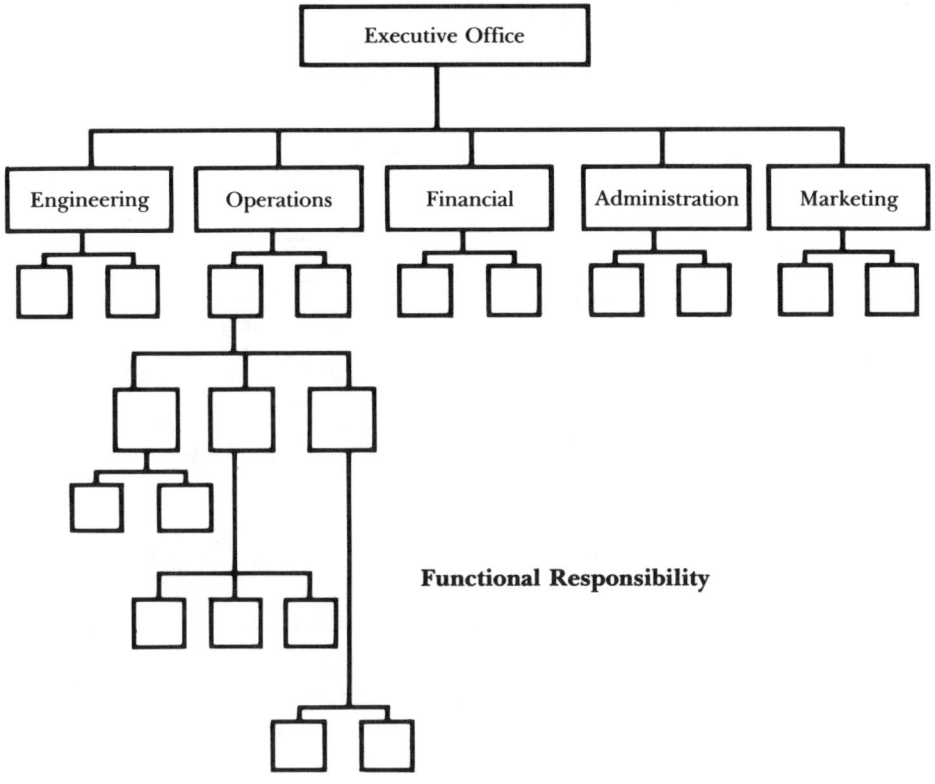

Source: Kerzner, 1984, p. 97.

came larger and more complex, however, the traditional structure began to falter. In particular, projects were difficult to manage and complete, as there was a lack of formal authority at the project level and an overall lack of responsiveness to the customer (Kerzner, 1984).

Various alternative organizational models were developed (Figure 10.2) with varying strengths and weaknesses. For project-driven organizations in particular, however, the best model that has been developed is the matrix organizational form. Figure 10.3 shows a typical matrix/management structure. Kerzner (1984) explains its features and benefits as follows:

> The matrix organizational form is an attempt to combine the advantages of the pure functional structure and the product organizational structure. This form is ideally suited for companies . . . that are "project-driven." . . . Each project manager reports directly to the vice president and general manager. Since each project represents a potential profit center, the power and authority used by the project manager come directly from the general manager. The project manager has total responsibility and accountability for project success. The functional departments, on the other hand, have functional responsibility to maintain technical excellence on the project. Each functional unit is headed by a department manager whose prime responsibility is to ensure that a

132 Design and Implementation

Figure 10.2. *Other organizational models.*

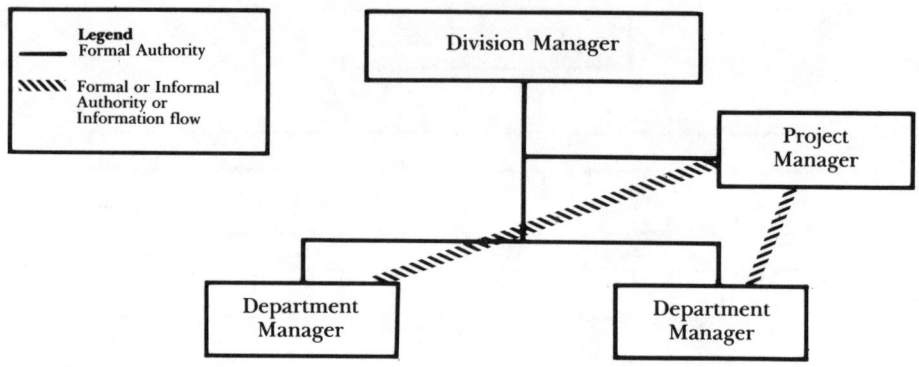

Line-Staff Organization

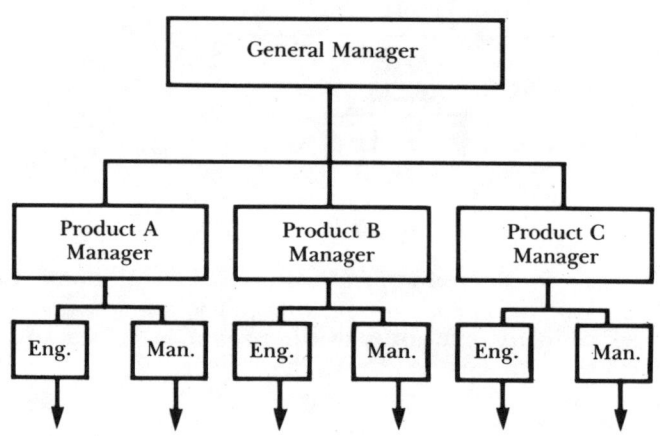

Pure Product Structure

Source: Kerzner, 1984, pp. 106–107.

unified technical base is maintained and that all available information can be exchanged for each project. Department managers must also keep their people aware of the latest technical accomplishments in the industry [p. 110].

Within this organizational model, an instructional design unit might be placed as shown in Figure 10.4. In point of fact, both Digital Equipment Cor-

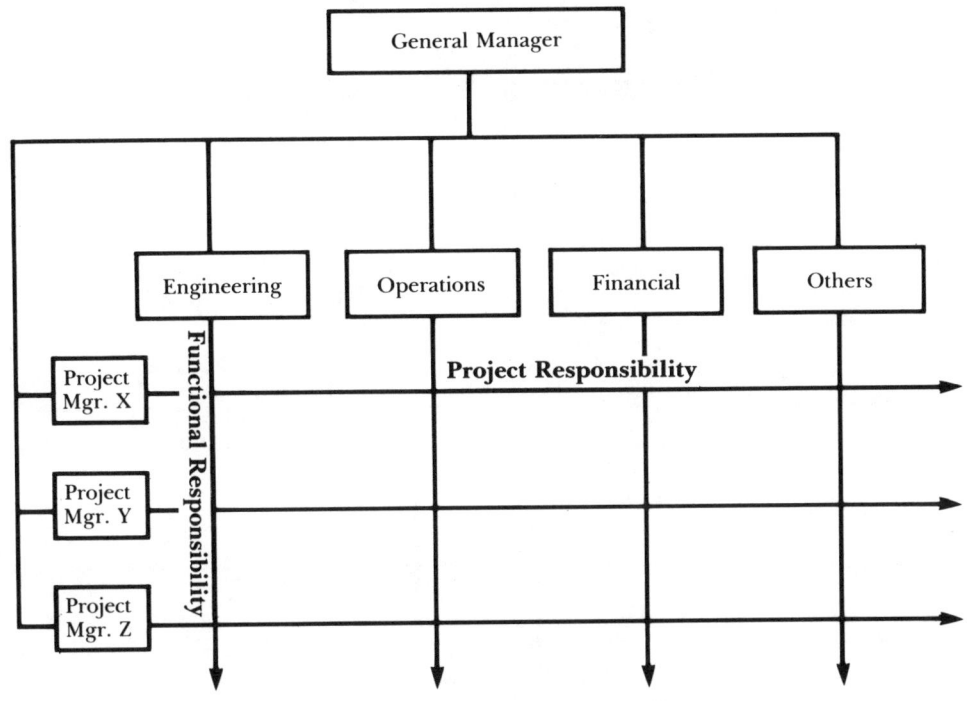

Figure 10.3. *Pure matrix structure.*

Source: Kerzner, 1984, p. 110.

poration and The University of Maryland have placed instructional design units in such a matrix relationship to a larger organization.

Focusing now on the instructional design unit itself: What does such a unit look like in a matrix organizational form? Figure 10.5 presents actual organizational models of two instructional design units, one designed to create print-based courses and the other producing interactive video courses. Both organizations serve a mix of internal and external clients. And both organizations also use external contractors as well as internal staff in completing their projects.

It is particularly interesting to note that the interactive video group depicted in Figure 10.5 had been initially structured as a functional organization. When it was restructured into the matrix form, productivity increased dramatically—from 1,200 hours to produce a finished hour of courseware to less than 300 hours. Meanwhile, the quality of the end products improved, and cost and time control also improved. In this case, some technical improvements and staffing changes contributed to these improvements, but here and elsewhere the matrix model has proven to be highly effective in the project-driven environment common to instructional design organizations.

Staffing and Management Challenges

Creating and staffing a given instructional design unit involves planning for a number of specific management issues. Sadler (1971) and Maister (1982)

Figure 10.4. *Structure with a director of project management.*

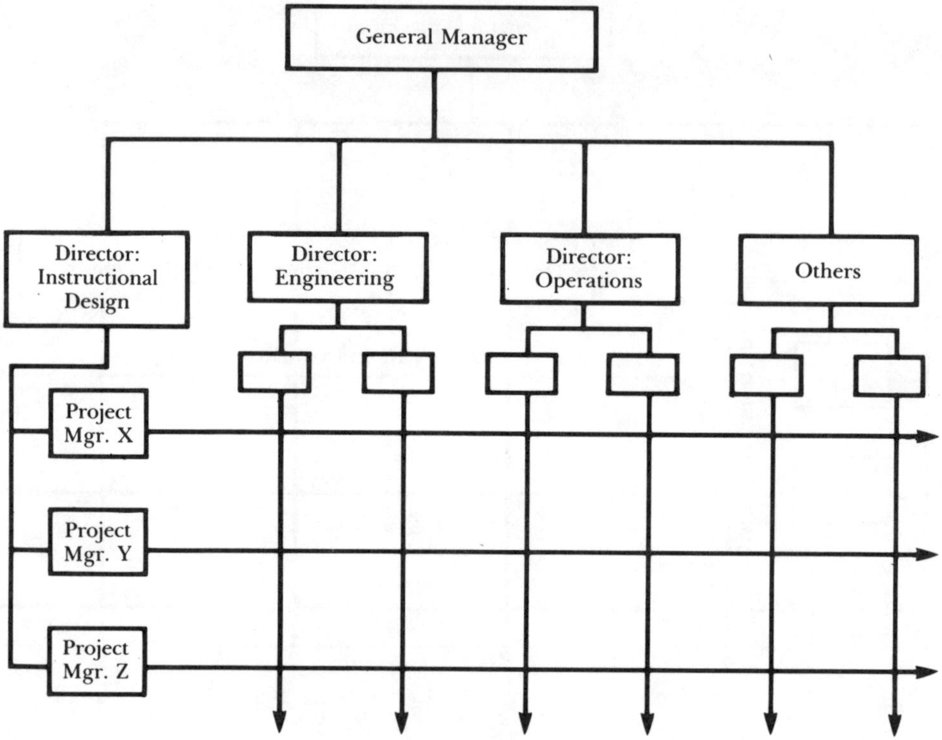

```
                        General Manager
         ┌──────────────┬──────────────┬──────────────┐
   Director:        Director:      Director:
   Instructional    Engineering    Operations      Others
   Design
      │
   Project Mgr. X
   
   Project Mgr. Y
   
   Project Mgr. Z
```

Source: Kerzner, 1984, p. 122.

have identified various considerations in planning an organization of this type. As interpreted and expanded for planning an instructional design unit, the key staffing and management challenges to be addressed are listed below.

- What is the desired mix of senior and junior technical professionals? What are the likely career paths within the organization?
- How will staff performance be measured and rewarded? How will individual goals be set? How will evaluation and incentive systems motivate staff to improve the quality and productivity of their work? How will a sense of ownership be promoted at both the project and the organizational levels?
- What natural social relationships and alliances can be expected to evolve within the organization? Will they be productive?
- How will the demands of long-range strategic projects be balanced against the immediate, tactical demands of today's priorities?
- How will the authority and responsibility of the project managers and functional managers be defined and maintained? Who is responsible for planning and specifying project budgets?
- What steps should be taken to ensure that the organization is a

Figure 10.5. *Matrix structures for instructional design units.*

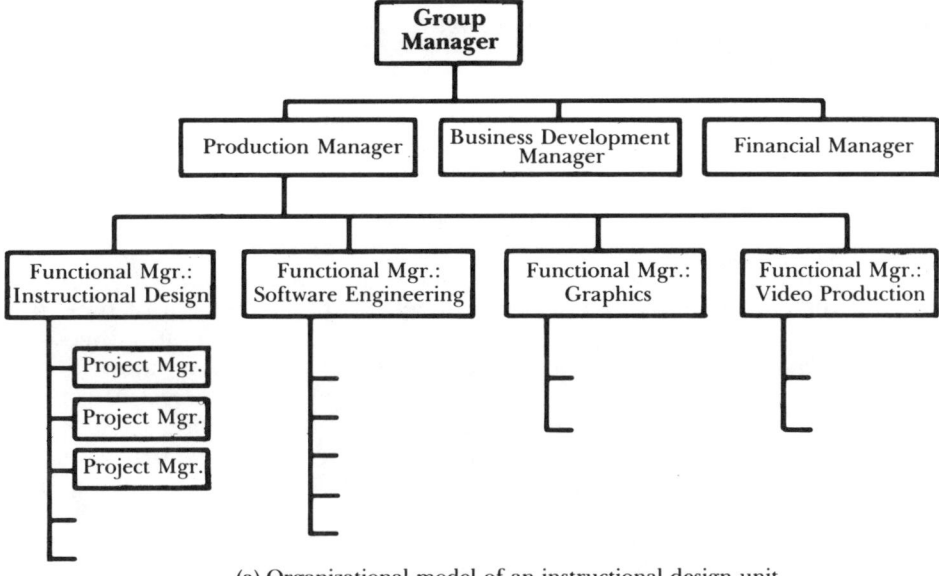

(a) Organizational model of an instructional design unit specializing in interactive video projects

(b) Organizational model of an instructional design unit developing print-based courses

productive environment for the mix of personalities it must contain, from the project managers who must have good customer skills and a high tolerance for ambiguity, to the technical specialists who must be detail-oriented and highly structured?
- How will individual responsibilities be varied to avoid "burnout" in the typically intense environment of project deadlines?

- How will changes in project scope be identified and evaluated for their effects on plans and budgets?
- How will the quality of the design unit's services to its customers be evaluated and maintained?
- What market and environmental changes are likely to affect the future direction of the parent organization's operations? How can the instructional design unit adapt and evolve over time?

CONCLUSION

Instructional design units present some unique management challenges. But for many organizations they are well worth the investment of time and resources. In developing an instructional design unit, consideration needs to be given first to identifying the primary client and what the nature of the service is that they want to buy. The experience of other project-driven organizations can be usefully applied to the design and management issues that occur during development. Finally, whether located within a corporation, a university, or the government, instructional design units seem to perform best in a project-driven environment.

REFERENCES

Bradford, D. L., and A. R. Cohen. 1984. *Managing for excellence: the guide to developing high performance in contemporary organizations.* New York: John Wiley.

Campbell, R. 1985. *Fisherman's guide: A systems approach to creativity and organization.* Boston: Shambhala.

Kerzner, H. 1984. *Project management.* New York: Van Nostrand–Reinhold.

Kidder, T. 1981. *The soul of a new machine.* Boston: Little, Brown.

Kotter, J. P. 1982. *The general managers.* New York: The Free Press.

Kouzes, J. M., and B. Z. Posner. 1988. *The leadership challenge: How to get extraordinary things done in organizations.* San Francisco: Jossey-Bass.

Lent, R. M. 1986. Courseware development. *National Forum* 66(3): 15–17.

Maister, D. H. 1982. Balancing the professional services firm. In *Course development and research profile.* Boston: Harvard University Business School, pp. 170–179.

Ohmae, K. 1982. *The Mind of the Strategist.* New York: Penquin Books.

Peters, T., and N. Austin. 1985 *A passion for excellence: The leadership difference.* New York: Random House.

Sadler, P. 1971. Designing an organizational structure. *Management International Review* 11(6): 19–33.

Sweeney, N. R. 1981. *The art of managing managers.* Reading, MA: Addison-Wesley.

SECTION III
Evaluation

CHAPTER ELEVEN

Evaluating the Instructional Designer
A Case Study of a Performance Appraisal System

Marcia A. Whitney

The Center for Instructional Development and Evaluation (CIDE) has two primary functions: (1) to provide instructional design and evaluation services to the larger, parent organization—in this case, a university; and (2) to provide instructional design and evaluation services, under contract, to federal and private-sector organizations external to the university. Because of this dual purpose, the center is similar both to a training department within either a corporation or an academic organization, and to an independent training company that markets its services to a broad client base.

CIDE management uses several criteria to determine what sort of external projects to pursue and accept. First, we must be convinced that a project we undertake will benefit our parent organization, the university. Our external projects have, through the years, brought new technology into our traditional curriculum, and have also prompted the university to move forward with innovative methods for delivering instruction. Because our particular mission within the university is to serve the adult learner, we also use this as a criterion for selecting external projects. Equally important, we seek projects that will match our strengths as an organization. We try to select new projects that build upon the base of our previous experiences, and we try to select projects that will challenge and tap the skills of our greatest resource, our staff members.

Our staff is large, and includes instructional designers, computer systems designers and programmers, and video production and quality-assurance personnel. Our center typically has many projects under way at the same time, and often a single staff member plays different roles simultaneously on one or more projects. Each project is managed by a project director who is an experienced staff member, and who, because of the nature of our center's projects, is usually an instructional designer. This director's responsibility is to balance project scope, deadlines, and resources.

As associate director of CIDE, I have learned that, to be effective, our instructional designers must not only understand and use the skill, art, and craft of the profession (as discussed in Chapter Two), but must also integrate these talents with an ability to respond appropriately to the three critical characteristics that define centers such as ours:

- We are a business, and we must recover all expenses associated with completing projects, which are usually awarded on a fixed-price basis.
- Our staff members work as individuals within larger teams on most projects.
- We serve clients whose needs may be minimally defined and whose real-world constraints may be restrictive.

Because these characteristics affect the designers, they define certain performance factors that differentiate a good designer from a poor one.

First, we are a business. If designers are too thorough or too rigid in their standards of excellence, our center will usually lose money on their work. For example, inexperienced designers often do not realize the programming complexities that may be associated with implementing a seemingly simple, but lengthy, computer-based lesson. We certainly do not encourage our designers to be sloppy, since we judge ourselves, and are judged by, our clients on the quality of our products. We do encourage designers to estimate realistically project scope, and the time and personnel costs necessary to produce what they design. A change in any one of these three—scope, deadlines, resources—mitigates a change in at least one other, also, if the project is to stay within budget.

The reverse of perfectionism also proves to be costly to our center: Designers who are careless about details can cause major problems. Particularly with respect to our computer-based projects, the designers must anticipate every path that might be followed, every mistake that might be made, and supply appropriate feedback and instruction. If the designers fail to do this, the personnel on the production phase of the project will necessarily be slowed, as lessons and the appearance of the lesson on each individual computer screen will continually have to be reviewed and revised by the designers.

The team orientation of our center makes yet another performance factor critical. Designers are generally accountable for meeting deadlines right from the beginning of a project. If they fail to meet even initial or interim deadlines, there is a cumulative effect on the rest of the project, and thus of course on the team. A delay of only one or two days at the beginning of a project can mean a delay of a week or more by the end of the project! Because each phase of a project typically is related to another, one unfortunate result of such delays often is that programmers and quality assurance personnel, whose work usually occurs at the end of the design process, are required to work overtime to meet final deadlines. This same team orientation makes it difficult, but essential, to separate an individual from the team, so that each person is accountable for his or her own performance within the context of the team's interdependency.

Finally, we work with the real world of clients. As plans begin to materialize, clients may decide that they wish to modify their original ideas, and thus the work statement. Designers must be alert to this, and must immediately bring any potential change in the scope of the project to the attention of the client and the project manager. Almost without exception, we have found our clients willing to negotiate contract changes that precede additional work involving a change in scope, but dissatisfaction and unwillingness usually characterize a client's response if we propose a renegotiation after the extra work has started. A clear value of interim deliverables—such as analysis reports, specifications, and draft materials—is the formal opportunity they provide to clarify understandings throughout the instructional design process. The client organization must also be thoughtfully studied by designers. Actual decision-makers must be identified and, to the extent possible, it is usually prudent to acquire some perception of political nuances within the client organization.

Our best instructional designers avoid the pitfalls. As Van Patton noted in a previous chapter, the instructional designer must create a design that "... meets the needs of the SME, the client, and the learner"—to which I would add "... within budget and on time."

After several years of informally appraising the performance of our staff members, our managerial staff decided to develop and implement a formal performance-appraisal system. This chapter documents the process we followed to develop that system, and describes the performance factors that we concluded were important to evaluate with respect to the instructional designer. We found (perhaps not surprisingly, given the systematic orientation of the design process) that our staff members were eager to participate in the development of this performance appraisal system, and have been advocates for its adoption and use. Rather than feeling threatened by such a system, our designers have welcomed clearly stated and agreed-on expectations for their performance. The starting point in this process was to define, accurately and explicitly, the roles that designers are expected to play in our Center.

ROLES OF THE INSTRUCTIONAL DESIGNER

An obvious function of instructional designers is to design effective learning materials. If their academic training has been thorough, it is this function for which they are probably best prepared. We expect designers to understand and be able to implement the phases of the instructional design process. To do this, they must have excellent analytical skills as well as creative ideas and design ability. They must also have the skills necessary to translate the ideas into the development and implementation of the actual instructional product. These skills usually are observable to others who work with the designer; hence they usually can be assessed.

Because each stage of the design process frequently culminates in a product, these, too, can be evaluated, just as an architect's blueprints can be reviewed and the final structure evaluated. But what if the resulting instructional product seems less than ideal? Is this an indicator of poor performance on the part of the designer? Perhaps not—because instructional design reflects a process as well as a product. Just as the architect works within client and budget constraints, so does the designer.

In addition to the design itself, there are other aspects of the designer's role that must be considered when appraising the final product. A good designer must be a client "manager." Our designers must gain a clear understanding of client expectations and budget, and often must persuade a client that these expectations are inconsistent with the budget. To master this role with the client, the designer must acquire the communication skills, persuasion skills, and timing of a good politician. The client should perceive that the designer is meeting her or his stated needs while, at the same time, the latter must remain firm regarding the scope of the project.

In today's workplace, many instructional design units are engaged in projects for multiple clients, frequently at an agreed-on cost related to project scope. Because changes in project scope may necessitate a change in deadlines and/or resources, they almost always require more money, and the negotiation of a new contract. As the person most likely to have ongoing, frequent contact with the client, it is the designer who must be sensitive to changes in scope, and who must inform project managers as these changes become apparent. Interpersonal sensitivity and effective communication skills are essential characteristics for the designer playing this role.

What if the client lobbies for a product that the designer knows is not instructionally sound? Then the designer must become a client educator as well as a manager. The designer must develop and justify an alternative, better position, with sound reasoning and clearly presented knowledge. Would an architect construct a building that will topple within one year? Not if the architect wants to remain in business. Neither should a designer settle for a product that contradicts the principles of learning and of instructional design. However, there is a difference between "instructionally sound" and "instructionally perfect." If the client's ideas will result in a good (but not necessarily the best) product, what is the designer's responsibility? Designers should discuss this with the client, but not lobby for perfection when the client has made another choice. Inexperienced designers, fresh from degree programs, often have difficulty accepting this reality. Designer unwillingness to shift standards of acceptability can create problems and confusion for the client as well as for the unit.

Designers need to be thorough documenters of meetings and decisions, because projects change and are redefined throughout the instructional design process. If these changes are not documented, they probably will not be recalled at a later time, should they be questioned. Documentation assures that everyone is aware of, and agrees to, decisions. It also makes it more likely that any shift in the balance of scope, deadlines, and resources affected by these decisions will be discerned. Designer documentation of meetings, discussions, and decisions represents an important source of information for appraisal ratings.

Generally our designers must work as part of, or even manage, a larger team of specialists to implement a project. The designer will almost always define content with the aid of at least one other person, a subject-matter expert or technical specialist who will be the primary source of information. On larger projects using more complex technology, such as computer-based or interactive videodisc instruction, the project team will include programming and video production personnel. As part of this larger team, the designer must live within the constraints imposed by a coordinated schedule and activities. If the designer also serves as project manager, he or she will need skills to resolve differences and conflicts, reward success, monitor expenses and budget, and report and summarize progress to unit administrators.

These, then, in our study are the roles our design staff identified as constituting their functions in the Center: The instructional designer is expected (1) to design and develop, and at times to produce, effective learner materials; (2) to maintain an effective working relationship with the client; (3) to solve problems, think critically, and communicate alternatives; (4) to define appropriate standards of acceptability; (5) to manage project scope and details; and (6) to be an effective member of a larger project team.

Unit administrators often assumed that designers had the adjunct skills necessary to fulfill these roles adequately—then became frustrated, angry, and discouraged when this proved not to be so. Just as we evaluate instructional products and revise them when it appears they are not functioning as intended or as needed, so, too, on-the-job performance of the designer must be evaluated, and appropriate development opportunities readily provided.

WHAT IS PERFORMANCE APPRAISAL AND WHY IS IT NEEDED?

Performance appraisal is the process by which an organization measures and evaluates an individual employee's behavior and accomplishments for a finite period of time (DeVries et al., 1986). As considered here, this process simultaneously involves the instructional designer, the designer's manager(s), and the unit management. To accomplish this process successfully, our managers needed to understand not only the goals and objectives of the Center, and of each individual project, but also what is required of the instructional designer to produce these outcomes. In turn, our managers needed to communicate these expectations to the designer, then compare actual performance with these expectations and give feedback to the designer. Just as instructional design attempts in a systematic way to assure instructional integrity and quality, a formal performance appraisal process in a systematic way seeks to assure a valid and reliable evaluation of an employee's performance.

In their earliest organizational use, performance appraisal ratings often were gathered on an ad hoc basis for administrative purposes—salary, promotion, retention, and discharge decisions. Through the years, these purposes have expanded and been adapted by a variety of organizations. Today, performance-appraisal ratings serve not only these earlier administrative needs, but also as a basis for counseling, employee training and development, and human resource planning. While all these are useful purposes, we chose to use a performance-appraisal system primarily as a means for giving feedback to, and improving the performance of, instructional designers.

As we have seen, designers do more than simply design, and even those who have graduate degrees in instructional design may not be prepared to react to all the variables operating in the workplace. Although trial-and-error learning inevitably takes place with experience, often it is demoralizing to the designer and costly to an instructional design unit. A preferable approach is to assess performance relative to identified standards. Where gaps exist, formal and informal in-service training and professional development can contribute to designer growth.

DEVELOPING A PERFORMANCE APPRAISAL SYSTEM

The necessary components of a performance-appraisal system are the same elements crucial to effective journalism: Who? What? When? Where? Why? (DeVries et al., 1986). The "Who?" in this instance has already been defined: instructional designers. The "What?" of a performance-appraisal system is critical to its effectiveness, as this is the heart of the process. Although we had identified the functions of our instructional designers, the actual and specific behaviors and skills to be evaluated remained to be identified. These behaviors, or performance factors, had to be observable, measurable, and essential to the effective performance of the designers in our unit. We did not want this list of performance factors to be lengthy, or cumbersome to use. Because the designers in our Center developed this list, they supported the implementation of the final system. We also included designers in the process of defining acceptable performance standards on these dimensions.

We derived nine instructional designer performance factors to be measured in our system. To develop this list, we identified all the performance factors associated with each function previously identified. Certain factors, such as communication skills, appeared often. Others, such as project management, were closely associated with only one or two functions. We then regrouped and synthesized all the factors, to arrive at the minimum number of essential factors. Thus, there is not always a direct relationship between each performance factor and the list of designer functions.

The nine factors are listed in the following paragraphs, with a brief description of each. The actual performance-appraisal form used at our Center, one of a series of pilot versions in an ongoing testing and developmental procedure, is included as Figure 11.1 at the conclusion of this chapter.

1. Project/Program Planning and Monitoring

This factor reflects the designer's ability to understand the client's needs, to meet deadlines, to use resources wisely, to analyze project needs, and to adjust plans as necessary to achieve objectives. As previously described, the balance among project scope, deadlines, and resources must always be known and maintained.

2. Leadership/Directing Others

This factor reflects the designer's role as a member, and often the leader, of a larger project team. The ability to motivate others, to direct their work, and to resolve conflicts when they arise are essential to the designer's success.

3. Collaboration

This performance factor recognizes that the designer works not only as a project team member, but also as a colleague to others within the larger organization. We expect each designer to collaborate with professional colleagues in order to enhance and achieve the goals and objectives of our unit and of the broader organization. To achieve this, the designer is expected to cooperate with others on project teams, and to take part in whatever organization-wide activities are asked.

4. Oral Communication and Presentation

We expect the instructional designer to communicate effectively and attentively with individuals and/or groups both within and outside our organization. This performance factor includes a willingness to invite and receive information and feedback, to present ideas and opinions in a clear and concise manner, to maintain discretion and confidentiality, to listen actively to others, and to communicate and negotiate effectively with clients. There are various forums in which supervisors can and should evaluate these skills.

5. Written Communication

Effective, thorough, and accurate written communication is expected of our instructional designers. Such communication includes reports, letters, proposals, memoranda, and project-related documentation and products.

6. Knowledge/Skills

We expect our instructional designers to remain up-to-date in their professional knowledge and skills. We expect them to apply the instructional design process in appropriate ways on all projects with which they work. We have an obligation to foster the development of this factor (and, by implication, strengthen performance in others) by providing opportunities for in-service training, and by encouraging and permitting designers to use time in this way.

7. Innovation

This performance factor comprises original thinking, creativity, and ingenuity in attaining work objectives. This might be considered the application of the craft and art of instructional design.

8. Personal Initiative, Effort, and Independence

The instructional designer is expected to systematically plan and follow through on activities without constant direction, and to assign appropriate priorities to daily, weekly, and monthly work activities. The designer must meet goals and deadlines, and delegate work when appropriate.

9. Problem Solving

This is the last major performance factor we evaluate. The designer is expected to recognize, and respond effectively to, problems—including foreseeing the possible consequences of proposed actions and/or recommendations.

Once we had identified the performance variables, we also had to identify data sources, and methods for measuring these variables. There are many ways to document the designer's actual performance on the critical dimensions, but our primary method is a rating scale. With this, each designer is rated on a seven-point (Likert) scale for each performance factor. We allow space for explanatory comments to accompany ratings, and the ratings and the comments are discussed with each designer. Our data sources include observations by team members as well as managers, written documentation, and interim instructional design products, or deliverables, as well as the final product.

These are initial steps in the performance-appraisal process. Our supervisors who complete the ratings are expected to become familiar with, and understand the dimensions of, the behaviors being rated. Practice in using the form and understanding the meaning of each rating-scale point has contributed to the ultimate validity and reliability of the system. Our supervisors have also had to be prepared to give feedback to the designer after performance has been monitored and evaluated, because the development cycle is incomplete unless the designer learns which aspects of job performance are being done well and which require improvement. Indeed, we have found that *managers* often have problems. Part of the design and development phase of our appraisal system has included skills training for managers on how and when to give feedback. Effective feedback sessions must also include the identification of development activities that will improve the designer's skills.

Our system provides an opportunity for self-appraisal as well. Each designer appraises his or her own performance, and then compares this appraisal with that of the supervisor who is completing the counterpart process. An advantage of this approach is that it requires the designer to invest something in the appraisal process, while at the same time enhancing the designer's ability to objectively and independently identify areas of needed improvement in his or her own performance.

The "When?" and "Where?" of performance appraisal depend entirely upon the particular unit and organization in which it occurs. At our Center, formal performance-appraisal ratings take place once a year, in conjunction with salary reviews. Each project manager also rates designers when projects are completed, since this occurs intermittently throughout the year. We believe that multiple ratings are preferable to single ratings, and that information regarding designer performance from varied supervisors will result in the most valid and reliable measure. Where responsibility for the performance appraisal system rests also is contingent upon the particular unit and organization. The performance appraisal plan for an instructional design unit should fit within any larger organizational plan.

Undergirding the entire performance-appraisal system is its ultimate purpose, or the "Why?" We have chosen to use performance appraisal to guide staff development and encourage professional growth. The use of a performance-appraisal system for this purpose suggests an obligation that the organization will release funds to meet designers' professional needs as determined by the appraisal process. We also use the performance-appraisal system as a method to assure both a formal recognition of each designer's contributions and achievements, and a personal accountability for performance. A formal performance-appraisal system has many benefits: It is consciously planned, it guides performance standards, it results in uniform documentation of performance both for the designer and for the unit management, and it permits a valid and reliable evaluation of performance.

COSTS AND BENEFITS OF PERFORMANCE APPRAISAL

Is it worth it to go to all this bother? The benefits of performance appraisal have been briefly discussed in this chapter—but what are the costs?

David L. DeVries and his colleagues at the Center for Creative Leadership (1986) have concluded that system development constitutes the largest initial cost of performance appraisal. These costs are primarily for staff time spent in analyzing, designing, and developing the system and its components. In our Center, it took a total of about three days for managers and designers to identify significant performance variables. In addition, it took about ten more days of senior management time to plan the process, gather information, meet with university personnel officials regarding the appraisal system, summarize the results of brainstorming meetings, and develop the final rating scale and system.

Immediately before its implementation, more staff time was required to introduce the system. We used one day to train managers and others who would be appraising performance. This day was used to review the rating scale and performance factors, to discuss their intended purpose, and to practice giving constructive feedback. Designers whose performance was being appraised, but who were newly arrived and hence had not been part of the planning process, were also introduced to the system, so that possible resistance could be ascertained and deflected. The actual implementation and maintenance of the system requires manager and designer time to conduct the appraisal and to give feedback.

Although not always direct costs, these are real costs that must be balanced against the benefits of appraising designer performance. To realize the staff development benefit generally requires a minimum of twelve months. These twelve months are used to set expectations, monitor performance, review performance with the employee, and make action plans for employee improvement. Performance appraisal results as described in this chapter can be used to identify unit-wide training needs, because they permit an organizational audit of performance trends.

One final key factor to consider before adopting a performance appraisal system for instructional designers is the likelihood that the system will be accepted at all levels of the organization. Managers should be willing to implement the system, and should believe that performance appraisal will be of some value to them in order to justify their investment of time. Designers should be shown how performance appraisals can be valuable to them, as important sources of data leading to their professional improvement. Finally, senior administrators in the parent organization must support the performance-appraisal process within the unit. Evidence justifying the costs relative to the benefits must be collected and presented to these administrators, to facilitate their decision-making about the plan.

CONCLUSION

If the benefits warrant the cost, and support to develop and implement the system is in place, performance appraisal can be a great asset to the institution, to the designer, and ultimately to the instructional design profession. There is neither curriculum time nor learner need during academic programs to justify the inclusion of all possible topics and skills to be learned by the instructional designer. Real needs occurring as a result of experience in the workplace serve as excellent motivators for continued learning. A performance-appraisal system gives shape to this "informal" and continuing curriculum for each designer. It provides a foundation for the logical extension of the learning cycle from academic preparation to continuing professional education. It also supports an instructional design unit's business operation, internal teamwork and morale, and ability to meet client needs.

REFERENCE

DeVries, D. L., A. M. Morrison, S. L. Shullman and M. L. Gerlach. 1986. *Performance appraisal on the line.* Greensboro, NC: Center for Creative Leadership.

Figure 11.1. *Pilot version of performance-appraisal form.*

PROFESSIONAL PERFORMANCE APPRAISAL & DEVELOPMENT FORM

Employee's Name _____ Date: _____

Employee's Position _____ Department _____

Supervisor's Name & Title _____

Performance Rating Period From: _____ To: _____

PERFORMANCE FACTORS

This section allows you to describe employee performance by indicating relative strengths and weaknesses against different factors. In a given position, some factors may be more important than others. Each factor is illustrated by examples. For each factor:

— Rate the IMPORTANCE of each factor to the employee's job by checking the appropriate box in the scale on the left side of the form. Check "NA" if the factor is not applicable.

— Rate the employee's overall EFFECTIVENESS for each factor, based on typical levels of performance during the review cycle, by checking the appropriate box in the scale on the right side of the form.

PERFORMANCE RATING SCALE						
1	2	3	4	5	6	7
UNACCEPTABLE	PARTIALLY ACCEPTABLE		ACCEPTABLE	MORE THAN ACCEPTABLE		OUTSTANDING

— Use the COMMENTS space to give specific examples of the employee's performance that illustrate the rating system.

PERFORMANCE FACTOR: Project/Program Planning & Monitoring	
DEFINITION	**COMMENTS**
Develops strategies to accomplish and monitor a specific goal. - Considers realistic timelines and resource availability when planning and monitoring specific projects. - Plans proper assignments of personnel and appropriate allocation of resources. - Analyzes needs, gathers information, and provides rational action plans. - Monitors progress towards objectives and adjusts action plans as necessary to reach objectives.	
FACTOR IMPORTANCE	**LEVEL OF EFFECTIVENESS ACHIEVED**
NA Low Medium High	1 2 3 4 5 6 7

Source: Adapted from a performance appraisal form developed by the American Council on Education.

Figure 11.1. *continued*

Page 2

PERFORMANCE FACTOR: Leadership/Directing Others	
DEFINITION Plans and directs that which is within responsibility in an effective and professional manner. - Recognizes and makes necessary decisions in a politic manner. - Balances professional goals of staff with departmental/unit goals. - Demonstrates enthusiasm for achieving specific goals. - Sets work plans and motivates staff through example and challenge. - Gains the understanding, support, and effective action of others to achieve specific goals. - Monitors staff performance & provides prompt feedback. - Promotes good personnel time management.	**COMMENTS**

FACTOR IMPORTANCE				LEVEL OF EFFECTIVENESS ACHIEVED						
NA	Low	Medium	High	1	2	3	4	5	6	7

PERFORMANCE FACTOR: Collaboration	
DEFINITION Collaborates with professional colleagues to enhance and achieve the goals and objectives of the employee's unit and of University College. - Works well with others in reaching specific goals. - Provides professional support to colleagues (e.g., demos, brainstorming, review of products/documents, advice).	**COMMENTS**

FACTOR IMPORTANCE				LEVEL OF EFFECTIVENESS ACHIEVED						
NA	Low	Medium	High	1	2	3	4	5	6	7

Figure 11.1. *continued*

Page 3

PERFORMANCE FACTOR: Oral Communication & Presentation	
DEFINITION Communicates effectively and attentively with individuals and/or groups both within and outside the organization. - Invites and receives information and feedback in a constructive manner. - Presents ideas and opinions in a clear, concise, and timely manner to the appropriate person(s). - Maintains discretion and confidentiality in communicating with others. - Actively listens to others, giving appropriate feedback, and makes others feel comfortable. - Communicates & negotiates effectively with clients and/or the public.	**COMMENTS**

FACTOR IMPORTANCE				LEVEL OF EFFECTIVENESS ACHIEVED					
NA	Low	Medium	High	1	2	3	4	5	6	7

PERFORMANCE FACTOR: Written Communication	
DEFINITION Communicates effectively, thoroughly, and accurately in writing. - Writes concise, organized and easy-to-read reports, letters, memos and/or project-related documentation. - Prepares accurate and meaningful proposals, reports, tables, charts and other documents. - Edits documents carefully; makes grammatical and substantive corrections (and/or seeks appropriate assistance). - Clearly expresses ideas in writing.	**COMMENTS**

FACTOR IMPORTANCE				LEVEL OF EFFECTIVENESS ACHIEVED					
NA	Low	Medium	High	1	2	3	4	5	6	7

Figure 11.1. *continued*

PERFORMANCE FACTOR: Knowledge/Skills	
DEFINITION Keeps up-to-date in one's field of expertise. - Serves as "resource person" on whom others rely for advice. - Uses all of the resources at one's disposal to be able to answer even the most difficult questions. - Keeps informed of the latest developments in area of expertise.	**COMMENTS**
FACTOR IMPORTANCE NA / Low / Medium / High	**LEVELS OF EFFECTIVENESS ACHIEVED** 1 2 3 4 5 6 7

PERFORMANCE FACTOR: Innovation	
DEFINITION Exhibits original thinking, creativity, and ingenuity in attaining work objectives. - Recognizes new needs and need for new approaches. - Analyzes existing systems/procedures and proposes more appropriate and innovative methods of operations/management. - Exhibits creativity in project/program planning and implementation. - Employs innovative problem solving to accomplish objectives.	**COMMENTS**
FACTOR IMPORTANCE NA / Low / Medium / High	**LEVELS OF EFFECTIVENESS ACHIEVED** 1 2 3 4 5 6 7

Figure 11.1. *continued*

Page 5

PERFORMANCE FACTOR: Personal Initiative, Effort, and Independence	
DEFINITION Organizes activities and devotes appropriate effort to insure proper completion in a timely manner. - Systematically plans and follows through on activities without continued direction. - Assigns priorities to daily, weekly, and/or monthly work activities. - Displays persistence and initiative in pursuit of job goals. - Meets commitments and deadlines. - Delegates work appropriately. - Self-starting, originates action rather than responds to actions of others. - Actively attempts to influence events to achieve goals.	**COMMENTS**
FACTOR IMPORTANCE NA — Low — Medium — High	**LEVEL OF EFFECTIVENESS ACHIEVED** 1 — 2 — 3 — 4 — 5 — 6 — 7

PERFORMANCE FACTOR: Problem Solving	
DEFINITION Recognizes and responds successfully to problem situations. - Recognizes when a problem is critical enough to require immediate attention. - Takes charge in problem situations. - Able to analyze situations and quickly provide an effective solution. - Foresees probable consequences of proposed actions and/or recommendations.	**COMMENTS**
FACTOR IMPORTANCE NA — Low — Medium — High	**LEVEL OF EFFECTIVENESS ACHIEVED** 1 — 2 — 3 — 4 — 5 — 6 — 7

Figure 11.1. *continued*

OVERALL PERFORMANCE

Page 6

Check the box that best summarizes the employee's overall performance against work expectations. Your rating should consider how well the work plan and objectives are achieved; how the employee goes about achieving them; their difficulty; and what other results are being achieved apart from planned objectives/assignments. When possible, take into consideration your experience with other employees in similar jobs and along the same factors. The rating scale includes three ranges of acceptable and one level of unacceptable performance, defined as follows:

Unacceptable:

Achievements do not meet the postion's key objectives or requirements.

Partially Acceptable:

Achievements partially meet the position's key objectives or requirements. With improvements in designated areas of the developmental plan, performance should become more acceptable.

Acceptable:

Achievements meet the position's key objectives or requirements.

More Than Acceptable:

Achievements consistently meet the position's key objectives or requirements. In some areas, accomplishments exceed work expectations.

Outstanding:

Achievements consistently exceed the position's key objectives or requirements.

Please check one:

1	2	3	4	5	6	7
UN-ACCEPTABLE	PARTIALLY ACCEPTABLE		ACCEPTABLE	MORE THAN ACCEPTABLE		OUT-STANDING

Comments:

Figure 11.1. *continued*

DEVELOPMENT PLAN

Page 7

This section should be used by the employee and supervisor to identify a future work plan. This plan may involve the clarification of goals and objectives; the possible addition of new duties; a recommended plan for training and development and/or specific actions to better utilize employee strengths.

Strengths:

Developmental Needs:

Possible Future Assignments:

(Over)

Figure 11.1. *continued*

Page 8

Employee Comments:

Overall Comments:

This appraisal has been reviewed and discussed with the employee.

_____   _____
Employee's Signature   Date

_____   _____
Supervisor's Signature   Date

CHAPTER TWELVE

The Role, Methods, and Worth of Evaluation in Instructional Design

Thomas C. Reeves

The reality of evaluation is that often it is undertaken simply because a funding source or other authority requires it. Evaluation, which many regard as nothing more than testing or measurement, inevitably consumes much of the energies and resources of instructional design teams, and may come to be viewed at best as a necessary evil, and at worst as an onerous hurdle to be circumvented whenever possible (Cronbach, 1980). Obviously, to be useful within the context of instructional design, evaluation must be grounded on a sounder rationale than the fulfilling of external requirements. Therefore, the general goal of this chapter is to provide a sound rationale for evaluation as part of the instructional design process. The chapter has the additional goals of providing an overview of evaluation methods that can be applied within instructional design, and of presenting recommendations for evaluating the process of instructional design itself.

To accomplish these purposes, the chapter is organized into three sections corresponding to the following three questions:

1. What is the role of evaluation within the context of instructional design?
2. What methods are available for evaluating the process and products of instructional design?
3. What is the worth of instructional design itself?

Caveats

The authors of other chapters in this book have pointed out that instructional design models cannot be applied as recipes that automatically yield effective, efficient instructional products, and that instructional design is just as much an art as a science. Similarly, it is important to stress that evaluation provides no automatic formulas for establishing truth, and that there is much more uncertainty involved in evaluation than the quantitative findings usually reported by evaluators might indicate. Evaluation cannot prove anything—it can only support or not support human conclusions and decisions. Furthermore, one must remember that evaluation does not make decisions, people do.

This last point is important because evaluation almost always occurs within a political context (House, 1980), and because evaluation findings must often compete with other sources to affect decision making (Cooley and Bickel, 1986). Perhaps an anecdote about the first evaluation I participated in as a graduate student at Syracuse University in 1974 will serve to illustrate this point. A new elementary mathematics program had been jointly developed by a large technology corporation and a prestigious research-and-development center. The instructional program was centered on the use of hand-held calculators manufactured by the sponsoring corporation, and featured attractive and expensively produced materials, including game boards, toy dinosaurs, workbooks, and teacher manuals. A year-long assessment in several school districts indicated that, while initial interest in the new materials was high, interest soon waned, and the materials yielded virtually no significant effects on mathematics achievement.

The results of the evaluation were presented to the sponsoring institutions with the expectation that major revisions, or perhaps a completely new development effort, would ensue. Instead, a few months later, two-page, full-color advertisements featuring pictures of children "learning" math with the calculators, game boards, dinosaurs, and other materials began to appear in educational magazines. The ads also included a bold footnote that stated: "These materials have been evaluated by Syracuse University." Clearly, there were other sources of influence on the decision to market these materials than the findings of the Syracuse evaluation!

THE ROLE OF EVALUATION WITHIN INSTRUCTIONAL DESIGN

Evaluation is the process of providing instructional design team members and others with timely, accurate information that will contribute to decisions about the improvement, continuance, and/or expansion of the instructional products (Anderson and Ball, 1978). This definition implies that the role of evaluation within instructional design is to provide those involved in design projects (instructional designers, subject matter experts [SMEs], production specialists, project managers, etc.) with any and all information that will support their conclusions and improve their decision making. The rationale for conducting this type of evaluation is the belief that informed decision making is better than uninformed or misinformed decision making.

This definition, role, and rationale for evaluation may seem to be just plain common sense and uncontroversial. However, two things have tended to limit the potential of evaluation within instructional design. First, the multiple conceptions and definitions of evaluation held by those involved in instructional design have led to misunderstanding and misuse of evaluation. Second, the linear representation of evaluation within most instructional design models and descriptions has resulted in underestimation of the power and scope of evaluation.

In the first instance, evaluation has been variously defined as: the determination of the degree to which objectives have been attained by a program (Tyler, 1942); measurement of the critical components of an instructional program or product (cf. National Study of Secondary School Evaluation, 1960); comparison of the effects of competing programs (Campbell and Stanley, 1963); judgment of a program's worth (Scriven, 1967); description of a program's inputs, processes, and outcomes (Stake, 1967); accounting for the use of project resources (Roueche and Herrscher, 1973); the ethnographic investigation of a program (Guba and Lincoln, 1981); and the critical analysis of a program's quality (Eisner, 1985).

While these and other definitions of evaluation and their accompanying methods may provide useful guidance and/or tools to the evaluator as information provider, the strict adoption of one or two narrow perspectives cannot possibly provide as much information as a broader perspective. Further, the evaluator as information provider may have difficulty communicating the findings of evaluations to those who hold more restrictive perspectives on evaluation. For example, it has been my experience that medical educators (particularly physicians) are reluctant to accept evaluation methods and findings that do not strongly resemble the experimental methodologies that they employ in their own research, even when their favored methods yield information of limited generalizability and utility.

In the second instance, most instructional design models and descriptions represent evaluation as a single step in a linear process generally beginning with analysis, proceeding through design and development, and ending with evaluation (Gustafson, 1981). The graphic representation of the instructional design process often takes the form of a modified flow chart, with the result that the instructional design process is perceived as being much more rigid and linear than is actually the case in the day-to-day progression of most development projects (see Figure 12.1).

The author prefers to adopt naturalistic representations of the instructional design process, such as the shape of a spiral galaxy or the Miraculous Thatcheria seashell (see Figure 12.1). These representations more accurately reflect the creative, experimental, and unpredictable aspects of the instructional design process than do flow charts or other technical schema. The latter representation is particularly illustrative of the role of evaluation within instructional design. Whereas the individual chambers of the seashell might be used to represent the various stages through which a product will progress during the instruc-

Figure 12.1. *Mechanistic and organic conceptions of instructional design.*

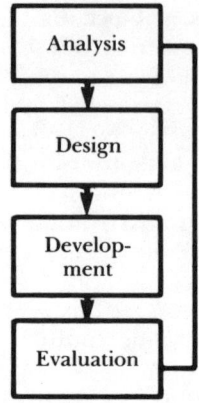

Linear ID model

Spiral Galaxy

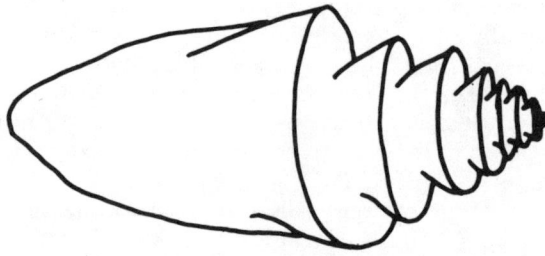

Miraculous Thatcheria Shell

tional design process, the shell itself can represent evaluation as a process that envelops and provides structure for each of the chambers or stages. Simply put, design without evaluation is no more than blind trial-and-error creation. Therefore, evaluation should be perceived as the structural force that holds the entire process of instructional design together.

The pervasive role that evaluation—when defined as the provision of information for decision making—should play within instructional design can be seen from another perspective. As described in earlier chapters, instructional design projects generally involve one or more representatives of the following areas of expertise. First and foremost, there must be an SME to provide the accuracy and structure of content within a field. Second, there is the instructional designer, who can apply the science derived from various theoretical perspectives (e.g., cognitive science, behavioral psychology, and information science) as well as the artist's creative tools. Next, there are representatives of the various media production areas required in a particular project—for example programmers, videographers, technical writers, or photographers. Ideally, there will also be a representative of management science, who will encourage communication among project participants, monitor budgets, and provide external support. Finally, there is the evaluator, the person responsible for providing information that will improve the decisions made by all project participants.

Of course, the reality of instructional design is that these areas often are not represented by separate people, but by the same individuals playing different roles at different times in a project. But whether represented by single or multiple persons, the team's success in developing effective, efficient instructional products depends on three bases of decision making: expertise, creativity, and evaluation. Expertise, whether theoretical or experiential, is woven together with the innovative ideas of creativity, and both are informed by the systematic and pervasive application of evaluation. All three elements must be constantly and deliberately applied for instructional design to be successful.

In summary, the answer to the first question posed in this chapter is that evaluation furnishes the information that instructional designers require to specify, develop, produce, and improve instructional products. Evaluation, in concert with expertise and creativity, provides the basis for the conclusions, decisions, and actions of those involved in instructional design. A fundamental assumption of this conception of evaluation is the belief that informed decision making is better than uninformed or misinformed decision making.

EVALUATION METHODS IN INSTRUCTIONAL DESIGN

What methods are available for evaluating the process and products of instructional design? The specific evaluation methods employed during any particular stage of the instructional design process depend on the types of decisions to be made during that stage. I suggest six major levels of evaluation activity that can be undertaken within instructional design efforts:

1. Project documentation
2. Assessment of the worth of project objectives
3. Formative evaluation

4. Immediate effectiveness evaluation
5. Impact evaluation
6. Cost-effectiveness analysis

These are an extension of an earlier conceptualization of evaluation levels for computer-based instruction described in Reeves and Lent, 1984. Figure 12.2 illustrates these six levels and lists some of the generic evaluation questions and design decisions addressed by each. It is important to understand that these six do not represent a strict hierarchy. Instead, they should be viewed as a menu from which evaluation options may be selected, depending upon the decisions that must be made and the questions that must be answered within the context of a particular instructional design project.

Project Documentation

This involves keeping records of when and where various project activities occur, what the activities cost, and who participates in them. Documentation is critical to an instructional design project for two reasons. First, documentation data are used to account for the use of project resources and to make decisions about resource allocations. Second, documentation data are required as baseline data for the other five levels of evaluation proposed for instructional design projects. The project evaluator is responsible for setting up the procedures, record forms, and data bases for project documentation, and all project staff are responsible for collecting documentation data. One example of a documentation strategy is requiring all design team members to maintain hourly project logs of all their instructional design activities (Reeves and Lent, 1984).

Without timely, accurate, and "user-friendly" documentation procedures, it is easy for instructional design team members to become so involved in the creative and logistical aspects of a design effort that information about project activities can go uncollected or become lost in the shuffle. Therefore, emphasis should be placed on incorporating documentation procedures into the normal work activities of team members through strategies and instrumentation such as automatically storing electronic communications and computer-based activity logs. Powerful microcomputer networks and commercial software can be combined to establish useful documentation systems (e.g., Goodman, 1988). There is even new software specifically developed to guide and track the instructional design process (e.g., Childs, 1988).

Assessment of the Worth of Project Objectives

This is defined as a separate activity because of the tendency of instructional designers to become so fixated on specifying objectives and then accomplishing them that they fail to adequately examine the worth or relationship to reality of their objectives. Ideally, instructional design projects will include a comprehensive needs assessment and contextual analysis, but more often than not are initiated on the basis of political, bureaucratic, or competitive agendas. Institutions of higher education often develop new curricula in response to funding opportunities rather than to an assessment of society's needs. Military personnel design new training activities in response to the idiosyncrasies of

Figure 12.2. *Levels of evaluation for instructional design with sample questions and decisions.*

Sample Questions	Levels	Sample Decisions
What are the delivery costs per unit of instruction? What are the development costs? What are the costs associated with different levels of achievement?	**Cost-Effectiveness Evaluation**	Should training products be disseminated? How should they be priced? How should training development proposals be budgeted?
What learning is transferred to the workplace? What performance changes are reported by the trainees? What performance changes are observed by supervisors? What is the impact on client services?	**Impact Evaluation**	Should job aids be developed? Should additional training be developed? Should training priorities be revised? Is liability insurance adequate?
What learning can be measured? What learning is reported by trainees? What are the trainee reactions? What learning is observed by instructors?	**Immediate Effectiveness Evaluation**	Should certification be awarded? How should products be marketed? Should instructor manuals be expanded?
How can the instructional product be improved? How can the delivery system be improved? How can the instructional design process be improved?	**Formative Evaluation**	Which colors should be used for screen commands? Text? Feedback? Which user interface should be adopted? Should a staff development retreat be initiated?
What are the relationships between project objectives and institutional needs? Who will benefit from the accomplishment of project objectives? Who will not benefit?	**Assessment of the Worth of Project Objectives**	Should the project continue, expand, or terminate design activities? Which clients should be represented in project needs assessment and planning? Should products be released?
What design activities are accomplished? By whom? When? At what costs? Who was trained? When? At what cost? What is product reliability?	**Project Documentation**	Which team members should be assigned to which tasks? Should additional staff be hired? Should additional funding be solicited? Should another delivery system be adopted?

ever-changing command structures. Businesses and industries produce new education and training programs to meet government regulations or to keep up with their competitors with respect to new technologies (e.g., interactive videodisc) or to training bandwagons (e.g., andragogy). Medical educators develop continuing medical education programs for the latest technologies (e.g., CAT scanners) whether or not more basic, but less exciting, needs exist.

Every experienced designer can describe specific examples of instructional design activities being carried out in relation to unexamined or poorly understood objectives. Ideally, all design decisions should be informed by an assessment of their relationship to the overall objectives for a project. For example, media selection decisions should be based on careful assessment of their appropriateness to the attainment of project objectives, but, all too often, instructional design activities are undertaken with the intent of developing a specific instructional medium, regardless of its relationship to project objectives.

Methods of assessing the worth of project objectives range from formal reviews involving expert or user panels to the periodic informal reviews of project goals by all team members. Even subtle environmental reminders of project goals can be beneficial. For example, posters throughout the training department of an innovative computer company repeated the theme that the ultimate goal of all training is to promote sales. The project evaluator should play the role of evangelist with respect to project objectives, constantly promoting them and exposing them to as wide a critical audience as possible.

Obviously there is some risk involved in looking too hard at the objectives of an instructional design project, because there is the potential for revealing that instructional design is an inappropriate activity for the goals at hand. Not many instructional design project sponsors want to be told that the project they are funding is an inappropriate response to the needs of the parties involved. In the final analysis, individual designers and evaluators must make personal decisions as to whether to pursue the review of objectives to the possibly logical conclusion of stopping the design process altogether. On the other hand, much more effective and efficient instructional products are likely to result from those projects in which objectives have been rigorously examined.

Formative Evaluation

This involves collecting the opinions, suggestions, and criticisms of project participants (team members, learners, sponsors, etc.) to revise and improve aspects of the project. Formative evaluation is the essence of good instructional design, and it should be carried out with respect to all aspects of the project—the processes as well as the products. Obviously, prototype products will be a major focus of formative evaluation during an instructional design project, but there should be equal emphasis on collecting formative information to improve the overall instructional design process used by the team so that the products of future efforts are enhanced. Simply put, the major emphasis of this third level of evaluation is to systematically answer the question, "How can we do a better job?" This question can just as well be asked with respect to management of a project as it can regarding the development of instructional products.

Formative evaluation often is set up so that it is little more than a "smiles index" used to find out whether users like an education or training activity. Or, as a slight improvement, formative evaluation sometimes takes the form of "key stroke testing" to reveal whether or not a medium functions as designed. However, these methods should not be the primary emphases of formative evaluation, because there are many more effective methods. Expert and user panels can be convened for the rigorous review of both the products and the processes of instructional design. In addition, systematic formative evaluation methods such as questionnaires, interviews, and observation can be used to collect data for improving the products at various stages of their development. For example, structured interview protocols (in person or via telephone) can be used to "debrief" users of prototype products at various intervals after product usage. Perhaps the richest source of formative evaluation information is the simple observation of individuals or small groups using prototype instructional products. Formative review logs with separate columns for (a) product references; (b) questions, comments, and recommendations; and (c) actions taken, can be used to record data during these intensive observation sessions (Reeves and Lent, 1984).

Information about variables, such as the scope and accuracy of content, quality of instructional interactions, and the sequencing and pacing of instructional events in instructional products, should be collected by formative evaluation methods and used to guide decisions that will increase the effectiveness and efficiency of the products. Further, even the most rigorously applied instructional analysis and design activities cannot yield instruction that is immune to installation and implementation problems. Thus, formative evaluation should be a major emphasis during the prototype testing and field testing phases of a project, as well as throughout the development and production phases. Additional sources for formative evaluation methods include Morris, Fitz-Gibbon, and Henderson (1978), May, Moore, and Zammit (1987), and Tuckman (1987).

Immediate Effectiveness Evaluation

This should be carried out to assess the instructional effectiveness and efficiency of instructional products within the immediate temporal and spatial contexts of their implementation. The goals and objectives of education and training programs can be classified as either immediate or long-term. Immediate goals/objectives can be accomplished within the time frame of the instructional program itself, whereas long-term goals/objectives may not be accomplished until some time after the completion of a program. For example, an immediate goal of a computer-based medical simulation might be to teach decision analysis strategies to physicians, while a long-term goal of the same program might be to increase the cost effectiveness of laboratory tests ordered by physicians in the context of their own practices.

Assessment of an instructional product's immediate effectiveness is most often considered to be a matter of subjecting users to pretests and posttests of the knowledge, skills, and attitudes engendered in the product's goals and objectives. However, though such tests may have value as diagnostic and motivational instruments, they often are inadequate indicators of the instructional effectiveness of an instructional product. Extreme care must be taken to guarantee the reliability and validity of the tests to be used for immediate effectiveness evaluation. These tests must not be too short to have adequate reliability, and the time between administration of the pretest and the posttest must not be so brief that user responses are based more on test familiarity than on new learning. Therefore, the evaluation of instructional products should involve multiple methods of assessing immediate effectiveness to promote "convergence" or "triangulation" of the findings (Mark and Shotland, 1987). In other words, the pretests and posttests commonly associated with effectiveness evaluation should be buttressed with enhanced assessment methods, including simulation-embedded tests, self-assessment, and peer assessment (Cronbach, 1982; Hunter, 1987).

There is ample evidence that the planned and actual uses of instructional products vary considerably (Cooley and Lohnes, 1976), and designers and evaluators are advised to make few assumptions about program implementation without careful assessment. For example, I recently served as a participant observer during a two-day training workshop on microcomputers. The training developers, located on the other side of the continent, had spent considerable energy and resources to produce what they thought were exemplary training manuals, but the field trainers seldom referred to them, and even deprecated their worth on numerous occasions. The traditional "smilometer" questionnaire distributed at the end of the workshop included questions about the manual, but no meaningful interpretation of the responses could be made without the knowledge of how the manuals actually were used. It is clear that all evidence for product effectiveness should be scrutinized in the light of implementation data. Additional sources for immediate effectiveness evaluation methods include Kosecoff and Fink (1982), Morris, Fitz-Gibbon, and Henderson (1978), May, Moore, and Zammit (1987), and Tuckman (1987).

Impact Evaluation

Although the ultimate intent of most evaluations of instructional products, this level of evaluation may be the most elusive. Determining, for example, whether physicians have learned methods of assessing the likelihood of drug interactions within the immediate context of an interactive videodisc training simulation is relatively simple. However, it is much more difficult to estimate whether the same product has resulted in decreased drug reactions in the elderly patients seen by the participating physicians. Even if improvements can be detected, it often is impossible to establish causal links between specific educational products and improvements in real-world performance because of the presence of plausible alternative explanations and numerous intervening variables.

Nevertheless, considerable effort should be expended to assess the long-term effect of the products of instructional design. Within the limits of project resources, methods such as interviews, examination of performance records, and anecdotal logs can be used to address questions about the transfer of knowledge from the context of the training products to the context of performance. For example, during the evaluation of an instructional program designed to teach functional literacy skills to military personnel, the first-line supervisors were interviewed to assess the degree to which on-the-job use of technical manuals had changed. If project resources do not permit direct evaluation of impact, instructional designers should be prepared to collaborate with external evaluators and researchers at multiple test and validation sites, to conduct impact evaluations.

Additional methods proposed for conducting impact evaluation include performance auditing (Gilbert, 1978) and program modeling (Borich and Jemelka, 1982; Wang and Walberg, 1983). Both of these approaches can be used to relate product inputs and processes to product outcomes in an effort to "explain" the effects of the instructional products. Such models can also be used to derive principles of program design and implementation that will guide the future development of other projects.

The performance audit is a systematic procedure that tracks trainee performance in the workplace and assesses the effects of that performance (Rummler, 1976; Crowley and Tillman, 1986). The formal audit procedure is complex, and its extensive use will probably require computer support.

Program modeling involves structured decomposition—breaking an instructional program into its component parts from the broad level of global conceptualization to the lowest level of generality at which meaningful decisions can be made. These program components, as well as input and output measures relevant to the educational context, can be analyzed using statistical procedures such as commonality analysis (Kenny, 1979). There are currently both technical and conceptual problems associated with "causal modeling" approaches, but they should be investigated, if only because other methods of impact evaluation have proven so elusive. Additional sources for impact evaluation methods include Rossi and Freeman (1985), Trochim (1986), May, Moore, and Zammit (1987), and Tuckman (1987).

Cost-Effectiveness Analysis

This is even more infrequently applied within the context of instructional design than is impact evaluation. Cost-effectiveness analysis involves the appraisal of instructional products to determine the costs of specific effects of a product. Cost-effectiveness analysis is usually conducted as a basis for comparing two or more competing products or programs, but its procedures can be applied within the context of a single design effort as well. The basic question to be addressed by this level of evaluation is, "What are the costs—financial, temporal, and personal—associated with the various effects of the instructional product?" Information about cost effectiveness is especially useful in making decisions about future design efforts or in preparing proposals for funding.

Since 1980, I have been increasingly involved in designing interactive videodisc programs, and frequently am asked such questions as, "What does it cost to make an interactive videodisc?" and "Is interactive videodisc cost-effective?" Responding to these types of questions is difficult because of the lack of a common metric for estimating instructional effects. In education and training, there is no widely accepted equivalent to the bottom line of profit used in commercial business. The best that can be done at this time may be to base cost-effectiveness analysis on some intermediate variable, such as student hours of instruction. If documentation data are carefully collected and matched by intensive efforts to evaluate immediate effectiveness and impact, these data can be integrated though cost-effectiveness analysis procedures to derive estimates of what various types of intermediate and ultimate instructional effects cost (Doughty, 1979; Lent, 1979; Orlansky, 1986). Additional sources for cost-effectiveness evaluation methods include Levin (1983) and Kearsley (1982).

In summary: Six levels of evaluation activity have been defined within the context of instructional design projects. It should be noted that the multipurpose, multimethod nature of these evaluation levels greatly expands the scope of evaluation as it is usually viewed in the context of the development and implementation of innovative instructional products.

In a series of reviews of evaluations of interactive videodisc education and training programs, I have found that most evaluations have tended to concentrate on only one level (at best two levels) of evaluation. The approach to evaluation in instructional design recommended here involves implementing all levels of evaluation to benefit fully from this most important activity. The six levels can help enhance specific instructional products and improve the design process itself. Of course, questions remain about the ultimate worth of instructional design—and the next section addresses these issues.

EVALUATING THE WORTH OF INSTRUCTIONAL DESIGN

What is the worth of instructional design itself? First, it is clear that looking to the educational research literature for an answer is an exercise in futility. Although cognitive psychologists and others have studied many topics related to instructional design, research investigating instructional design directly is largely absent from the field. Hannafin (1986) described barriers to research in instructional design, and Driscoll (1984) recommended adopting alternative paradigms for conducting this needed research. Unfortunately, there is little evidence that there have been, or will be, increases in basic or applied research in this field. A few evaluations support the worth of instructional design, but these are largely in the form of testimonials (cf., Miles, 1983).

Evaluating the Process by the Product

Though relatively few systematic research and evaluation studies have been undertaken, support for the conduct of instructional design can be derived from evaluations of products that have been the objects of intensive instructional design. In other words, we can infer the worth of the design processes from evaluations of the products that result from their use. This might be seen as analogous to the situation faced by modern physicists studying subatomic particles. Unable to observe the phenomenon directly, physicists have verified the existence of these particles by investigating their traces and paths.

The importance of finding evidence in support of systematic instructional design seems more critical than ever. As described by Wildman and Burton (1981), most educational products are not the result of systematic instructional design. The need is especially great if one considers how much education and training occurs daily in public and higher education as well as in business, industry, and the military. In another chapter of this book, Foa refers to the underutilization of instructional design in higher education, and many can testify to its equally poor diffusion in public education. Instructional innovations do not enjoy a positive press, and prominent national education leaders continue to call for a return to basics in the classroom (Bennett, 1988), not understanding that even instruction in the basics could benefit greatly from sound design techniques. Therefore, if instructional design is to have the effect advocated by its proponents, evidence of its worth must be found.

If it can be accepted that we must look to instructional design products for evidence of the worth of the process, which type of products should be investigated? As noted above, I have been heavily engaged in designing and evaluating interactive videodisc training programs—primarily for military training, continuing medical education, and adult literacy. Complex interactive products are seldom, if ever, the work of an isolated trainer or lonely "hacker."

Interactive videodisc products generally are produced by teams of specialists who have used systematic instructional design models. Therefore, if support for the effectiveness of these products across multiple criteria can be presented, the inference that instructional design is a worthwhile endeavor is supported.

Drake (1987) summarized the major findings of existing research-and-evaluation studies comparing interactive videodisc with "traditional instruction" as supporting three conclusions:

1. Trainees in a wide variety of settings generally like interactive videodisc training.
2. Use of interactive videodisc training often significantly reduces training time.
3. Interactive videodisc training has equivalent or improved effectiveness in a wide variety of applications.

This section attempts to broaden Drake's perspective on the effectiveness of interactive videodisc products to include other dimensions of training, and by implication to establish criteria for assessing the worth of the instructional design processes employed to develop these products. Evidence for the validity of the statements supporting the effective dimensions of interactive videodisc is presented through six illustrative case studies, as well as through the research and evaluation results of additional studies. (A more in-depth treatment of this topic can be found in Reeves, 1988.)

Six Common Dimensions

Interactive videodisc can be compared with other training approaches in reference to a set of common dimensions: experience, cost, safety, flexibility, efficiency, and instructional effectiveness. Obviously, there are many more training approaches than classroom training, interactive videodisc, face plate simulators, and hands-on training, but these four are among those most frequently employed in training and education. Following are definitions of these four training approaches:

1. *Classroom training methods* involve instructional strategies such as texts, lectures, and demonstrations, and often are referred to as "traditional" or "platform" training.
2. *Interactive videodisc* is a laser videodisc program, under the control of a microcomputer, allowing the student to interact with the training program's flow and content by responding to questions, options, and/or problems presented at predetermined points.
3. *Face plate simulators* refer to combinations in physical form of technical equipment and instructional interactions, such as a Link flight simulator.
4. *Hands-on training* refers to any type of on-the-job training in which students learn by using real equipment or from interacting with real people under the supervision of a trainer or supervisor.

The next few paragraphs of this section describe my assessments of the relative effectiveness of the four training methods defined above, with respect to six dimensions: experience, cost, safety, flexibility, efficiency, and instructional effectiveness. These assessments are supported by research and evaluation findings wherever possible, and illustrated by case studies from varied education and training contexts. The summary assessments are stated in the form of propositions or hypotheses with respect to each dimension.

1. Experience Dimension

In comparison with traditional training methods (text, lecture, demonstration), interactive videodisc is more concrete and realistic for technical and process-skills training (see Figure 12.3).

The experiential value of a training approach is probably related to students' positive or negative attitudes toward it. As Drake (1987) states, students in a wide variety of settings have expressed positive attitudes about interactive videodisc. Comments such as "it's just like being there" and "felt like I was actually making decisions" are not uncommon when interviewing users of interactive videodisc. Sircus (1986) claims that the experiential nature of interactive videodisc actually represents a return to the earliest type of training, the apprenticeship. The student (as apprentice) works with the interactive videodisc program (as expert or teacher) to master skills by observation, action, and feedback in a continuous loop until the skills are attained. Sircus contrasts this apprenticeship model of training with the mass-production model of training inherent in most "platform" or classroom training methods, and makes a strong case for the experiential value of interactive videodisc.

The case study presented for the experience dimension of interactive videodisc is the "Advanced Combat Trauma Life Support" (ACTLS) case simulation produced by Dr. Joseph V. Henderson for the Computer-Assisted Medical Interactive-Video System (CAMIS) of the U.S. Naval Health Sciences Education and Training Command (Henderson, Pruett, Galper, and Copes, 1986). This interactive videodisc program (which won the award for "Best Overall Achievement" at the 1987 Nebraska Videodisc Awards) presents five highly realistic, even gripping, patient management problems for training military physicians in critical care skills. These interactive case simulations have several features that contribute to their high experiential value, including: (a) the events and outcomes of the simulation are not predictable; (b) the primary problem-solvers in the simulation are the medical personnel using the simu-

Figure 12.3. *Experience dimension of effectiveness for four training methods.*

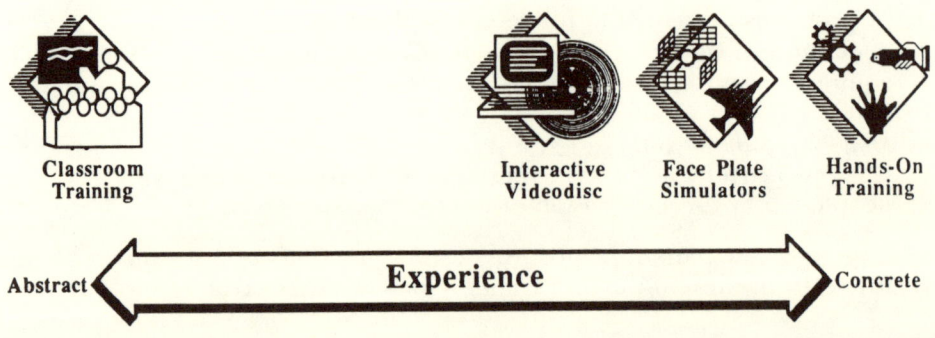

lation; (c) the interactions are based on actual case histories; and (d) the video is clinically and dramatically lifelike. Formative evaluation of the ACTLS program under field training conditions at Fort Sam Houston, Texas, indicated that over 90 percent of the users judged it to be a highly effective training system (Reeves and Marlino, 1987).

Patient-management simulations have been a major factor in medical education for many years, but interactive videodisc represents the first training approach that permits these simulations to approach the realism of actual patient–physician exchanges. The following is a typical voice-controlled interaction between user and simulated patient in another interactive videodisc case simulation, "The Case of Frank Hall," which was developed at the National Library of Medicine (Harless, 1986):

> *User:* "What's your problem?"
> *Frank Hall:* [Looking directly out at the user.] "I'm sick. I've been throwing up blood. I'm afraid I might have cancer." [Wait state.]
> *User:* "When did it begin?"
> *Frank Hall:* "Well, it started last week. I was in this restaurant. . ."

Both the ACTLS and the "Frank Hall" interactive videodisc simulations represent highly experiential training treatments that provide concrete learning opportunities beyond the capabilities of most traditional classroom procedures. Furthermore, because of their safety, flexibility, and efficiency, they may offer advantages in some instances over "hands-on" clinical experiences. Other examples of interactive videodisc products with noteworthy experiential value are the Military Operations in Urban Terrain simulation that trains officers in certain battle tactics (Reeves and King, 1985), and the Individualized Management Development System that trains middle managers to develop conflict-resolution skills in interpersonal relationships (Watson, Kemph, and Steele, 1985).

2. Cost Dimension

When compared with face plate simulators and hands-on training with real equipment, interactive videodisc is less expensive (see Figure 12.4).

Cost is often the first dimension criticized with respect to interactive videodisc programs. The expense of equipment such as computers and laser videodisc players, combined with the high labor costs involved in video production and programming, frighten many would-be adopters of this approach. Industry estimates for development costs *per hour* of training time run as high as $25,000, and certain prototype programs have cost much more. However, a closer examination of these costs, and of amortization of the expenses across large numbers of students, can result in a very favorable cost case for interactive videodisc. This advantage is strongly supported with respect to simulators and hands-on training, and, in some cases involving large numbers of students, interactive videodisc can cost less to develop *and* deliver than classroom training.

The case study presented for the cost dimension of interactive videodisc is the "Principle of the Alphabet Literacy System (PALS)" jointly developed by Dr. John Henry Martin, the International Business Machines Corporation, and the Department of Instructional Technology at The University of Georgia (Reeves and King, 1986). The PALS interactive videodisc program trains adolescents and adults in the basic functional literacy skills required for success

172 Evaluation

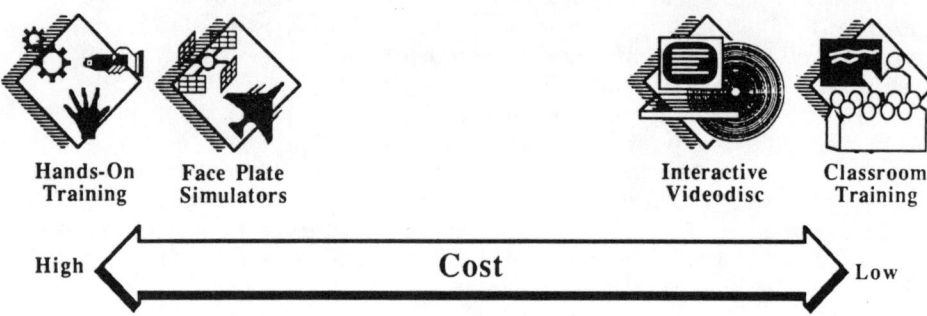

Figure 12.4. *Cost dimension of effectiveness for four training methods.*

in virtually every work context. The PALS program is delivered via a special interactive videodisc laboratory in which sixteen students per hour go through functional literacy training. By operating the lab for twelve to sixteen hours per day, estimated delivery costs for the 100 hours of training fall to a very low cost-per-hour rate over a two-year period.

Illiteracy is a major problem throughout most of the world, but it seems particularly shocking in the United States of America. Authorities estimate that 25–60 million adult U.S. citizens are functionally illiterate. This situation presents enormous and expensive training problems for schools, industries, businesses, and the armed forces. Traditional approaches to reducing illiteracy have included one-on-one tutoring, and classroom instruction. Whereas the latter has proven to be generally ineffective in meeting the individual needs of beginning readers, the former has been ineffective because of drastic shortages in trained and motivated tutors. The PALS project represents an IVD-based alternative functional literacy training system that permits the efficiency of group instruction while including the individualization of tutoring. While the development costs of the 100-hour program may at first seem high, its amortization over large numbers of installations and many students will result in an attractive cost-effectiveness ratio.

Additional examples of interactive videodisc programs representing cost savings include the TTC-39 Switchboard program that trains soldiers to maintain sophisticated satellite control stations. By the early 1980s, this program reportedly saved the U.S. Army more than $118 million in training costs (Ketner, 1982). Examples also include the Simulated Aircraft Maintenance Trainers that combine partial simulators with interactive videodisc to train U.S. Air Force pilots to fly F-16 aircraft (Gitt and Keskey, 1987).

3. Safety Dimension

When compared with real-equipment training, interactive videodisc is safer for students *and* equipment (see Figure 12.5).

Safety is an important concern in many training contexts—especially those involving technical skills such as equipment operation or computer maintenance. Safety in training often has two concerns: safety of the students, and safety of the equipment with which the students are being trained. In the former (and obviously more important) case, training must be conducted so that no bodily or psychological harm can come to the students. For example,

Figure 12.5. *Safety dimension of effectiveness for four training methods.*

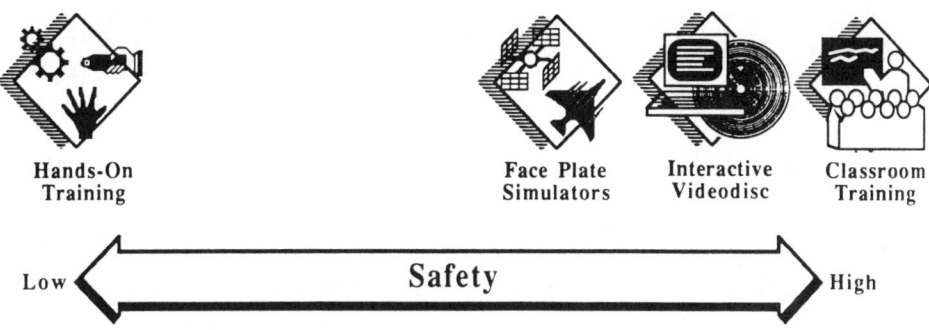

students learning to troubleshoot electronic equipment are susceptible to electric shocks. In the latter case, students may damage the equipment while they are learning to operate or maintain it. For example, the Digital Equipment Corporation (DEC) reported that large numbers of disk drives were damaged when students attempted to install them (Lent, 1984).

Provided that a sufficient level of experiential value or operational fidelity can be attained, interactive videodisc can provide students with technical-skills training free of hazards to themselves or the equipment they are learning to use. At the same time, interactive videodisc can be used in process-skills training settings to provide risk-free environments in which students can try new behaviors that they would be unable or afraid to try in many face-to-face training situations.

The case study presented for the safety dimension of interactive videodisc is "The Academy of Aeronautics Welding Simulator" developed by Ixion, Inc. (Hon, 1986). This high-fidelity interactive videodisc simulation trains workers to weld without any text-based instruction. Students use three-dimensional replicas of welding tools to conduct simulated welding exercises, thus eliminating the high burn risks associated with traditional hands-on training of novice welders.

The interactive videodisc oxyacetylene welding simulator not only eliminates danger to trainees, but it also has decreased training time and expenses for novice welders. Evaluation of the innovative system has indicated a high degree of transfer from the simulator to the actual first welding exercise. Welding is a basic construction skill needed around the world, and the lack of on-screen text in the simulator should facilitate its transfer from country to country.

Additional examples of the safety dimension in interactive videodisc include the Transistor Amplifiers program that employs an "electronic workbench" to train students to troubleshoot electrical circuits (Taplin, 1987); and the chemistry videodisc series developed at the University of Nebraska–Lincoln to provide college students with risk-free laboratory experiences (Nugent, 1986).

4. Flexibility Dimension

When compared to real equipment, simulators, and even lecture/demonstrations, interactive videodisc is more flexible (see Figure 12.6)

Figure 12.6. *Flexibility dimension of effectiveness for four training methods.*

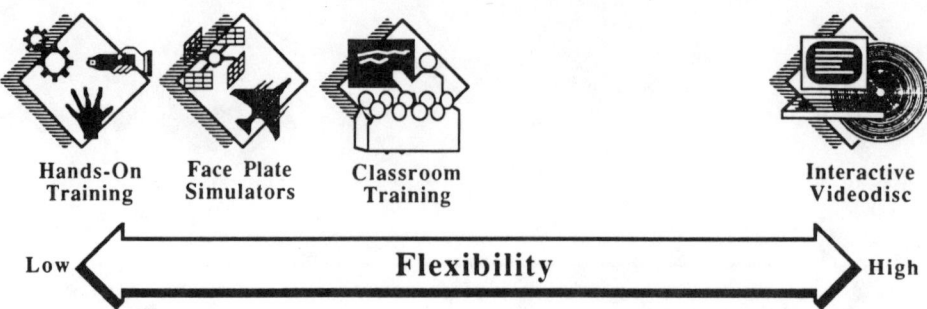

The term "training flexibility" refers to both the ease of scheduling and the physical logistics required to implement a particular training approach. Training may be brought to students at the workplace, or they may be required to leave the workplace to complete training. In many, if not most, technical and process-skills training contexts, training is located apart from the setting of actual job performance either because the presence of training is perceived as disruptive to the normal work flow, or because large numbers of students from different locations must be trained at one time. In either case, the removal of training from the workplace often results in a lower level of learning transfer from the training program to actual job performance. In other words, skills demonstrated in the classroom often are not implemented on the job site.

The case study presented for the flexibility dimension of interactive videodisc is the "Chrysler Hazardous Chemical Training" program developed by MetaMedia Systems, Inc. (Held and Davis, 1986). The interactive videodisc delivery system used for the Chrysler program is built into a rugged cabinet that is lifted by a fork-lift truck and moved from one position to another along an automobile assembly line. This innovative delivery approach permits students to complete government-mandated safety training with minimal interference to the work flow and maximum transfer to the job site.

Automobile workers may use scores, and even hundreds, of potentially harmful chemicals every workday, but many have been oblivious to the health and property damages that can occur when such chemicals are handled incorrectly. The hazardous-chemical interactive videodisc program trains workers in such important skills as how to recognize potential hazards in the workplace, and how to handle spills and other mishaps. Most importantly, the modular design and kiosk-based delivery system permit the training to occur in the same locations where the newly learned skills will be applied. This high degree of flexibility ensures that workers will be trained when their motivation is strong and their learning will be easily reinforced.

Additional examples of the flexibility dimension of interactive videodisc programs include the "Space Time Army Reconnaissance" (STARS) program that teaches basic functional literacy skills to enlisted soldiers stationed at remote sites (Reeves, Aggen, and Held, 1982) and the "An Ounce of Prevention" program that trains day-care professionals in their workplaces to recognize, report, and prevent child abuse (Murray, 1987).

5. Efficiency Dimension

When compared to traditional methods, interactive videodisc has resulted in a consistent 25–50 percent savings in training time (see Figure 12.7).

Efficiency of training is essentially a matter of the amount of time required by different training approaches to deliver equivalent training effectiveness. The efficiency of interactive videodisc has been demonstrated in numerous technical-skills training contexts and a few process-skills training settings. For example, John Hirschbuhl of Computer Knowledge International reported that field engineers took 40 percent less time to learn the same technical skills as did students completing instructor-led training (Drake, 1987). A large medical training facility in San Antonio, Texas reported a 33 percent reduction in training time when teaching medical students to prepare and administer an intramuscular injection (Drake, 1987). The Digital Equipment Corporation of Burlington, Massachusetts (Lent, 1984) has reported consistent 25–45 percent time savings for numerous interactive videodisc programs in both technical and process-skills training contexts.

The case study presented for the efficiency dimension of interactive videodisc is "Decision Point: A Living Case Study," which trains midlevel managers in decision-making skills (Digital Equipment Corporation, 1985). This program uses first-person simulations to present the student manager with numerous problems requiring the application of high-level decision skills within an intense period of training time.

Within the overall problem context of a sales force that is not meeting its sales projections, the "Decision Point" simulation includes ten decision points that confront the manager/user with making recommendations for conflict resolutions. Users interact with the program to interview key members of a simulated corporation, review documents, and investigate possibile consequences of alternative actions. Most middle managers cannot afford the time required to learn alternative management strategies via traditional classroom-oriented methods. Furthermore, even the best managerial internships would be unlikely to present the manager with the range of problems and decision-point options presented in the interactive videodisc program. It is clear that "Decision Point" provides an extremely efficient alternative to other types of management training programs.

Figure 12.7. *Efficiency dimension of effectiveness for four training methods.*

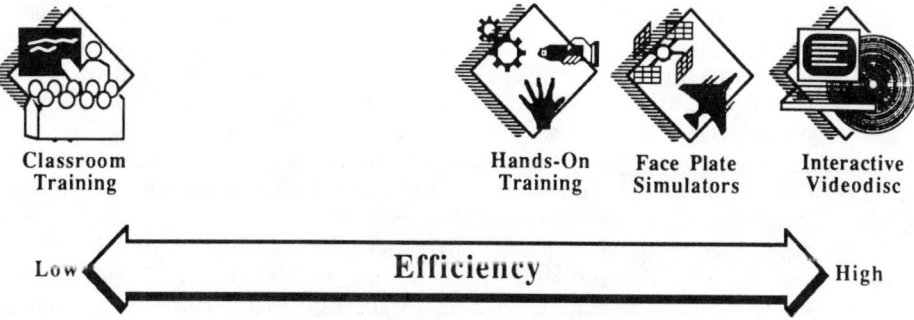

176 Evaluation

Additional examples of the efficiency dimension of interactive videodisc programs include the "Aid to Families with Dependent Children" program, which reduced social-worker training time by 25 percent (from 160 to 120 hours) (Smith, 1984); and Digital Equipment Corporation's internal training applications of its IVIS system (May, 1984).

6. Effectiveness Dimension

Interactive videodisc has been shown to be an effective training and educational approach in numerous settings for both technical and process-skills training (see Figure 12.8).

Effectiveness is the bottom line for any training approach—no matter how much the method may be liked. Effectiveness can be evaluated at two levels: immediate effectiveness within the context of the training program itself, and long-term effectiveness with respect to the transfer of the skills from the training context to the workplace. The latter is obviously more important, but assessment of training impact often is elusive. In fact, despite individual studies of note, there is a lack of solid research and evaluation evidence to support interactive videodisc (or any other training innovation).

A notable exception to the general findings of "no significant differences" in effectiveness among training methods is a recent study conducted by the International Business Machines Corporation (Vadas, 1986). IBM compared traditional classroom methods with interactive videodisc designed to train executives in employee management skills, and reported that the interactive videodisc resulted in as much as a 50 percent increase in immediate retention of management knowledge and skills over traditional instructor-led courses.

The case study presented for the effectiveness dimension of interactive videodisc is "Cash Flow Planning," developed by the Cooperative Extension Service at the University of Nebraska (Rockwell, 1986). This program trains farmers to prepare a cash-flow plan for use on family farms. Preliminary evaluation results indicate a high level of training effectiveness for this interactive program.

Small family farms have suffered from a host of reversals in recent years, and the decline in the numbers of family-owned-and-operated farms in the U.S. has reached a critical rate. Existing professional trainers, such as cooperative extension agents, have been unable to provide struggling family farmers with sufficient training in financial assessment and planning strategies to enable them to survive. The interactive videodisc program provides farmers with an efficient, effective, and confidential alternative for learning better farm financial management.

Additional examples of the effectiveness dimension include the Hawk Missile Air Defense programs that effectively train soldiers to solve integration check problems (Kimberlin, 1982); the American Heart Association cardiopulmonary resuscitation (CPR) training system (Hon, 1982); the Railroad Worker Safety program (Fedewa, 1983); the "Variable Venturi Carburetor" program that trains Ford Motor mechanics to repair engine components (Marx and Edwards, 1985); and the foreign-language programs developed by the Defense Language Institute (Rowe, 1984).

In summary: Interactive videodisc products that have been developed by using systematic instructional design for a wide variety of applications have been shown to be effective with respect to six significant dimensions when

Figure 12.8. *Instructional effectiveness dimension of effectiveness for four training methods.*

compared with training products that have not been the objects of systematic instructional design. Therefore, the inference that instructional design has worth in developing effective products for education and training seems warranted. On the other hand, this warranted assertion does not "prove" the value of instructional design. Much research and evaluation remains to be done (Reeves, 1986).

CONCLUSION

This chapter addresses three questions about the role, practice, and value of evaluation within instructional design. My answers to these questions can be summarized as follows:

1. The role of evaluation is to provide information to improve decision making, but this role is generally underused in instructional design because of conflicting perspectives on the meaning of evaluation, and its limited representation in models and descriptions of instructional design.
2. Evaluation methods and tools can be selected from six levels of evaluation, depending on the type of decisions that the evaluative activities are intended to influence.
3. The worth of instructional design is demonstrated by the effectiveness of design products measured across multiple criteria.

REFERENCES

Anderson, S. B., and S. Ball. 1978. *The profession and practice of program evaluation.* San Francisco: Jossey–Bass.

Bennett Report Card. 1988. *AP News File* 258, February 25.

Borich, G. D., and R. P. Jemelka. 1982. *Programs and systems: An evaluation perspective.* New York: Academic Press.

Campbell, D. T., and J. C. Stanley. 1963. *Experimental and quasi-experimental designs for research.* Chicago: Rand McNally.

Childs, J. 1988. *Instructional design and development system* [Computer program]. Detroit: Microsys.

Cooley, W. W., and W. Bickel. 1986. *Decision-oriented educational research*. Boston: Kluwer–Nijhoff.

Cooley, W. W., and P. R. Lohnes. 1976. *Evaluation research in education: Theory, principles, and practice*. New York: Irvington.

Cronbach, L. J. 1980. *Toward reform of program evaluation*. San Francisco: Jossey–Bass.

———. 1982. *Designing evaluations of educational and social programs*. San Francisco: Jossey–Bass.

Crowley, J. R., and M. Tillman. 1986. Performance audit in the selection and management of personnel in the physician's office laboratory. *Primary Care* 13: 617–631.

Digital Equipment Corporation. 1985. *Decision point: A living case study* [Interactive videodisc program]. Bedford, MA: Digital Equipment Corp.

Doughty, P. L. 1979. Cost-effectiveness analysis tradeoffs and pitfalls for planning and evaluating instructional programs. *Journal of Instructional Development* 2(4): 17, 23–25.

Drake, S. 1987. Does IVI really work? *Data Training* (May), pp. 16–19.

Driscoll, M. P. 1984. Alternative paradigms for research in instructional systems. *Journal of Instructional Development* 7(4): 2–5.

Eisner, E. W. 1985. *The art of educational evaluation: A personal view*. Philadelphia: Falmer Press.

Fedewa, L. J. 1983. Safety training for railroad operating employees. *Proceedings of the Fifth Annual Conference on Interactive Instruction Delivery*. Warrenton, VA: Society for Applied Learning Technology.

Gilbert, T. F. 1978. *Human competence*. New York: McGraw–Hill.

Gitt, A. P., and L. C. Keskey. 1987. Interactive videodisc training for F-16 electronics. *Proceedings of the Fifth Annual Conference on Interactive Instruction Delivery*. Warrenton, VA: Society for Applied Learning Technology.

Goodman, D. 1988. *Focal point: The ultimate organizer* [Computer program]. Mountain View, CA: Activision.

Guba, E. G., and Y. S. Lincoln. 1981. *Effective evaluation: Improving the usefulness of evaluation results through responsive and naturalistic approaches*. San Francisco: Jossey–Bass.

Gustafson, K. L. 1981. *Survey of instructional development models*. Syracuse, NY: ERIC Clearinghouse on Information Resources.

Hannafin, M. J. 1986. The status and future of research in instructional design and technology. *Journal of Instructional Development* 8(3): 24–30.

Harless, W. G. 1986. An interactive videodisc drama: The case of Frank Hall. *Journal of Computer-Based Instruction* 13: 113–116.

Held, T. H., and J. C. Davis. 1986. *Interactive videodisc in chemical hazard awareness training for manufacturing employees*. Paper presented at the Second Interactive Videodisc West Conference, Los Angeles (May).

Henderson, J. V., R. K. Pruett, A. R. Galper, and W. S. Copes. 1986. Interactive videodisc to teach combat trauma life support. *Journal of Medical Systems* 10: 271–276.

Hon, D. 1982. Interactive training in cardiopulmonary resuscitation. *Byte* 7(6): 108–138.

———. 1986. *Oxyacetylene welding simulator* [Interactive videodisc program]. Seattle: Academy of Aeronautics, and Ixion Inc.

House, E. R. 1980. *Evaluating with validity*. Beverley Hills: Sage.

Hunter, J. E. 1987. Multiple dependent variables in program evaluation. In M. L. Mark and R. L. Shortland (eds.), *Multiple methods in program evaluation*. San Francisco: Jossey–Bass.

Kearsley, G. 1982. *Costs, benefits, and productivity in training systems*. Reading, MA: Addison–Wesley.

Kenny, D. A. 1979. *Correlation and causality*. New York: Wiley.

Ketner, W. D. 1982. Videodisc interactive two-dimensional equipment training. *Videodisc for Military Training and Simulation*. Warrenton, VA: Society for Applied Learning Technology.

Kimberlin, D. A. 1982. The U.S. Army Air Defense School distributed instructional system project evaluation. *Videodisc for Military Training and Simulation*. Warrenton, VA: Society for Applied Learning Technology.

Kosecoff, J., and A. Fink. 1982. *Evaluation basics: A practitioner's manual*. Beverly Hills: Sage.

Lent, R 1979. A model for applying cost-effectiveness analysis to decisions involving the use of instructional technology. *Journal of Instructional Development* 3(1): 26–33.

Lent, R. M. 1984. *Case studies: Cost justification of interactive video in key industries*. Paper presented at the Sixth Annual Conference on Interactive Videodisc in Education and Training, Washington, DC (August).

Levin, H. M. 1983. *Cost-effectiveness: A primer*. Beverly Hills: Sage.

Mark, M. L., and R. L. Shotland. 1987. *Multiple methods in program evaluation*. San Francisco: Jossey–Bass.

Marx, R. J., and S. Edwards. 1985. Variable Venturi carburetor: Overview and field evaluation of an intelligent video learning system. *Proceedings of the Fifth Annual Conference on Microcomputers in Education and Training*. Warrenton, VA: Society for Applied Learning Technology.

May, L. S. 1984. Corporate experience in evaluating interactive video information system courses. *Proceedings of the Second Conference on Interactive Instruction Delivery*. Warrenton, VA: Society for Applied Learning Technology.

———, C. A. Moore, and S. J. Zammit. 1987. *Evaluating business and industry training*. Norwell, MA: Kluwer Academic.

Miles, G. D. 1983. Evaluating four years of ID experience. *Journal of Instructional Development* 6(2): 9–14.

Morris, L., C. Fitz-Gibbon, and M. Henderson. 1978. *Program evaluation kit*. Beverly Hills: Sage.

Murray, R. A. 1987. On-site interactive instruction for day care staff on child abuse and neglect. *Proceedings of the Fifth Annual Conference on Interactive Instruction Delivery*. Warrenton, VA: Society for Applied Learning Technology.

National Study of Secondary School Evaluation. 1960. *Evaluative criteria*. Washington, DC: U.S. Government Printing Office.

Nugent, R. W. 1986. The interactive videodisc instruction: Alternative science laboratories project. *Proceedings of the Fourth Annual Conference on Interactive Instruction Delivery*. Warrenton, VA: Society for Applied Learning Technology.

Orlansky, J. 1986. The productivity of training. In J. Zeidner (ed.), *Human productivity enhancement*. New York: Praeger.

Reeves, T. C. 1986. Research and evaluation models for the study of interactive video. *Journal of Computer-Based Instruction* 13: 102–106.

———. 1988. Effective dimensions of interactive videodisc for training. In T. Bernold and J. Finklestein (eds.), *Computer-assisted approaches to training: Foundations of industry's future*. Amsterdam, NR: Elsevier Science.

———, W. D. Aggen, and T. H. Held. (1982). The design, development, and evaluation of an intelligent videodisc simulation to teach functional literacy. *Proceedings of the Fourth Annual Conference on Video Learning Systems*. Warrenton, VA: Society for Applied Learning Technology.

Reeves, T. C., and J. M. King. 1985. *Final report of the military operations in urban terrain (MOUT) interactive videodisc test and evaluation*. Fort Eustis, VA: Army Communication Technology Office.

———. 1986. Development, production, and programming of an interactive videodisc adult literacy program. *Proceedings of the Eighth Annual Conference on Interactive Videodisc in Education and Training*. Warrenton, VA: Society for Applied Learning Technology.

Reeves, T. C., and R. M. Lent. 1984. Levels of evaluation for computer-based instruction. In D. F. Walker and R. D. Hess (eds.), *Instructional software: Principles and perspectives for design and use*. Belmont, CA: Wadsworth.

Reeves, T. C., and M. R. Marlino. 1987. *Final report of the evaluation of the Advanced Combat Trauma Life Support interactive videodisc case simulation*. Bethesda, MD: Naval Health Sciences Education and Training Command.

Rockwell S. K. 1986. *Cash flow planning* [Interactive videodisc program]. Lincoln, NE: Cooperative Extension Service, University of Nebraska–Lincoln.

Rossi, P. H., and H. E. Freeman. 1985. *Evaluation: A systematic approach* (3d ed.). Beverly Hills: Sage.

Roueche, J. E., and B. R. Herrscher. 1973. *Toward instructional accountability: A practical guide to educational change*. Palo Alto: Westinghouse Learning Press.

Rowe, A. A. 1984. Interactive language simulation systems: Technology for a national language base. *Proceedings of the Second Conference on Interactive Instruction Delivery*. Warrenton, VA: Society for Applied Learning Technology.

Rummler, G. A. 1976. The performance audit. In R. L. Craig (ed.), *Training and development handbook*. New York: McGraw–Hill.

Scriven, M. 1967. The methodology of evaluation. In R. E. Stake (ed.), *Curriculum evaluation*. American Educational Research Association Monograph Series on Evaluation, No. 1. Chicago: Rand McNally.

Smith, R. C. 1984. Full-scale pilot testing of Florida's videodisc training project. *Proceedings of the Second Conference on Interactive Instruction Delivery*. Warrenton, VA: Society for Applied Learning Technology.

Stake, R. E. 1967. The countenance of educational evaluation. *Teachers College Record* 68: 523–540.

Sircus, J. 1986. *Greek vases* [Interactive videodisc program]. Los Angeles: J. Paul Getty Museum, and Interac Corp.

Taplin, P. 1987. *Transistor amplifiers: The interactive workbench*. Paper presented at the Annual Nebraska Videodisc Symposium, Lincoln, NE (October).

Trochim, W. M. K. 1986. *Advances in quasi-experimental design and analysis*. San Francisco: Jossey–Bass.

Tuckman, B. W. 1987. *Evaluating instructional programs* (2d ed.). Rockleigh, NJ: Allyn and Bacon.

Tyler, R. W. 1942. General statement on evaluation. *Journal of Educational Research* 35: 492–501.

Vadas, J. E. 1986. Interactive videodisc for management training in a classroom environment. *Proceedings of the Eighth Annual Conference on Interactive Videodisc in Education and Training.* Warrenton, VA: Society for Applied Learning Technology.

Wang, M. C., and H. J. Walberg. 1983. Evaluating educational programs: An integrative causal-modeling approach. *Educational Evaluation and Policy Analysis* 5: 347–366.

Watson, M., J. Kemph, and J. Steele. 1985. Marketing muscle and the videodisc. *Business Marketing* (June).

Wildman, T. M., and J. K Burton. 1981. Integrating learning theory with instructional design. *Journal of Instructional Development* 4(3): 5–14.

CHAPTER THIRTEEN

Chaos, Connectivity, and Computers

Kerry A. Johnson

THE NATURE OF SCIENTIFIC THOUGHT

As we learned in the first chapter of this book, instructional design is derived from various members of the family of basic and applied social sciences—psychology, sociology, communication, and management. Because a major goal of social science theory development has been to emulate the approaches of the physical sciences, instructional design theorists have also been attempting to apply traditional scientific methods to the various questions and problems associated with learning and teaching.

Some progress has been made, but slowly. For example, social science, which has tried to be as deterministic and reductionist in intent as physical science, has come to recognize the usefulness of looking at events and phenomena from the perspective of probabilities rather than absolutes. Similarly, social science has understood the implications of relativity theory for explaining human behavior, especially in terms of multivariate, multidimensional representations of that behavior. Even given these contributions, however, social science is still far short of its goal of understanding how individuals and social systems behave. Indeed, their complexity and unpredictability sometimes suggests a randomness and lack of causality that runs counter to the basic assumptions that can be observed and described.

Several of the preceding chapters, while they have pointed out many of the useful results that instructional design has achieved, have nevertheless been sprinkled with caveats and exceptions. Certainly, the major difficulty in developing instructional design theory and practice has been on the research side—that is, in conducting sophisticated, multivariate research leading to verifiable findings. Present models of learning based on these traditional scientific methods are still too linear and limited. And, while there is consensus about the complexity of learning, there is frustration with oversimplified explanations of it.

In this concluding chapter, I would like to point beyond some of these present-day frustrations, to suggest how some of the new findings in the physical sciences may strongly influence the future effectiveness of instructional design, as well as lead to improvements in the management of education and training. The physical sciences have traditionally provided models for the development of the social sciences. It is reasonable, therefore, to assume that some of the approaches presently being developed in physics, chemistry, and mathematics will find their way into social science, and eventually might be useful to instructional design.

One of the difficulties in applying the ideas of the physical sciences to questions in the social sciences has had to do with levels of abstraction. Events, phenomena, and things traditionally described by physical scientists were physical, visible, and concrete. In the recent decades, however, this has changed. New areas of inquiry focus on concepts that are rarely concrete, seldom visible, and in some senses so temporal as to hardly be physical. As physical scientists begin to deal with smaller, faster, and more abstract concepts, their approaches become more and more useful for social scientists—levels of abstraction are transcended, the concrete gives way to the abstract, the seen to the unseen, the real to the imagined.

However, it takes a long time for the techniques and approaches of physics and chemistry to move through biology into psychology, sociology, economics, and management. This is due largely to the lack of strong mathematical understanding among social scientists. When they are not concentrating on abstract, pure mathematics, mathematicians focus their energy on the physical sciences. Breakthroughs in applied mathematics are generally made first in the realm of physical science, and only later, if ever, do those few concepts make their way to the social sciences.

Human behavior is complex. It requires rich description, sophisticated modeling, and dynamic representation. If high-quality mathematics is not applied to social-science phenomena, representations of that complexity remain simplistic, linear, and limited. Researchers rely on regression techniques, for example, hoping to describe the subtleties of human behavior by collapsing observations about a mean, by reducing complexity to a linear equation. Variations around the mean, the complexities, the fabric of the phenomena, are estimated using a sleek, linear representation.

While this situation does not escape the ironic understanding of most social scientists, the mathematical tools to explain human behavior, to deal with complexity, remain either inaccessible or unavailable to the majority of them. Even now, as new methods are becoming accessible and available, they will only slowly reach into the various social science fields, because they require sophisticated mathematical thinking.

The main point, however, is that these new mathematical tools are in fact rapidly becoming available in the physical sciences. Both the tools and the mathematicians will eventually have an impact on the social sciences. Furthermore, these new tools will change the way computers are used for the effective design, delivery, and management of education and training.

CHAOS AS A SCIENTIFIC APPROACH

What are these new mathematical tools? A significant set derive from a new form of science: chaos. Basic science has proposed that everything can be explained in simple terms, reduced to a fundamental set of laws. Fundamental laws of physics, for example, are generally expressed as simple, linear functions. Elegance in physics and mathematics is defined by expressing complex phenomena in simple mathematical statements (e.g., $F = ma$, $E = mc^2$). Once such functions are derived they can be used to predict future events, a basic goal of all science.

A drawback with traditional scientific explanations has often been the apparent need to begin with fundamental assumptions that limited the utility of the function. For example, many of the basic laws of motion rest on the assumption that friction and air resistance are negligible or nonexistent. This is seldom the case. In truth, the very existence of such resistors, according to a new breed of scientists, defines dynamic motion and creates conditions in which there is neither equilibrium nor total randomness. Instead, there is chaos—regular, predictable irregularity.

Chaos, as a science, attempts to describe the world in all its complexity, and is careful not to rely solely on linear relationships. Chaos is careful to consider basic assumptions and exceptions. It accepts multivariate, nonlinear descriptions of events and processes. It fosters multidimensional perspectives unlimited by Euclidean parameters.

It is also a science derived from a strong sense of the visual. Scientists in this new field tend to create visualizations of the phenomena they seek to describe. They use geometrical concepts—primarily non-Euclidean but recognizable, visual, and manipulable.

According to Gleick (1987), chaos is a science of process rather than of state, of becoming rather than being. Clearly, learning is a process, not a state, and learning is a fundamental activity of growing and becoming.

While the effect of this new science on instructional design could be significant and relatively obvious, it will probably not be felt for some time, for several reasons. First, there is the essential need to attract high-quality mathematicians to the problems of instructional design. Second, there is still the need to organize some of the basic knowledge of the field, to prepare it for analysis using the new techniques. Third, there are less abstract levels of social-science problems that need to be addressed before those of instructional design—issues of the more basic social sciences.

In short, while there is no question of the effect of chaos as a way of conceptualizing social science phenomena in general, and questions of instruction and learning in particular, it will likely be felt first in a more roundabout way. The most probable scenario is that it will affect the tools of instructional design first; and foremost of these is the computer.

CONNECTIVITY—"THE SOCIETY OF MIND"

The computer is perhaps the most significant invention of the century, and it may prove to have even greater importance as it develops beyond its infancy. Current computers provide only a small glimpse of their own significance. The present limiting factor of computers is that they process information serially. That is, they deal with one instruction at a time, finish it, and move on to the next one. A convenient measure of computing power is actually a measure of speed—MIPS, or millions of instructions per second. The unit of measure itself provides ample evidence that speed is the computer's principal strength.

However, two requirements by the scientists and mathematicians of the new field of chaos bring the adequacy of this speed into question. First, they require a powerful graphics engine. They tend to make extensive and unusual use of graphics to describe, represent, and simplify their concepts. Second, they rely on nonlinear representations of phenomena. In both cases, they require enormous processing capability and, hence, even greater speed from the computer. And, except in the largest machines, this is not readily available.

The approaches of the science of chaos are allowing glimpses of such new ways of thinking about thinking and learning, at least at a philosophical level, that new developments in computers are being conceived. These new developments involve the concepts of parallelism and connectivity.

Parallelism is the notion proposed by Minsky (1985), among others, that, rather than consisting of a single, major central processing unit, a computer is constructed of millions of processing units each doing a specific task. The critical design factor is that these millions of processes all are interconnected. They work in concert. They pass information freely and instantly in any order. They create bridges.

Minsky and his colleagues at MIT have developed a machine that they call the Connection Machine, which does just that—it processes in parallel. More importantly, it achieves connectivity by passing information from one processor to each of the others. Its architecture is based on the human neurological model—millions of brain cells, each with a specific capability connected by a vast network to provide a coordinated, integrated, efficient, dynamic, regenerative thinking tool.

Computing speed, as a result of this approach, is now measured in *billions* of instructions per second. Processing speed increases many million fold. The implications of that increased speed are multiplied yet again because, with connectivity and parallel processing it becomes possible (a) to do graphical analysis in quality and quantity to support the new scientific approaches, and (b) to support the development of artificial intelligence (AI).

GRAPHICS AND LEARNING

Graphics, broadly conceived to mean visual materials, have always been widely regarded as a valuable aid to learning. However, connectivity (and hence parallelism) will make possible phenomenal access to control of visual information by both designers and users of computer systems. Digitized video (and audio)—the process by which a picture is stored in a computer memory as manipulable numerical data—allows complete user control, and parallelism makes digitizing technically possible. At a most basic level, and as an indicator of the impact of digitized video, consider the following question: Who owns the rights to a photograph entered digitally into a computer and subsequently rethought, manipulated, rotated, enhanced, or whatever?

The effect of very high quality, manipulable graphics on instructional design will be substantial. First, it means that complex concepts can be visualized, supplementing typical verbal descriptions. Second, visual models will take on new significance because they will be interactive. Learners will be able to add to, change, store, retrieve, or select from them, to create new ways of exploring abstract concepts and developing personalized study tools. In the sciences, for example, learners will be able to have their own interactive model of complex topics like heat exchange, reactor kinetics, or differentiation, which they tie into both their own cognitive structures and their personal organization of the content. Third, these visualizations will be rich in detail where necessary. Layers of visual data will be built up to create multidimensional models that can be used as laboratories. Concepts will peel away like layers of an onion. Nested thoughts and elaborate sequences will unfold, providing even deeper insights into a given subject area.

Visualizations of complex concepts will also be easier for designers to create because they will have access to more sophisticated design tools and more comprehensive learning models. In fields like biology, for instance, computer modeling has allowed biologists to project the consequences of various biological conditions on crop yield, reforestation, and water resource management. Design engineers in various industries using computer-aided design (CAD) techniques can simulate the way a new design will perform under typical conditions. In much the same way, instructional designers will be able to simulate and test new instructional designs, modifying and extending them to better meet learner needs.

ARTIFICIAL INTELLIGENCE AND LEARNING

Artificial intelligence (AI), the science of making machines that think, provides two major directions for instructional design and learning. First, it provides a rational, measured, and fresh way to examine learning and thinking as human activities. Far from being counterhuman or nonhumanist, the scientists exploring AI focus on the most basic of human thinking and learning skills. They are providing new and valuable insights into the way human beings think and learn, by trying to make machines that think and learn. They are also emphasizing, through their own appreciation of the richness and complexity of the process, how very profound thinking and learning really are.

Second, AI will be a useful design and delivery tool for instruction. It will provide ways to deliver remarkably flexible, personal, and adaptive instruction. It will provide tools to create structures for knowledge that grow and change with their users, with the learners. In essence, it will make possible the development of learning systems that learn about the learner and adapt to the learner's needs, progress, and insights.

COMPUTERS AS DESIGN, DELIVERY, AND MANAGEMENT TOOLS FOR THE FUTURE

The use of the computer as an instructional design and delivery tool seems to have become generally, if grudgingly, accepted. Major concerns persist over (for instance) dehumanizing and depersonalizing education and training; control and flexibility; access; and limited instructional approaches. However, the directions that the computer revolution is taking, including graphics and AI, seem to be addressing many of these concerns. In an article in *Scientific American,* Peled (1987) argued that: (1) computing will grow more powerful, sophisticated, and flexible during the next decade; (2) computing will become easily accessible and ubiquitous, like an information utility; (3) visual, verbal, and other natural interfaces will allow users to access machines more easily; and (4) flexible, high-capacity networks will be capable of linking individuals worldwide. As these changes occur, computers will become an integral part of *all* instructional environments. Increases in computer power and speed, combined with insights from the concepts of chaos and connectivity, will be passed on to instruction and learning either through research, or directly through the design, delivery, and management of instructional systems.

In summary, the science of chaos will directly influence connectivity, parallelism, and computing (see Figure 13.1). It will contribute to greater understanding of the ways in which human beings gather and process information. These understandings will, in turn, influence the design of parallel processors and connected computing.

Design Tool

As a design tool, computers affect instructional design in two major ways: (1) through research on instruction, and (2) directly by providing a specific, replicable, flexible design tool kit. In the development of instructional design research and theory, a limiting factor has always been the ability to consider multivariate phenomena in meaningful ways. The influence of the combined forces of chaos, connectivity, and computers is apparent in dealing with that issue.

In using computers as design tools, several lines of inquiry currently are being, or soon will be, pursued. Knowledge engineering, information mapping, and other approaches to information science are rapidly finding their way into the standard lexicon of instructional designers. This trend can only increase. The amount of information required to be proficient in any field is increasing at rates that challenge the abilities of professionals in a field to learn it. Therefore, information scientists are increasing their efforts to find better ways to organize that information and to provide better, easier-to-use tools to access it. Accessing, rather than memorizing, information will be emphasized.

A second major line of inquiry is in the use of AI and expert systems to do some of the design themselves. Expert systems simulate the thinking and decision-making behavior of experts. This takes the form of design templates, accompanied by decision models, that allow for subtle modifications in instructional goals and objectives, and prescribe appropriate learning strat-

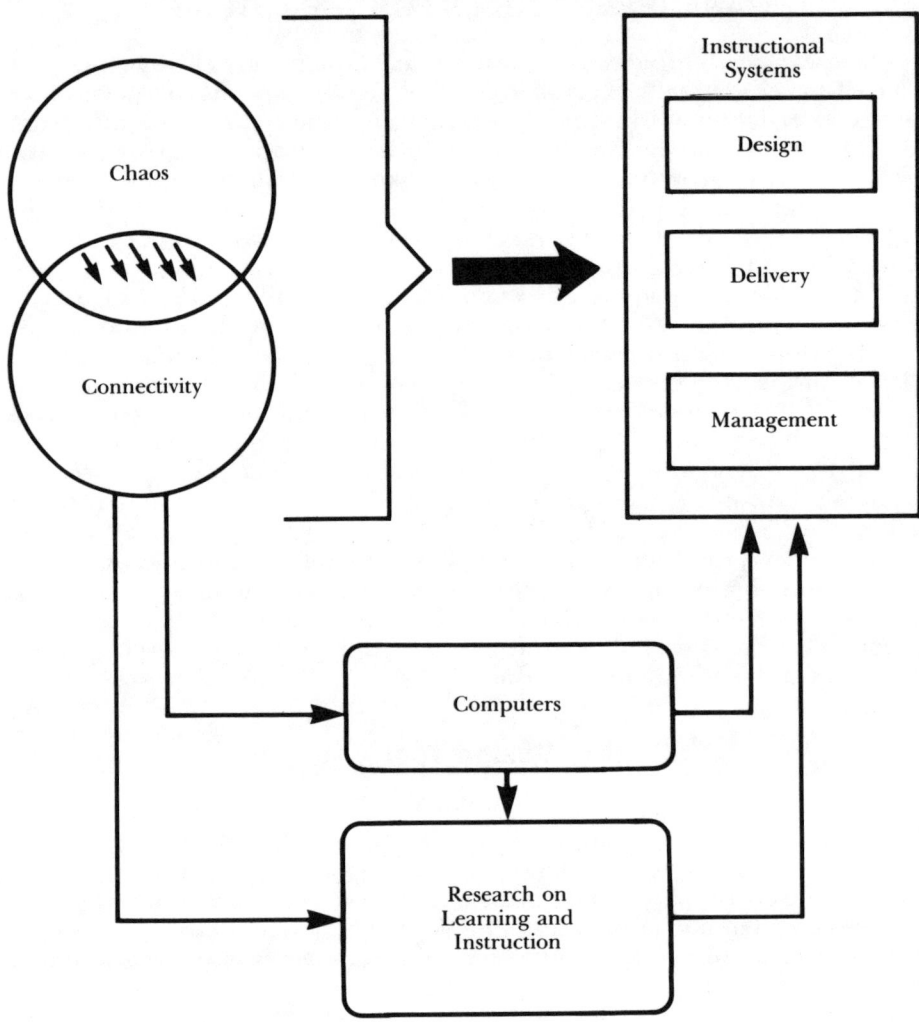

Figure 13.1. *Chaos, connectivity, computers, and instructional systems.*

egies. Given a specific, categorizable instructional problem, the system suggests a format and a set of instructional approaches. These can then be fine-tuned or modified to meet individual learner needs or specific delivery conditions.

Delivery Tool

As the computer revolution speeds up, one of the clearest indicators of its influence is the amount and variety of information about it available to everyone. The power of knowledge is becoming an ever more significant fact of life. Control of information—both its development and its delivery—is of significant concern, but there are some very interesting and potentially powerful individualizing trends under way that give hope that this power of knowledge will be put into the hands of the individual. The university and the corporation must each recognize, however, that their competitiveness in the next decades will depend in large measure on whether or not their employees understand how to access, use, and affect information.

One of the clearest trends is the availability of information. Everything from telephones to television to computers allows immediate and extensive access to large amounts of information. Ease of access to computerized information will approach that of one of today's most basic communication instruments—the telephone. Computers are fast becoming the information utility they promised to be.

New computer techniques also are providing for completely flexible and interactive information resources. *Hypermedia,* for example, combines all forms of visual, audio, and text information into a single, easy-to-use data base or information storehouse. This data base is generally organized along natural, hierarchical knowledge structures that allow the user free and complete access to all information in any combination of media. With windowing capabilities (the ability to show parts of one activity superimposed on another), high-quality graphics, and optical data-storage media, large quantities of information can be integrated into a single system.

Students learning about biological determinism, Greek mythology, or physiology, for example, will have at their command a vast resource of visual and print materials. They will be able to browse, examine in detail, and try out various and far-reaching concepts in the given field. They will know where they are in the system, and the system will know where they are. The system will, in fact, respond to the needs and interests of each user, and adapt subsequent sessions to the individual student's style and performance.

In fact, at the Media Lab at MIT, they are designing personalized newspapers and personalized network newscasts. These approaches to popular press and media are made possible by creating what are essentially "intelligent" newspapers and news shows. The papers or the television programs are delivered over "intelligent" television systems that remember the tastes and interests of their users and provide them with complete control. The individual who wants to hear headlines first, for instance, and then select stories to hear or see in detail, will have that option. It is also possible to see background material that typically would not make the evening news. Libraries of visuals, and audiotape archives, can be called up to see what led to a given story, to provide detailed background stories. It will even be possible to individually edit the evening news, tape it, and keep it for future reference.

Applied to education and training, this level of interactivity becomes a powerful learning tool. Each learner could, in essence, create his or her own library of useful study materials. The computer, keeping track of them, could then even suggest possible situations in which additional materials would be relevant, if not essential, or in which specific study strategies should be used. Reference notebooks that are significantly more powerful, flexible, and interesting can be created by students as they grapple with the complexity of their studies.

Management Tool

A major innovation in the way instruction is designed, developed, and delivered will be in the way it is managed and financed. Already, the cost of producing computer-based instruction and interactive video has created unusual consortia of supporters and backers. Production costs are high, and the costing models differ from those for traditional instruction. In essence, costs are front-end loaded, creating a need for a venture capital mentality. Because the benefits are clear, many government agencies, universities, and industry training departments are willing to explore inventive methods for cost-sharing. Costs include creating materials for use with one organization and marketing them to another—possibly even to a competitor. However, it is clear that such explorations are still the exception when, in fact, they will need to become the rule.

The area of creative financing is a natural point of collaboration for industry and academia. The experience of business in creative finance generally surpasses that of the university. Businesses, for example, are beginning to explore training as a profit-and-loss activity as opposed to a cost activity. This means that even training should be pushed to make money, to create revenue instead of simply spending it.

This has design implications in that instructional customizing will more likely be done at the local or individual level. Designers will create modularized learning packages structured around a central core of required materials and activities. Users will move through these mental environments according to their own abilities and needs, taking what they need and leaving the rest. This packaging paradigm will allow greater user flexibility and improve profitability because the market for the materials is automatically expanded by its greater user base.

Computers will also make cost-benefit analysis much more reliable and useful. At present, the research on cost-benefit analysis is limited by the same set of factors that affects social science in general. However, as the techniques and tools improve, our ability to collect and understand cost data and to relate them to the complexity of training benefits will also improve—yielding clearer cost-benefit models. Understanding the factors that affect cost, and their relationship to training benefits, will greatly enhance our ability to deal with those factors, to manage them, and to use the relationship between cost and benefits to justify further improvements to education and training. Both are driven by market sensitivity. Both require a verifiable return on investment.

Building on the obvious benefits of presently available management tools such as spreadsheets, expert systems, and artificial intelligence, chaos and connectivity will influence the development of sophisticated forecasting, modeling, and contingency tools with which to manage projects, people, and profits. These enhanced tools will allow quicker, more complex processing. They will encourage "what if" thinking. They will track past performance and predict future performance. If used carefully, they will be capable of improving management performance at all levels.

CONCLUSION

Chaos, connectivity, and computers will each, separately and in combination, have a significant effect on future education and training. They will contribute to a greater understanding of how people learn. They will provide tools to improve the design, development, and delivery of instructional systems. They will improve accountability and management practices. As an important byproduct of their direct effect, they will also challenge designers and managers to perform at higher levels. Whatever form their influence takes, the changes will be significant, pervasive, and, with careful planning, positive.

Seeing psychological and social situations in chaotic pattern—like seeing, from an airplane window, clouds or the sea surface extending into the distance in rolls and mounds and ripples and waves—allows new perspective. As artists and poets have learned to capture the essence of complex humanness, learning psychologists will use the contributions of the new sciences, with their new perspectives and new scale, to sketch designs for learning. Using intuition, validated by new methodology, they will sense the rhythms of learners, anticipating outcomes and adapting systems to meet learner needs.

That chaos exists predictably, that it explains much that has been a mystery, and that it leads to new insights and new visions of human potential, ultimately will contribute to the design of more effective learning systems. If these concepts guide the development of new techniques and new tools, greater instructional design and management efficiencies and effectiveness will be achieved. Developing these keys to improved education and training suggests a challenging and rewarding future for us all.

REFERENCES

Brand, S. 1987. *The media lab: Inventing the future at MIT.* New York: Viking.

Davis, D.D., and Associates. 1986. *Managing technological innovation.* San Francisco: Jossey-Bass.

Drexler, E. 1986. *Engines of creation.* New York: Doubleday.

Gardner, H. 1987. *The mind's new science: A history of the cognitive revolution.* New York: Bantam Books.

Gleick, J. 1987. *Chaos: Making a new science.* New York: Viking.

Goodman, D. 1987. *The complete hypercard handbook.* New York: Bantam Books.

Johnson, G. 1986. *Machinery of the mind.* Redmond, WA: Tempus.

Kline, M. 1980. *Mathematics: The loss of certainty.* New York: Oxford University Press.

Kline, M. 1985. *Mathematics and the search for knowledge.* New York: Oxford University Press.

Minsky, M. 1985. *The society of mind.* New York: Simon and Schuster.

Papert, S. 1980. *Mindstorms: Children, computers and powerful ideas.* New York: Basic Books.

Peled, A. 1987. The next computer revolution. *Scientific American* 257, No. 7 (October).

Schank, R.C. (with Childers P.G.). 1984. *The cognitive computer: on language, learning and artificial intelligence.* Reading, MA: Addison-Wesley.

Searle, J. 1984. *Minds, brains, and science.* Cambridge, MA: Harvard University Press.

Turtle, S. 1984. *The second self: Computers and the human spirit.* New York: Simon & Schuster.

Glossary

artificial intelligence (AI)—the science of making machines that think; the product of such machines.

deliverable—the product, or portion thereof, designed to meet specific standards and due on a specific date.

distance education—formal instruction delivered mainly to remote locations and/or asynchronously.

distance learning—the achievement of learning by students geographically separate from the instructor.

electronic mail—the system whereby users can send asynchronous messages to each other via computer.

evaluation—the process of providing timely, accurate information that will contribute to decisions about the inprovement, continuance, and/or expansion of instruction and instructional products.

formative evaluation—an assessment of a "deliverable" or product during the process of development. Results of formative evaluations are used to make decisions about any problems, and to formulate subsequent steps.

front-end analysis—the definition of the exact nature of the training problem and all the contingencies that will affect the design of the solution.

hyper-environment (or "hypermedia")—a system of interrelated data bases (text, visuals, audio, etc.) that allow for maximum exchange of information between components of the system.

information science—the discipline that studies the structure, organization, and management of information.

instructional design—a systematic process that creates efficient and effective instructional programs based on an analysis of learners, content, and the learning environment; an academic discipline and body of knowledge.

instructional systems design (ISD)—the name given to the formalized system of instructional design developed for the military in the 1960s and still used as a standard.

instructional technology—the study of the uses of technology in teaching and learning.

interactive video—a medium that combines the power of the computer to control, manage, and organize information, with the power of video to represent visual data.

learning outcomes—strictly, the concept that learning tasks can be categorized and that the accomplishment of those tasks can be measured. In a more generalized sense, learning outcomes are the result of any instruction.

needs assessment—the process that is part of the front-end analysis aimed at identifying the difference between current performance levels and desired performance levels.

storyboard—a draft of graphics and text used to plan a video, computer-based, or interactive video program.

subject matter expert (SME)—the content expert who provides the core of relevant subject matter information used in instructional design projects.

summative evaluation—the assessment that occurs at the end of an instructional design project.

technology transfer—the means by which new inventions or research discoveries are applied as processes or products in a new context.

teleconferencing—the system whereby students at different locations may view the same live instruction (delivered by satellite) and call in their questions over special telephone hookups.

Index

A

"Academy of Aeronautics Welding Simulator" program, 173
Accountability, 80–81
Active learning, 8
Adults, motivation and, 48–49
"Advanced Combat Trauma Life Support" (ACTLS) program, 170–171
Aggen, W. D., 174
"Aid to Families with Dependent Children" program, 176
Allama Iqbal Open University, Pakistan, 93
American Demographics, 36
American Heart Association cardiopulmonary resuscitation (CPR) training system, 176
Analysis phase, 22–23
Anderson, S. B., 159
Andrews, D. H., 13
Annenberg/CPB Project, 96
Anthropology, 12
Appeal, 50
Applied learning, 76–78
Apprenticeship, 170
Architecture, 4, 18–20, 27

ARCS Model of Motivation Design, 51, 55
Arendt, Hannah, 17
Artificial intelligence (AI), 10–11, 186, 187, 190
Assessment, 80–81
AT&T Company, 11
Athabasca University, Canada, 93, 97
Attitudes of designers, 30
Ausubel, D. P., 8

B

Baath, J. A., 98
Baldwin, A. L., 47
Ball, S., 159
Bandura, A., 48
Bates, A. W., 95, 98, 101
Bayard-White, Claire, 110, 111, 114
Behavior modeling, 8
Behavior modification, 6
Behavioral psychology, 4–6
Bennett Report Card, 168
Berlyne, D. E., 57
Bickel, W., 158
Biology, 26, 42, 186

Birth rate, 35
Borich, G. D., 166
Bottomley, J., 100
Briggs, L. J., 4, 65
British Open University system, 79, 92, 96, 99, 108, 109
British Telecom, 110
Brookfield, S. D., 48
Brophy, J., 50
Bruner, J. S., 8, 11, 65
Burge, E. J., 98
Burton, J. K., 168
Butler, F. C., 77

C

Calvert, Joyce, 92–105
Campbell, D. T., 159
Carp, A., 49
"Cash Flow Planning" program, 176
Catchpole, M. J., 95
Center for Instructional Development and Evaluation (CIDE), 139–147
Chabay, R. W., 56
Challenge, 57
Chandler, Daniel, 109
Chaos, science of, 184, 185, 187, 190, 191
Chemistry, 183
"Chrysler Hazardous Chemical Training" program, 174
Citizenship, education for, 41, 43
Classroom extension model, 94–96
Classroom training methods, 169–177
Clyde, A., 98
Cognitive psychology, 4, 5, 7, 8, 27
Cognitive strategies, 65
Cohen, P. A., 56
Coldeway, D. O., 97
Commonwealth Open University Network, 93
Communications, 4, 5, 7, 11
Community colleges, instructional design and, 85–91
Component Design Theory (CDT), 58, 64, 66
Componential subtheory, 8–9
Computer-aided design (CAD), 186
Computer-assisted learning (CAL), 108, 109
Computer-based instruction (CBI), 64–68, 70, 98
Computer-based interactive videodisc: *see* Interactive video

Computer-based training (CBT), 108, 109
Computer science, 4, 5, 7, 10–11
Computers
 as delivery tool, 188–189
 as design tool, 187–188
 as management tool, 190
 motivation and, 55–57
Computing speed, 185
Connection Machine, 185
Connectivity, 185, 187, 190
Contextual subtheory, 8–9
Contingency management, 6
Continuing education, 39, 42, 78
Continuing motivation, 50
Cooley, W. W., 158, 166
Copes, W. S., 170
Correspondence study, 95–96, 98
Cost-benefit analysis, 190
Cost-effectiveness analysis, 162, 163, 167–168
Cox, Margaret, 109
Crawford, G., 97
Creative financing, 190
Critical path analysis, 10
Cronbach, L. J., 157, 165
Cropley, A. J., 98
Cross, P. K., 74
Crowley, J. R., 167
Curiosity, 57

D

Daniel, J. S., 98
Davis, J. C., 174
de Charms, R., 48
Deakin University, Australia, 93
Deci, E. L., 48
"Decision Point: A Living Case Study" program, 175
Defense Language Institute, 176
Demographic changes, 33–35
Descriptive science, 26
Design specifications, 23–24, 28
Designers
 attitude of, 30
 knowledge of, 18, 21, 29
 performance appraisal of, 139–156
 skills of, 20–21, 28–30
Development phase, 24
Developmental psychology, 4–8
DeVries, David L., 143, 144, 147
Dewey, John, 8

Dick, W., 13
Digital Equipment Corporation, 126, 132–133, 173, 175, 176
Digitized video, 185–186
Distance learning, instructional design for, 92–105
Dodds, A. E., 98
Doughty, Philip L., 77, 167
Doulton, Angus, 106–120
Drake, M., 93
Drake, S., 169, 170, 175
Driscoll, M. P., 12, 168
Dropout rates, 33, 34
Drucker, Peter, 124
Duchastel, P. C., 98
Duplication phase, 25

E

Economics, 183
Education Utility, 11
Edwards, S., 176
Eisner, E. W., 159
Elaboration Theory of Instruction, 51, 58, 64–66
Elaborative sequence, 65
Electronic publishing, 101–102
Elman, S. E., 76, 77
Elsner, Joyce K., 85–91
Engineering process, 18
Ethics, 82
Evaluation in instructional design, 157–181
  methods, 161–168
  role of, 158–161
  worth of instructional design, 168–177
Everyman's University, Israel, 93
Experiential subtheory, 8–9
Expert systems, 187, 190
Extension model, 94–96
External accountability, 80
External linkages, 82–83

F

Face plate simulators, 169–177
Faculty development research, 78–79
Faculty guides, 79
Faculty rights, 81
Faculty-as-authority model, 75
Fales, A. W., 98

Fantasy, 57
Fedewa, L. J., 176
Fink, A., 166
Fitz-Gibbon, C., 165, 166
Foa, Lin J., 72–84, 168
Foreign-language programs, 176
Formative evaluations, 21, 161, 163–165
Freeman, H. E., 167
Front-end analysis, 22

G

Gagne, R. M., 4, 65
Gagne-Briggs Theory, 50
Galbraith, John Kenneth, 124
Galper, A. R., 170
Gardner, H., 8
Garrison, D. R., 98
General education revisions, 90–91
Gilbert, T. F., 166
Gitt, A. P., 172
Gleick, J., 184
Global competitiveness, 37
Goodson, L. A., 13
Gooler, D. D., 11
Graphics, 185–187
Grossman, David M., 81
Gruber, Howard E., 3
Guba, E. G., 159
Gustafson, K. L., 159

H

Hands-on training, 169–177
Hannafin, M. J., 168
Harless, W. G., 171
Harry, K., 93
Hawk Missile Air Defense programs, 176
Held, T. H., 174
Henderson, Joseph V., 170
Henderson, M., 165, 166
Herrscher, B. R., 159
Hirschbuhl, John, 175
Hodgkinson, Harold, 33
Holmberg, B., 93, 98
Hon, D., 173, 176
House, E. R., 158
Hunter, J. E., 165
Hypermedia, 189

I

IBM Corporation, 110, 171, 176
Illiteracy, 34, 35, 172
Image-enhanced software, 67
Immediate effectiveness evaluation, 162, 163, 165–166
Impact evaluation, 162, 163, 166–167
Implementation, 25
Indira Gandhi National Open University, India, 93
Individualized Management Development System, 171
Information management, 4, 5, 7, 10, 11
Information science, 4, 5, 7, 10–11
Instructional design
  case study, 85–91
  community colleges and, 85–91
  compared to architecture, 4, 18–20, 27
  compared to traditional instruction, 12–14
  defined, 4, 16–31
  designers: see Designers
  for distance learning, 92–105
  evaluation in: see Evaluation in instructional design
  foundations of, 3–15
  historical development, 6–11
  in interactive video development, 106–120
  motivation and, 49–51
  needs assessment: see Needs assessment
  new teaching technologies and, 63–71
  organization: see Instructional design organization
  process, 18, 21–26
  product, 19–20, 26–28
  research findings, 12
  universities and, 72–84
Instructional design organization, 121–136
  benefits of external resources, 126–127
  benefits of internal resources, 124–126
  costs of, 127
  defined, 121–122
  functional versus matrix organization models, 130–135
  necessity of, 123–124
  project-versus-nonproject driven, 129–130
  staffing and management challenges, 133–136
  structure, 128–129
Instructional Systems Design (ISD), 9, 21–25
Instructional theory, 27
Instructional transformation model, 95–96
Interaction, 98
Interactive video, 64, 66–68, 70, 78, 82
  compared with other training approaches, 169–177
  instructional design in development of, 106–120
Internal accountability, 80–81
International Council for Distance Education, 93
International University Consortium, 93, 96, 101
Intuition, 18, 21
Ixion, Inc., 173

J

Jemelka, R. P., 166
Jenkins, J., 97
Jevons, F., 93
Johnson, Kerry A., 3–15, 63–71, 182–191
John-Steiner, V., 14

K

Kahl, T. N., 98
Kaye, A., 97, 98, 101
Kearsley, G., 167
Keegan, D., 93
Keller, J. M., 51, 55
Kelly, M. E., 99
Kemph, J., 171
Kenny, D. A., 167
Kerr, S. T., 99
Kerzner, Howard, 129–135
Keskey, L. C., 172
Ketner, W. D., 172
Kimberlin, D. A., 176
King, J. M., 171
Knowledge
  brokering, 40, 41, 43
  changing structures, 75–76
  of designers, 18, 21, 29
  shifting demands, 38–44
Knowledge Network (Canada), 100

Knox, A. B., 48
Konrad, A., 93
Koop, T. W., 51, 55
Kosecoff, J., 166
Kulik, C. C., 56
Kulik, J. A., 56

L

Labor Department, 35
Lasker, Harry, 67
Laurillard, D., 110
Lawrence, J. A., 98
Learner autonomy, 98
Learner control, 65–66, 68
   motivation and, 58–59
Learning constituencies, emerging, 38–44
Learning environment, 6
Learning theory, 4
Learning-prerequisites sequence, 65
Lent, Richard M., 121–136, 162, 167, 173, 175
Lepper, M. R., 56
Leslie, J. D., 95
Levin, H. M., 167
Levin, T., 48
Lewis, R., 110
Life enhancement education, 41, 43–44
Life expectancy, 35
Lincoln, Y. S., 159
Link flight simulators, 169
Listening skills, 29
Ljosa, E., 97
Lloyds Bank, 110
Lohnes, P. R., 166
Long, R., 48
Lynton, Ernest A., 76, 77

M

McClean, P., 93
McClelland, D. C., 48
McCombs, B. L., 13, 14, 58, 59
MacGregor, A. A., 95
McIntosh, N. E., 93
Maehr, M. L., 48
Maintenance, 25
Maister, D. H., 133
Malone, T. W., 57
Management theory, 4
Management/engineering science, 4, 5, 7, 9–10

Manpower Services Commission (MSC), 108
Maricopa Community Colleges, 85–91
Mark, M. L., 165
Marlino, M. R., 171
Marquis, C., 98
Martin, John Henry, 78, 171
Marx, R. J., 176
Massey University, New Zealand, 101
Mathematics, 42, 183, 184
Matrix organization model, 130–135
May, L. S., 165–167
Media, 4, 5, 7, 10
Media Lab (MIT), 189
Medicine, 18, 26
Merrill, M. D., 58, 64, 66, 68
MetaMedia Systems, Inc., 174
Miles, G. D., 168
Military Operations in Urban Terrain simulation, 171
Minorities, demographic changes and, 33–35
Minsky, M., 185
Monson, M. K., 95
Moore, C. A., 165–167
Moore, M. G., 97, 98
Morariu, Janis, 10
Morris, L., 165, 166
Motivation, 47–60
   adults and, 48–49
   computer-based education and, 55–57
   instructional design and, 49–51
   learner control, 58–59
   models, 51–55
Mugridge, I., 93, 100
Murray, R. A., 174

N

National Alliance for Business, 44
National Center for Education Statistics, 42
National Information Utilities Corporation, 11
National Interactive Video Centre (NIVC), 106–119
National Study of Secondary School Evaluation, 159
National Technological University, 93
Navy Health Services Command, 82
Needs assessment, 32–46
   demographic changes, 33–35
   future design and delivery of adult programs, 44–45

Needs assessment (*continued*)
  global competitiveness, 37
  shifting knowledge demands and emerging learning constituencies, 38–44
  technological innovation and, 35–37
New Liberal Arts Program, 76
New University, Ulster, 108
New York Times Magazine, The, 32, 33, 36
Nichol, John 109
Noncredit education, 42, 45
Nonproject-driven organizations, 129–130
Norman, 65
Nugent, R. W., 173
Nutrition, 42

O

Objective setting, 4
Observation, 18, 21
Off-campus sites, 79–80
On-the-job training, 169–177
Open College, United Kingdom, 108–109
Open College of the University of East Asia, Macao, 101
Open Learning Institute, Canada, 93, 101
Open University, 79, 92–93, 96, 99
Operations research, 4, 5, 7
Organization: *see* Instructional design organization
Organizational development, 4, 5, 7
Organizational effectiveness, 125
Organizing principles, 27–28
Orlansky, J., 56, 167
"Ounce of Prevention, An" program, 174

P

Parallel processing, 11
Parallelism, 185–187
Parker, L. A., 95
Part-time faculty, 78
Peled, A., 187
Penland, P., 48, 50
Perelman, L. J., 80
Performance appraisal of instructional designers, 139–156
Performance audit, 166–167
Perseverance, 50

PERT charting, 10
Peruniak, G. S., 97
Peterson, R., 49
Physics, 183, 184
Piaget, Jean, 6, 8, 57
Pilot test, 24–25
Plato system, 82
Prescriptive science, 26
"Principle of the Alphabet Literacy System" (PALS), 78, 171–172
Procedural prerequisites, 65
Production phase, 25
Program comparability, 79
Program modeling, 166, 167
Programmed instruction (PI), 6
Project documentation, 161–163
Project management, 5, 7, 9, 10
Project objectives, assessment of worth of, 161–164
Project REDEAL, 97
Project-driven organizations, 129–130
Proprietary information, control of, 125
Pruett, R. K., 170
Psychology, 26, 183

Q

Quality control, 125
Questioning skills, 29

R

Railroad Worker Safety program, 176
Reeducation, 40, 42
Reeves, Thomas C., 12, 157–181
Regression techniques, 183
Reigeluth, C. M., 49–51, 58, 64, 66
Reinforcement, 6
Relativity theory, 182
Relicensure, 42
Revision, 24–25
Richey, R., 4, 12
Riley, J., 93
Rockwell, S. K., 176
Roelfs, P., 49
Rossi, P. H., 167
Rothwell, J., 110
Roueche, J. E., 159
Rowe, A. A., 176
Rowntree, D., 97, 101
Rumble, G., 93
Rummler, G. A., 167
Ryan, R. M., 48

S

Sadler, P., 133
Sagan, Carl, 124
Salomon, G., 10
Scheffler, I., 4
Schramm, W., 97
Scriven, M., 159
Seaborne, K., 99
Self-control of learning, 58
Self-pacing, 56
Sesame Street, 80
Shale, D., 93
Shaw, B., 99
Shotland, R. L., 165
Simulated Aircraft Maintenance Trainers, 172
Sircus, J., 170
Skills of designers, 20–21, 28–30
Skinner, B. F., 5, 6
Sloan Foundation, 76
Small, J. M., 93
Smith, R. C., 176
Smith, R. M., 49
Smith, W. A. S., 98
Social psychology, 4, 5, 7, 8
Social science, 4–9, 182–184
Sociology, 183
Socrates, 124
"Space Time Army Reconnaissance" (STARS) program, 174
Sparkes, J., 96
Speaking skills, 29
Specialized programs and services, 125–126
Spencer, 97
Spender, Stephen, 14
Spiral curricula, 65
Spreadsheets, 190
Stake, R. E., 159
Stanley, J. C., 159
Steele, J., 171
Stein, F. S., 49, 58, 64, 66
Sternberg, R. J., 8–9
Strategic planning, 90
String, J., 56
Structure of instructional design organization, 128–129
Subject matter experts (SMEs), 17, 24, 28–30, 89, 99
Sukhothai Thammathirat Open University, Thailand, 93
Summarizer, 65
Summative evaluations, 21
Suzuki, K., 55
Synthesizer, 65

Syracuse University, 77, 78, 158
Systems analysis, 4, 5, 7, 9–10
Systems model, 18

T

Taplin, P., 173
Task analysis, 65
Taylor, E., 98
Taylor, J. C., 99
Technological innovation, needs assessment and, 35–37
Technology transfer, 43, 45
Telecommunications, 101, 102
Telecourses, 80
Thompson, G., 93, 97, 98
Tight, M., 93
Tillman, M., 167
Time Continuum Model of Motivation, 51–55
Timmers, S., 100, 101
Tough, A., 48
Traditional instruction, 38–39, 44, 45, 74, 75, 169–177
  compared to instructional design, 12–14
Traditional management structure, 130–131
Transformation model, 94–96
Transistor Amplifiers program, 173
Triarchic theory, 8–9
Trochim, W. M. K., 167
TTC-39 Switchboard program, 172
Tuckman, B. W., 165–167
Tyler, R. W., 159

U

Uguroglu, M., 48
Universitas Terbuka, Indonesia, 93, 96
Universiti Sains Malaysia, 93
Universities, instructional design and, 72–84
University of California extension system, 42
University of Georgia, 77–78, 171
University of Maryland, 133
  Center for Instructional Development and Evaluation, 126
  International University Consortium, 93, 96, 101
  University College, 79, 82
University of Nebraska, 173, 176

University of Waterloo program, 95
University of Wisconsin, 95

V

Vadas, J. E., 176
Value, 50
Van Patten, James, 4, 13, 16–31, 141
"Variable Venturi Carburetor" program, 176

W

Walberg, H. J., 48, 166
Walshok, Mary, 32–46
Walson, M., 171
Wang, M. C., 166
Web learning, 65
Weiner, B., 48
Whitaker, Janet, 85–91
Whitney, Marcia A., 139–156
Wildman, T. M., 168
Wlodkowski, Raymond J., 47–60
Workforce 2000: Work and Workers for the Twenty-first Century (Labor Department), 35
Workplace changes, reeducation and, 40, 42
Writing skills, 29

Z

Zammit, S. J., 165–167
Zuckernick, A., 99